The

LIFE and CAREER

of

DR. WILLIAM PALMER

of **RUGELEY**

ALSO BY BILL PESCHEL

The Illustrated Life and Career of William Palmer
(The Rugeley Poisoner, Vol. 1)

The Times Report of the Trial of William Palmer
(The Rugeley Poisoner, Vol. 2)

The 223B Casebook Series
The Early Punch Parodies of Sherlock Holmes
Sherlock Holmes Victorian Parodies and Pastiches: 1888-1899
Sherlock Holmes Edwardian Parodies and Pastiches I: 1900-1904
Sherlock Holmes Edwardian Parodies and Pastiches II: 1905-1909
Sherlock Holmes Great War Parodies and Pastiches I: 1910-1914
Sherlock Holmes Great War Parodies and Pastiches II: 1915-1919
Sherlock Holmes Jazz Age Parodies and Pastiches I: 1920-1924
Sherlock Holmes Jazz Age Parodies and Pastiches: II 1925-1930
The Cases of Blue Ploermell
The Best Sherlock Holmes Parodies and Pastiches: 1888-1930

Annotated Editions by Bill Peschel
The Complete, Annotated Secret of Chimneys
By Agatha Christie
The Complete, Annotated Murder on the Links
By Agatha Christie
The Complete, Annotated Secret Adversary
By Agatha Christie
The Complete, Annotated Mysterious Affair at Styles
By Agatha Christie
The Complete, Annotated Whose Body?
By Dorothy L. Sayers

Career Indie Author Series
Career Indie Author by Bill Peschel and Teresa Peschel
Career Indie Author Quote Book by Bill Peschel

The Casebook of Twain and Holmes
Writers Gone Wild (Penguin Books)
The Dead Man: Hell's Casino
Man Out of Time

The

LIFE and CAREER

of

DR. WILLIAM PALMER

of RUGELEY

(The Rugeley Poisoner, Vol. 3)

Together with a Full Account of the Murder of John P. Cook
and a Short Account of his Trial in May 1856

By GEORGE FLETCHER, M.D. (CANTAB.)[1]
Formerly Scholar of Clare College, Cambridge; Visiting
Magistrate[2] at Pentonville Prison[3]

Edited by BILL PESCHEL, B.A. (UNC)
Formerly Copy Editor at The Patriot-News, Harrisburg
ILLUSTRATED

PESCHEL PRESS
HERSHEY, PA.

---

[1] Signifying he earned a degree from Cambridge University. The term is derived from *Cantabrigia,* the medieval Latin name for the university. Clare College is the university's second oldest, founded in 1326.

[2] A judge who hears summary offences such as drunk and disorderly, motoring violations and minor criminal charges. For more serious charges, a magistrate would order the case to be heard at the quarter sessions or the twice-yearly Assize Courts.

[3] A prison built in 1842 in the Islington borough of North London. Known for holding murderers Charlie Peace and Hawley Crippen, Oscar Wilde (briefly), convicted traitor Roger Casement, historian David Irving, and musicians Pete Doherty, Boy George, and George Michael.

First published in 1925

Cover Design by Bill Peschel. Art based on William Palmer's death mask

www.peschelpress.com

ISBN-13: 978-1-950347-06-3

Third printing: March 2021

TO

MY FORMER PARTNER

DR. A. MILNE HENDERSON

AT WHOSE HANDS FOR OVER FORTY YEARS
MY FAMILY AND I HAVE RECEIVED
INNUMERABLE KINDNESSES

CONTENTS

CHAPTER XI

CHAPTER XII

CHAPTER XIII

CHAPTER XIV

CHAPTER XV

APPENDIX

LIST OF MAPS AND ILLUSTRATIONS

London, Liverpool, and Rugeley

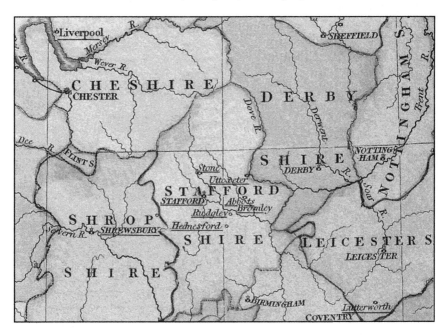

Dr. Palmer's World
(Villages and cities mentioned in the book are underlined)

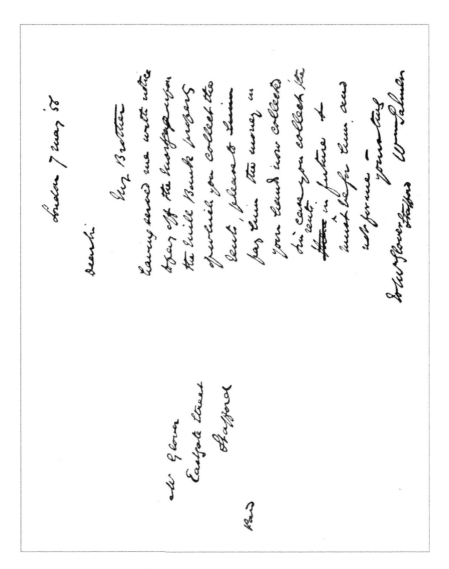

William Palmer's Letter (Facsimile)

(Editor's Note: Fletcher published from his collection this letter sent by Palmer while awaiting trial in London to a rent collector in Stafford. The transcription was added.)

LONDON 7 MAY '58

DEAR SIR

My Brother having served me with notice to pay off the mortgage upon the Mill Bank property of which you collect the rents, please to pay him the money in your hand now collected. In case you collect the rents in future it must be for him and not for me.

YOURS TRULY,

WILLIAM PALMER

DATES

Aug.   6, 1824. William Palmer born.
Oct.   21, 1824. William Palmer baptized.
Oct.   8, 1836. Joseph Palmer died.
        1827. Anne Thornton (Mrs. Palmer) born.
Aug.   1846. Palmer qualified M.R.C.S. (Eng.).
Oct.   1847. Palmer and Anne Thornton married.
Oct.   1848. Wm. Brookes Palmer born.
Jan.   18, 1849. Mrs. Thornton died.
May   13, 1850. Leonard Bladen died.
Sept. 29, 1854. Mrs. Anne Palmer died.
June   26, 1855. Eliza Tharm (housemaid) confined, a boy;
        he died Dec. 13, 1855.
July   5, 1855. Worcester Races.
Aug.   16, 1855. Walter Palmer died.
Nov.   21, 1855. Cook murdered.

        1855.
Tues., Nov. 13. To Shrewsbury Races with Cheshire.
        Cook's horse "Polestar" won S/R. Stakes.
        Palmer returned home alone.
Wed., Nov. 14. To Shrewsbury.
        Cook's illness commenced with brandy at
        The Raven.
Thurs., Nov. 15. Palmer lost heavily on "The Chicken."
        Cook and Palmer to Rugeley 9.30 p.m. after
        the races.
Fri., Nov. 16. Cook dined with Palmer 2-6 p.m.
Sat., Nov. 17. Cook very ill in bed.
Sun., Nov. 18. Chambermaid Mills very ill after broth.
Mon., Nov. 19. Palmer to London to collect Cook's
        winnings.
        Returned 8.45, Stafford.
        Drove to Rugeley.
        Obtained 3 grains strychnine from Newton,
        10 p.m.
        Cook very ill at midnight.
Tues., Nov. 20. Cook rallied at 2 a.m.
        Palmer bought 6 grains strychnine at
        Hawkins's at 11 a.m.

		Dr. Jones came 2 p.m.
Wed.,	Nov. 21.	Cook died 1 a.m.
Fri.,	Nov. 23.	12.30 p.m., Stevens arrived.
		Lunch at Talbot Arms.
Sat.,	Nov. 24.	Palmer to London; travels back with Stevens.
Sun.,	Nov. 25.	Palmer sends for Newton; chat on strychnine.
Mon.,	Nov. 26.	Post-mortem on Cook.
Thurs.,	Nov. 29.	Inquest on Cook.
Fri.,	Nov. 30.	Funeral of Cook.
Wed.,	Dec. 5.	Cheshire opens letter. Adjourned inquest held.
	Dec. 12.	Adjourned inquest held.
	Dec. 13.	Palmer writes to Coroner, sends £10 note.
	Dec. 14.	Taylor's evidence at inquest.
	Dec. 15.	Inquest—verdict. Palmer arrested 11 p.m.
	Dec. 22.	Bodies of Anne Palmer and Walter Palmer exhumed and viewed by jury.

1856.

Wed.,	Jan. 9.	Inquest on Mrs. Palmer.
Sat.,	Jan. 12.	Verdict.
Mon.,	Jan. 14.	Inquest on Walter Palmer.
Tues.,	Jan. 15.	Inquest on Walter Palmer.
Wed.,	Jan. 23.	Taylor's evidence—verdict.
	Jan. 21.	Palmer gives evidence at the trial at Westminster on forged bills.
	March.	Grand Jury, Stafford, returned true bill in case of Cook and Mrs. Anne Palmer.
	May 14	Trial at Central Criminal Court.
	to 27.	Verdict — guilty.
	June 14.	Execution at Stafford.

TRIAL & EXECUTION OF WM. PALMER.
For Poisoning at Rugeley,
MR. JOHN PARSONS COOK.

PREFACE

IN 1925, AN ELDERLY George Fletcher listened to the advice of his associates and published his notes on the William Palmer case. He was in a unique position to contribute a wealth of fascinating details to the story of the country doctor who poisoned at least 11 victims, and probably more, before his 32nd year. That's quite an accomplishment.

As you will read, Fletcher's interest in the case was sparked as a boy. His father knew John Parsons Cook, and was there when his dad warned him that he was risking ruin by associating with a black-leg reprobate such as Palmer.

And he was right; within a few months, Cook would die in agony of strychnine poisoning at the Talbot Arms with Palmer at his side. His stepfather's decision to investigate the circumstances of Parson's death would reveal Palmer's activities as a serial killer who destroyed his family and his gambling partners in his quest for greed and lust.

Soon after his execution in 1856, a flood of books on Palmer's life and crimes appeared. Two of the better works — *The Illustrated Life and Career of William Palmer of Rugeley* and *The Times Report of the Trial of William Palmer* — were republished by Peschel Press. While there are editions already out there, they are reproductions from the original pages and of dubious quality. The Peschel Press editions are expanded editions, the text edited, proofread and annotated and the illustrations cleaned up.

To these I added Fletcher's biography, which went out of print after its first edition and has never been reprinted. The resulting trilogy — with their stories about the shady world of horse racing, vignettes of rural life in the early Victorian era, and portraits of the horrible sociopath at the center of it all — will be a revelation for readers interested in true crime and the Age of Victoria.

The Rugeley Poisoner series was created with an eye toward recreating the feel of opening these books for the first time. The authors' idiosyncratic way with words were retained. Archaic spellings were kept, such as strychnia for strychnine and per cent. (an abbreviation of the pseudo-Latin *per centum*). Words, idioms and now-forgotten references were defined in the footnotes.

Some changes were made, however. Any confusion with dates and names were silently amended — a "he" replaced with a name, for example — or the information added in square brackets [like this]. Editor's notes were also added where needed. Fletcher's footnotes were identified. To make the ebook edition easier to read, the order of the book was altered, and left out were page numbers referring the reader to other parts of the book.

Bill Peschel
Hershey, Pa.

William Palmer at "The Oaks" (1854)

THE LIFE AND CAREER OF
DR. WILLIAM PALMER

CHAPTER I

Rugeley and Dr. Palmer—Pamphlets and stock pictures—My reasons for writing—Cook's visit to Bromsgrove—My many opportunities to gain information—My first visit to Rugeley, seeing Mrs. Palmer—Cook's grave, massive stone with texts—Palmer vault—Names of interest on tombstones.

TO MANY PEOPLE NOW LIVING the name of Rugeley, a small town in Staffordshire, at once associates itself with the career of William Palmer, Surgeon, and the many victims he poisoned, now nearly seventy years ago.

A few books and copies of the trial and pamphlets have been written about him and his crimes. Sunday papers, monthly magazines, have articles periodically, and almost fables, about him and his career, and the interest is still very great wherever the English language is spoken.

Even within the last few months an article has appeared in the *Sunday Times,* and in two different books published lately on various murders and motives (by Miss Tennyson Jesse and Harold Eaton),[1] a chapter is given in each book with a slight sketch of Palmer the Poisoner, and will repay the reading.

But no connected history of his life and career and various murders has ever been published since the year of his execution, though many short extracts appear from time to time in magazines and newspapers, chiefly about his trial, and only a few lines alluding to his previous career. But this book

---

[1] Fletcher is referring to Jesse's *Murder and Its Motives* (London: Harrap, 1952) and Eaton's *Famous Poison Trials* (London: W. Collins Sons & Co., 1923). The bibliography provides details about these and other books he mentioned.

is meant to give a history of Palmer's early life and general career, as well as a full account of his murdering Cook, and only a very slight account of his trial, as that can be read easily elsewhere. And as his career is of such remarkable interest, so he stands out prominently above all murderers in the last century. And from the age of eighteen, when it is generally supposed he poisoned his first victim, till he was hanged at thirty-one for killing Cook, his eleventh victim, every year of his career is full of interest in his many deep villainies and as far as possible I have endeavoured to give the remarkable events of his life.

The whole trial was published soon after his execution: an illustrated copy by Ward & Lock with his career, also choicely illustrated with STOCK sketches and portraits, as, for example, portraits used in Palmer's career (p. 72); Dr. Waddell, who attended Walter Palmer—the same picture does duty for Mrs. Yelverton's father (Yelverton Trial, p. 23); and the "Leading Counsel" (p. 104 in Yelverton Trial) does duty in a small account of Palmer's trial for Dr. Harland; also "The First Call" in Palmer's Life does duty for the same call in Yelverton (p. 32), and "The Proposal" in Yelverton Trial (p. 53) does duty for Palmer imploring his wife to forge his mother's name.[2] A capital verbatim account of the trial by Angelo Bennett (1856) is well worth reading. Both books are out of print now.

I have received many letters and requests asking for some authentic details and the results of my personal investigations and labours. Many hope that I will write fully my notes, and publish this remarkable Life and Career. So at last, in my old

---

[2] It was actually the Yelverton book that reused art from the Palmer book. *The Yelverton Marriage Case* was published in 1861, five years after the Palmer trial. In 1861, Theresa Longworth, a nurse serving in the Crimean War, sued Major William Yelverton for support. They had met at Balaklava and because she was Roman Catholic and he a Protestant, they were married in a Catholic "renewal of consent" ceremony that was not recognized by the state. When she became pregnant, he abandoned her and remarried, claiming that his marriage to Longworth was not legal. The trial was notorious for its details of numerous seductions and reinforced popular prejudices that nurses indulged their passions. Yelverton won his case after an appeal to the House of Lords, but a law was passed in 1870 that legalized mixed marriages before a Catholic priest.
The Bennett book is *The Queen v. Palmer: Verbatim Report of the Trial of William Palmer* (London: J. Allen, 1856).

age,[3] I have decided to give my knowledge of this "Prince of Poisoners," together with a few details not alluded to in magazines and newspaper articles. Some details are of small value and of little interest, yet to many friends, and to listeners at my lectures on Palmer, and to myself, all details, large and small, are of absorbing interest.

It certainly does seem almost unnecessary to inflict on the public a book on the notorious Palmer's Life and Career, where a qualified surgeon was condemned and hanged sixty-eight years ago for murdering his friend and companion John Parsons Cook. There are several other murders laid to his charge. Two more coroner's inquests had found him guilty of wilful murder. But no *book* has been written on Palmer for sixty years, except the book on his trial in the Notable Trial Series in 1912.[4]

My difficulty is to know what to write, and a greater difficulty what to omit, for the matter has been thrashed out by all sorts of writers over and over again in magazine articles and in short collections of trials, often with many errors, and omitting details which are most interesting to those who have studied the case.

My reminiscences and the results of my investigations and study may be said to appeal to two sets of the reading public. One set will be those who know all the details of Palmer's life, his many murders, his trial and execution, and do not care to read again what will be to them superfluous details. The other set of readers will be those to whom the trial of Palmer has a hazy meaning of an interesting career, and will want to learn some details of his murders, which the others do not require. Thus my task is very hard to decide what to omit.

I think the simplest and best plan will be to give my own investigations, and notes of my various visits to Rugeley and many enquiries there, extending from 1859 to 1920. Then a

---

[3] Born in February of 1848, Fletcher was 77 when he published this book in 1925.

[4] The *Trial of William Palmer* was published in two editions, the first edited by barrister George H. Knott in 1912 and the second by Eric R. Watson in 1923. John Buckingham in *Bitter Nemesis* had harsh words for the first edition: "[the account] plays up Padwick, describing him as a 'notorious racing man and moneylender,' makes light of Pratt's involvement, and does not even mention the money owing to Wright. The legal profession looking after its own."

general history of Palmer's family and life and murders, ending
with the murder of John Parsons Cook when he was only
thirty years old, for which he was tried at the Central Criminal
Court and hanged in June 1856.

I have not only made a lifelong study of the whole of
Palmer's life and various murders, as well as his trial, but I
have had exceptional opportunities of looking into the whole
matter, and perhaps not made as good a use of my chances as
I now wish I had.

My earliest recollections begin with Cook coming to
Bromsgrove (where my father practised as a doctor), when I
was a schoolboy, and I carried his cricket-bag to the ground in
the summer of 1855. And I remember my father strongly
upbraiding him, a fine young man about twenty-seven years of
age, telling him he was wasting his substance and his health
in riotous living, racing, and general dissipation, adding, "Even
now you are on your way to Worcester Races with a set of
blacklegs and idlers, the worst of whom is that dissolute Dr.
Palmer, who will rob you again and again"; and mother chimed
in with a lot more to the same effect.

This Mr. Cook was the last of Palmer's victims, and it made
a great impression on my elder brother and myself, when we
heard only a few months later how treacherously he had been
robbed and poisoned by this very Dr. Palmer.

And here let me add the trial was fixed for ever in my mind
from the fact that my father sent me to buy any daily paper at
Birmingham New Street Station during the trial, for which I
had to pay fabulous prices, especially the last four days of the
fortnight's trial in London—often 3s. or 4s. a copy[5] of The
Times, as so few could be had except by regular subscribers.

There have been relations of mine living in the suburbs of
Rugeley for over two hundred years, and some live there still, and
staying with them and with a distant connection in the town a
few years ago, I have been able to keep up my interest in this
remarkable case.

Another opportunity of learning some details was at one of
my visits to Rugeley. I found the Vicar was a former

---

[5] Three or four shillings, of which 20 of them made a pound.
Estimating the value of yesteryear's currency in today's prices
involves too many variables to make it 100 percent accurate. The
relative value calculator at the Measuring Worth website
(www.measuringworth.com) shows that the purchasing power of
three shillings then is equal in 2013 to £12.23 or $18.60 USD.

schoolmaster of mine, and he helped me with access to the register of burials preserved in the vestry of the Parish Church.

The private diary for 1855 of Hatton, the Chief Constable of Staffordshire, was given to me some years ago, and I still possess it.

I had several interviews and long chats with two or three residents in Rugeley who had served on the coroner's juries for Palmer's victims, and with a few of the witnesses at the trial.

Then my former partner in Highgate was a surgeon who was helping (at the time of the trial) Dr. Bamford in Rugeley, the surgeon called in by Palmer to all his victims.

Before I add one line I must record my thanks for the unfailing courtesy and kindness I have met with on all sides at Rugeley and in the neighbourhood, and also from the last and present Vicar, from the Clerk of the Church of St. Augustine's, and from the shopkeepers and many others too numerous to mention. This courtesy extends from 1859 down to my last visit five years ago.

Many were amused; many wondered why I asked questions on details which, to them, appeared so insignificant, yet all added to my store of information concerning the life and history of the man Mr. Justice Stevens described as "cruel, as treacherous, as greedy of money and pleasure, as brutally hard-hearted and sensual a wretch as it is possible even to imagine. It shows me that atrocious wickedness is consistent with good education, perfect sanity, and everything, in a word, which deprives men of all excuse for crime. If he had been the lowest and most ignorant ruffian that ever sprang from a long line of criminal ancestors, he could not have been worse than he was."

I fear many will think most of these records contain much of a trivial nature. Let them skip the trivial and throw this on one side.

I must begin with my early visits to Rugeley before I start on Palmer's career.

My first visit was in 1859—cheap trip trains were running from Birmingham, and I went as a lad about twelve years old. Determined to see and learn all I possibly could in Rugeley, I carefully studied before I started Ward & Lock's fully illustrated book of the "Life and Trial, and Pictures of Rugeley connected with Palmer," which copy I still possess.

Walking from the station, I came to the Parish Church on

the left-hand side of the road, exactly opposite to the house where Dr. Palmer was born in 1824 and brought up, and where his mother was still living (*vide* p. 89).

I was staring, with many other trippers, through the bars of a small iron gate into her front garden, when she suddenly came out of the front door and, walking down to the gate, said, "Well! I am Mrs. Palmer, the mother of Dr. Palmer. The Judges hanged my saintly Bill, and he was the best of my lot," evidently proud of her notoriety in the case where her saintly son William had forged her name to documents and robbed her of some thirty thousand pounds.[6]

I crossed the road into the churchyard, and close by the boundary wall and near the path leading from the gate up to the west door was a large, well-kept mound, between two trees (of which one is still there), over a grave (a picture of it is in Ward's book, p. 46). The grave is exactly opposite Mrs. Palmer's house. This was shown me, by the sexton and people standing round, as the grave of John Parsons Cook, murdered by Dr. William Palmer in 1855.

I remarked strongly about there being no stone over it, and finally two or three said, "Why, my lad, not go and explain your opinion to the Vicar?"

I took the hint, and as the churchyard joins the Vicarage garden, I called on the Vicar, who seemed to agree with my youthful complaint.

I mention this in full as a large stone was subsequently placed over the grave, and though I have tried many sources, yet I cannot find out who placed it there;[7] but the next Vicar told me he had learnt from the Parish Clerk, Mr. Frith, that it was placed there about 1859 or 1860. He had made a model of the stone out of wood from one of the yew trees which grew over the grave at the time. The grave is still frequently visited, for a well-beaten track from the path to the tomb shows the interest taken.

---

[6] It's doubtful that she lost so much as a pound. As we'll see, the one recorded suit against her over a £2,000 loan was dismissed after Palmer testified that his wife forged his mother's name on the bill. The forgeries were so blatant and the moneylenders had never met Mrs. Palmer so she wasn't held responsible.

[7] Mr. Stevens, Cook's stepfather, testified at Palmer's trial that he had intended to bury his stepson's body next to his mother in London. One wonders what happened to change his mind and why (or even if) a public subscription was needed to bury Cook.

COOK'S GRAVE, RUGELEY CHURCHYARD.
From a drawing done in 1856.

COOK'S GRAVE.
Present day.

A few years later I called again at the Vicarage, and heard that the last Vicar, the Rev. T. D. Atkinson, had chosen the texts on the stone, but I am sorry to say the inscription, cut so deeply on the top of the slightly convex stone, is wrong in two respects, and I went to the then Vicar, the Rev. R. M. Greer (1865 to 1887), who turned out to be an old schoolmaster of mine, but he could not alter the errors, so they still remain.

One error—"the night of the 22nd November, 1855." Cook died just before 1 a.m. 21st November. The second error—"Calthorpe" should be spelt "Catthorpe."

The texts round the four sides of the stone are most admirably chosen, and were selected by the Vicar, the Rev. T. D. Atkinson, who, I believe, wrote the whole inscription. The text and inscriptions are printed on a large postcard and sold in the town. A copy is on the next page.

I am sorry to say that moss and lichen, together with the passing of over sixty years, have rendered the inscriptions almost illegible.

A photograph I have by me, taken in 1868, shows a clear, well-placed oblong stone about 9 ft. by 3 ft., the top slightly arched, and the inscriptions then were clearly legible.

In the churchyard I found the Palmer family vault, standing at the north-east corner of the church, the old-fashioned, large top of heavy stone, and surrounded by iron palings; but it is a remarkable fact that, from its erection in 1836, when old Joseph Palmer (aged 59) was buried there, only two other names are inscribed on the vault: George Palmer (the second son), died 1866, and Eliza Catherine, his wife, died 1870. Yet the register in the vestry gives the following seven more: Elizabeth (1851), Henry (1852), Frank (1853), John (1854)— infants; Anne (Dr. Palmer's wife), aged 27 (poisoned 1854); Walter, aged 32, third brother (poisoned?), 1855; and finally, Mrs. Sarah Palmer, aged 67, died 1861, mother of Dr. Palmer.

There is a picture (on p. 141, of Ward & Lock's book) of the vault, which now is sadly out of repair, and only just escaped demolition when the new chancel of the church was erected thirty years ago, so close is it to the end walls of the church.

In walking round the churchyard, I noticed many names on gravestones of witnesses in the Palmer trial, and of others connected with his career—all familiar to those who studied this trial Amongst them are the following:

Thornton, Mary, aged 50, mother of Dr. Palmer's wife; buried January 22, 1849 (*vide* p. 47).

"His own iniquities shall take the wicked himself, and he shall be holden with the cords of sin."

"Enter not into the path of the wicked, and go not into the way of evil men; avoid it, pass not by it, turn from it and pass away; for they eat the bread of wickedness and drink the wine of violence."

SACRED TO THE MEMORY

OF

John Parsons Cook,

LATE OF CALTHORPE LODGE,

IN THE COUNTY OF LEICESTER,

Whose Life was taken away at Rugeley,

On the Night of the 22nd Nov., 1855,

IN

THE 29th YEAR OF HIS AGE.

AMIABLE AND AFFECTIONATE IN HIS DISPOSITION, KIND AND GENEROUS IN HIS CONDUCT.

He was sincerely beloved, and will long be lamented by his kindred and friends.

"Keep thy heart with all diligence; ponder the path of thy feet; lest thou give thine honour unto others and thy life unto the cruel; lest thou mourn at the last, when thy flesh and thy substance are consumed."

"Whoso hearkeneth unto Me shall dwell safely, and shall be quiet from fear of evil."

Bladen, Leonard, aged 49 ("From London"); died in Palmer's house May 13, 1850 (*vide* p. 51).

Masters Thomas aged 75, landlord of the Talbot Hotel when Cook died there; buried November 20, 1857.

Bamford, Sarah, aged 80, wife of Dr. Bamford; buried February 7, 1855

Bamford, William, aged 88, the aged doctor who was called

in to most of the victims; buried April 21, 1859 (*vide* p. 84).

Newton, Charles, aged 30, a very important witness at the trial; buried April 15, 1863 (*vide* p. 100).

Newton, Louisa, widow of the above; buried July 1863.

Boycott, John, clerk to solicitors Landor & Gardner, served Palmer and his solicitor with many legal notices, writs, etc.

Bonney, Rev. C., Headmaster of Rugeley Grammar School when Palmer was a pupil there; buried 1853.

Bonney, Mrs., widow of the above; buried 1895.

Bonney, Mrs., wife of Professor Bonney; buried 1923.

Bonney, Professor T. G., F.R.S., aged 90, brought from Cambridge to be buried here, 1924.

Thirlby, Ben, aged 54, took over Palmer's practice, buried September 1866.

Thirlby, Jane (*née* Mrs. Turnock), widow of above; buried 1879.

Myatt, George, a saddler, aged 65, boon companion of Palmer's, important witness for the Defence; buried 1865 (*vide* p. 33).

Myatt, James (postboy), aged 64, refused Palmer's bribe to overturn the cab and smash the jar; buried 1871 (*vide* p. 159).

Rowley, Ann, charwoman to Palmer, laid out the body of Cook and other victims; buried 1866 (*vide* p. 60).

Freer, Dr. Richard, aged 80, present at the post-mortem on Cook, grandfather of Dr. Richard Freer, now in Rugeley; buried 1882.

Smith, Jeremiah, aged 47, Solicitor, mixed up with Palmer in many shady transactions; buried January 1, 1858 (*vide* p. 86).

Atkins, Rev. T. D., born May 1792, for 32 years Vicar of this parish; buried November 1865.

Atkinson, Mrs., widow of the above, aged 78; buried July 1875,

Salt, Dr., at whose surgery Palmer obtained the strychnine on November 19, 1855; buried 1873.

CHAPTER II

My second visit to Rugeley, 1865—Subsequent visits—Palmer's house and the Talbot Arms—Taylor's lecture—Original letters of Palmer—Vicar my old schoolmaster—Two packets of poison in surgery—Superintendent Hatton's Diary—The Jane letters, unfit for publication—My special opportunities for acquiring details.

I PAID MY NEXT VISIT OF INVESTIGATION in the summer of 1865, and well remember every detail of it. I was on the point of leaving school for Cambridge, and was not accustomed to lunch at an hotel, but I bravely ordered lunch at the Talbot Arms, and at once commenced a series of questions about Dr. Palmer and his victim, John P. Cook.

The waitress took me to the room where Cook died, and showed me *all* she could. There is an upper assembly-room close to Cook's bedroom, where the post-mortem was made on November 26, 1855, the Monday after Cook's death; and with much pride she showed the big schoolboy some blood on the floor from the examination. Then she showed me the two doors in the room about which a great deal was made at the trial. Then the half-circle wooden reading-chair, in which Dr. Palmer sat from 1 a.m. on the morning of Tuesday, November 20, watching Cook die, as he thought. But, as I shall subsequently relate, the strychnine was poor stuff, not strong enough, and Cook rallied while Palmer slept in the chair. The waitress had been a servant in the hotel at that time, and a well-laid-out tip brought me much information.

May I add the sequel to the lunch and chat? I had some cider, which was a pleasant drink to me, and when, in the churchyard after lunch on the summer afternoon, I sat down at the end of Cook's grave to make some notes, I fell asleep for nearly two hours, lost my train, and had to go to relatives at Stone[1]—and wire home. But my notes of that day are full of information and most interesting to me.

Subsequent visits to Rugeley only confirm and enlarge on this visit of 1865.

My next visit was forty years later, early in this century. I

---

[1] A market town about 7 miles north of Stafford and 14 miles north of Rugeley.

went over from Stafford, and, walking up from the station, easily found Cook's grave in the churchyard with the large stone over it, which helped to point out Cook's resting-place to the many visitors who went to see it, fifty years after the murder, as part, and not the least interesting part, of Rugeley.

In the centre of the town, the house where Palmer had lived and practised had been much altered. The front was all pulled down, the front rooms built out over the little piece of garden up to the line of the street, and a large post-office had been erected there which included Palmer's dining-room and drawing-room, much enlarged, making a post-office hall for the public—very different from the little post-office up Albion Street where Cheshire was post-master in 1855, before he went to prison for opening and reading a letter at Palmer's wish. But the back-premises of Palmer's original house had not been touched, nor the upper storey, and the bedrooms were exactly as in Palmer's time.

From them I could see across the road into the room at the Talbot Arms, where Cook died. The post-office officials kindly gave me leave to go all over the premises. The kitchen was exactly the same as in Palmer's time, where he sat on the Sunday evening after Cook's death, with Newton, discussing strychnine poison and the dose, and what could be seen or found on analysis after death. The room upstairs had not been altered by the new building for the central post-office.

There was Mrs. Anne Palmer's bedroom and with her door left open, and from the position of the wardrobe with plate-glass panels, it was plain how she saw by the mirror, when lying ill in bed, what was going on when she saw Palmer kissing the pretty housemaid Eliza Tharm, on the landing at the top of the stairs. The post-office has been removed, and a motor-garage now occupies what was Palmer's house.

From friends and relations in Rugeley I was able to obtain some details of Palmer's career, though fifty years after his execution.

I was taken to see the last man alive of those who had served on the local coroner's juries fifty years previously. But he was not able to help me much, being well over eighty-four years of age.

I went to various relations of some of the witnesses at the trial, amongst them two sisters of the man George Myatt, the saddler (he went occasionally to races with Palmer). They told me many details of Palmer's life, and knew him well, as he frequently came to the saddler's shop when they both were living there with their brother.

These visits and the opportunities afforded by them, and with the following exceptional chances of picking up details, and with relatives living there, helped me greatly.

I subsequently went to hear Professor Taylor lecture at Guy's Hospital[2] on strychnine. Three-quarters of his lecture was taken up with his account of Cook's case and the terrible state in which he found the contents of the one jar (of which more hereafter, when we come to the post-mortem on Cook). His animosity against Professor Herapath[3] was very evident and *would* come out, off and on, all through the lecture.

The lecture left no doubt on my mind that no analyst in the world could have had a more difficult task to detect any poison, owing to the careless, disgraceful state in which the mangled stomach and part of the bowel had been sent up. And as strychnine was at that time a poison scarcely known, the task was intensified for Professor Taylor. But the antimony[4] must have been in great abundance for Professor Taylor to find what he did.

At St. Thomas's Hospital a fellow medical student, William S. Mavor by name, told me his father was foreman of the jury which convicted Palmer at the great trial in 1856 (Central Criminal Court), and a few details I learnt from him.

I have two original letters of Palmer's in my desk. He wrote an excellent hand, and the letters are well expressed.

An old schoolmaster of mine was Vicar of Rugeley (Rev. R. M. Grier) for twenty-three years (1865-87), and gave me many

---

[2] A London hospital built by Thomas Guy (1644/45-1724) from the proceeds of his investment in the South Sea Bubble, a notorious financial scandal that beggared thousands but from which he profited handsomely. It is one of the two oldest teaching hospitals in Britain.

[3] William Bird Herapath (1820-1868), then professor of toxicology at Bristol Medical School, testified at Palmer's trial that Taylor should have been able to discover strychnine in Cook's stomach. The defense used this to imply to the jury that he thought there was no strychnine to be found, but cross-examination by the attorney-general revealed that Herapath had said publicly that Cook had been poisoned, and that he was suggesting that Taylor was not competent in applying the Marsh test. No wonder years later he was still sore.

[4] A naturally occurring chemical element used since ancient times for cosmetics. It is also poisonous, causing symptoms similar to arsenic. It can also be used as an emetic and to treat animals.

details I wanted.

The Rev. M. F. Alderson, formerly Rector of Lutterworth, a grandson of one of the Judges at Palmer's trial (Baron Alderson), lent me his grandfather's original MSS. book with the notes and evidence which he took down at the Central Criminal Court, and I read them all with special interest. A connection of mine in Stafford told me that a great friend and neighbour of his went into Palmer's house when the Sheriff's officers had taken possession on Padwick's bills (December 12, 1855) and had arrested Palmer, remaining in charge of his person. He went over all the premises with the officers after Palmer was arrested for the murder of Cook, and said he saw in a nest of drawers, in what was used as a surgery, two packets not yet unwrapped—one of laudanum[5] and one of prussic acid[6]; probably two out of the three parcels Palmer had bought at Hawkins's shop on November 20, 1855, three weeks previously—twelve hours before Cook was poisoned—but the third packet, bought at the same time, the six grains[7] of strychnine, was not there!!!! (*vide* p. 98).

Superintendent Hatton, Chief Constable of the County of Stafford during the years 1855-56, went to live at the "Big House" in the village where I practised in Suffolk. He left just before I settled there. But his landlord had some of his goods, and amongst his books was Hatton's personal diary for 1855 when he first heard of the suspicion of murder, and he was present at every adjournment of the inquest up to the arrest on December 15, 1855, of Palmer for the wilful murder of Cook; and was present at the inspection of the bodies of Mrs. Anne Palmer and Walter Palmer in December 1855 and at the inquests on both.

Thus my friends thought I had had exceptional opportunities and chances of studying the case.

Fifty years after the trial I paid two or three long, quiet visits to Rugeley, and from the variety of items and facts I picked up from several of the Coroner's jurymen whom I interviewed then and on previous visits, I found my collection

---

[5] A liquid extract of opium.

[6] A poisonous liquid containing hydrogen cyanide. Today, it is called hydrocyanic acid.

[7] A obsolete unit of weight based on the size of a cereal seed. Five grains made up a common aspirin tablet. As little as a grain of pure strychnine was fatal, but as we'll see, quality control was negligible in the Victorian era.

was worth working out, and after giving a few lectures on the case I was asked by many, amongst them by Sir Richard Webster (Lord Alverstone[8]) and Baron de Worms (Lord Pirbright[9]), to publish my reminiscences and collections. So I make this attempt, hoping it will be interesting to my readers.

Later on in this volume will be found several matters not met with in other "Palmer" books, or only slightly alluded to, such as a summary of thirty-four letters written by Palmer to Jane Bergen, in the early months of 1855 up to the time of Cook's death. I have had the original letters submitted to a great expert in handwriting, and he says they are undoubtedly all in Palmer's writing. They are called the "Jane letters[10]," alluded to in the Notable Trial Series by Mr. Knott after seeing them in my library.

They consist of thirty-four letters written to a Miss Jane Bergen, in a most lascivious, degrading style. They are not mentioned in any account of Palmer's life, except in the introduction to the trial in *Notable Trials*. They show unmistakably the nature of the illicit intercourse existing between them both, and Palmer gives the name and address of a doctor in Stafford, who, he says, would be *"silent as death,"* and who performed an illegal operation successfully on her.

She kept all the letters—much to his surprise—and when he was unable to help her with much (or any) money she threatened to show these letters all round, unless he sent her £50 (after asking for £100). He sent £40 the very day he and Cook returned from Shrewsbury races.

I need scarcely say the letters are not fit for publication. But they are well written and clear, showing a man of education, though of a most disgusting nature.

Also I am giving a full account of the murder of and inquest on Mrs. Anne Palmer, and of the suspected murder of and inquest on Walter Palmer. I cannot find these are published in any account of Palmer's trial, and I obtained them from local papers.

---

[8] Richard Webster (1842-1915) was a barrister, politician and judge. He served as the country's Attorney-General from 1885 to 1900 and Lord Chief Justice from 1900 to 1913.

[9] Henry de Worms (1840-1903) was a Conservative politician who served in the House of Commons from 1880 to 1885 and was Under-Secretary of State for the Colonies from 1888 to 1892.

[10] Reprinted in *The Illustrated Life and Career of William Palmer* (Peschel Press, 2014).

I am also giving a complete account of the post-mortem on Cook, and a few remarks on the operators and the spectators there. I have a few remarks to make that neither side called the driver of the "fly" from Stafford station on the night of November 19, and a very full discussion on the pills given on the Monday night. I next give a full account of Palmer as a witness in a civil trial in January 1856, when brought in custody from Stafford jail to give evidence at Westminster.

Then I make a strong comment on the fact that Palmer was never able to give evidence, nor his version in any court, as he was never present at any inquest, nor taken before any magistrate (*vide* p. 134). And prisoners were not allowed in the witness-box till forty years later.

Also I make an allusion to Serjeant Shee[11] not being allowed to sum up his evidence for the Defence, no second speech being allowed till Denman's Act of 1865; and a summary of Royalty who were present every day at the trial. All these items, fully described, add some interest to the narrative, and to the career of Dr. Palmer, which I at once commence.

---

[11] William Shee (1804-1868) was appointed to an order of barristers called Serjeants-at-Law, a position that dated back to the 1300. Serjeants were part of an a elite group allowed to work in the central common law courts. Their slow decline in status began with the appointments of Counsels (Queen's or King's depending on the gender of the dominant monarch, of course) beginning with Elizabeth I. Under the rules of precedence, the most junior Q.C.s or K.C.s still ranked above the eldest Serjeant. By 1875, changes in the law made the position irrelevant and no more were appointed.

CHAPTER III

Palmer's parentage—Brothers and sisters—Mr. Timmis's recollections of his schoolfellow—Palmer qualified M.R.C.S., 1846—Doctors Pritchard, Smethurst, Lamson, and Cross.

IT WOULD CERTAINLY HAVE BEEN very surprising and contrary to all expectation if William Palmer had grown up and become an honest member of society.

Both his parents leave much to be desired as regards their moral character, so that he started handicapped, as it were, in honesty and uprightness, and he was spoilt by his mother more than any of his brothers.[1]

Many of his relations on both sides appear to have been low-class drunkards and sexual degenerates.

His father, Joseph Palmer (born 1777, died 1836, buried at Rugeley in the family vault), was by trade a sawyer[2], living at King's Bromley, where there was also residing a man named Bentley, who had come there a few years before with a very bad character from a bad house in Derby which he and his wife had managed for a few years. They brought with them a daughter, Sarah (born 1793), who was useful to her father, carrying farm produce to Lichfield market and saving the expense of a general servant.

She also had a loose character, and the Marquis of Anglesey's steward, named Hodson, paid her marked attention, as did also several other men in the neighbourhood,

---

[1] There were five sons and three daughters born to Joseph and Sarah Palmer, and they lived lives of widely varying respectability. Here is a summary:

* Mary Ann (1816-1853) scandalized Rugeley with her behavior, never specified, at least in print, and died an alcoholic;

* Joseph (1818-c. 1853) became a timber merchant in Liverpool;

* Twins George (d. 1866) became an attorney, and Sarah (1821-1822) died at 11 months;

* Walter (1823-1856) was a bankrupt alcoholic;

* William (1824-1856);

* Thomas (1827-1877) became a minister;

* Sarah (1832-1907) became a respectable vicar's wife and left eight children.

[2] One who saws trees.

amongst them this young forester, a sawyer named Joseph Palmer, who, seeing many rivals, especially Hodson, married her in a hurry about 1818.

Joseph Palmer remained on good terms with Hodson after the marriage, and the pair managed to rob heavily the Marquis of Anglesey's estate[3], Palmer taking by far the greater share— selling and cutting down trees, while Hodson was courting his wife, Mrs. Sarah Palmer. Joseph Palmer, with a bad reputation, died suddenly in October 1836, aged fifty-nine, leaving an unsigned will, a widow with seven children, and over £75,000.

The eldest son, Joseph, agreed to forgo his claim on all the freehold property, and arranged that each of the seven children should have £7,000 and the widow nearly £25,000 provided she did not marry again. Perhaps this clause was one of the excuses for her subsequent life. The lawyer who drew up the deed told Joseph he was sure he would live to regret his liberality—and he did bitterly repent.

Of the seven children (five sons, two daughters), in spite of their parentage and example, some of the family seem to have held respectable places in the world. Joseph, the eldest son (born 1819), was a timber merchant, following his father's trade, but moved early to Liverpool, where he held a good position and reputation (died about 1853).

The next son, George Palmer (born 1821), was a solicitor, and helped with the family matters, and had a fair practice at Uttoxeter, where he married a Miss Flint, daughter of Mr. A. A. Flint, the Coroner. George Palmer died 1866, aged forty-six, and his wife, Eliza Catherine, died 1870. Both were carried to be buried in the family vault at Rugeley.

The next son, Walter (born 1823), drank heavily, was an all-round loafer, and was poisoned by his brother William in 1855 (aged thirty-two).

The next son was a doctor—William, the famous poisoner (born 1824).

The next son, Thomas (born 1827), was in Holy Orders, supposed to be the writer of a scurrilous pamphlet, abusing the Lord Chief Justice after the trial. I do not believe Thomas

---

[3] The title was created in 1815 for Henry Paget (1768-1854), who served with distinction at the battle of Waterloo and served in several major government posts, including twice Lord Lieutenant of Ireland.

was the author.[4] He was for twenty-seven years Rector of Trimley St. Martin, near Felixstowe (died 1887). He told his churchwarden, a friend of mine, that he felt certain his brother never killed Cook.

But when asked to account for the purchase of strychnine on each of the two days before Cook died, and the finding of his wife's body saturated with antimony, and heavily insured only a few months previously, he said he could not discuss the details, but he believed in his brother's innocence.

Two years after his death in 1887, his widow married a friend of mine, Dr. W. Elliston, a physician in Ipswich.

The elder daughter, Mary Ann, married Mr. Thomas Hayward, and went to live at Heywood,[5] near Rugeley, where her brother William was pupil of Dr. Tylecote. Her character was not of the best and she died early in 1853.

The younger sister, Sarah, married two years after the trial a Scotchman, Mr. Brodie. She was a regular attendant at the chapel in Rugeley, and much given to good works. She was twin sister with George, the solicitor.

When William was about ten years old he was sent to the Rugeley Grammar School, the buildings adjoining his mother's house. He was there under the Rev. Thos. Bonney, M.A., whose tombstone in Rugeley Churchyard says: "Born 1802, died 1853. For 28 years Master of the Free Grammar School in This Town." On the same stone we read: "Eliza Ellen Bonney, born 1813, died 1895."

Within the last few months their son, the Rev. T. G. Bonney, F.R.S.,[6] Fellow of St. John's College, Cambridge, was carried to Rugeley to be buried, about ninety years of age.

For Palmer's schooldays and early life I cannot do better than quote verbatim an interview I had with Mr. John Timmis at Marston Vicarage, his son's residence, in 1907.

---

[4] The pamphlet, published as *A Letter to the Lord Chief Justice Campbell*, was attributed to the Rev. Thomas Palmer. Thomas Palmer disavowed any connection with it. In his memoirs, Campbell says that an unnamed barrister was the true author.

[5] A town that was part of Lancashire in Palmer's time, located seven miles north of Manchester and 77 miles north of Rugeley.

[6] Fellow of the Royal Society of London for Improving Natural Knowledge. Founded in 1660 as a way for physicians and natural philosophers to share knowledge, it has grown to become a major authority on scientific issues.

"I am five months younger than William Palmer" (Timmis was born February 1825, Palmer was born September 1824). "We were at Rugeley Grammar School together for three years. He was a thoroughly bad boy, and did not mind how he cheated, He would get other lads to write his thesis and many of his exercises. He was not cruel to small boys, but very cruel to animals and sneaking in every detail. He was a great deal too flush with money, and could often show three or four Sovereigns which, to us boys, seemed a fortune. He used to rob his sisters' pockets and his mother's purse, and steal any cash lying about.

"From school he was sent as apprentice to Evans & Co., chemists, Lord Street,7 Liverpool, and was bad and lazy all his time there. He was detected robbing from letters, bringing them from the post. Two or three times he was seen fingering the envelopes, feeling for coins, then more frequently sent in the post than now. Two letters with marked coins were posted, which did not arrive, and the marked coins were found in his pocket. At the end of six months, Evans & Co. dismissed him.8

"He then went as pupil to Dr. Tylecote at Heywood, nearly opposite where his married sister lived, and here he was, if possible, more vicious than at Liverpool. He formed the acquaintance of the young daughter of a small farmer in a neighbouring village and took her about to different village and town fairs, often using his master's dog-cart. He had the fee for a physician (who had been called in consultation) given him to hand to the doctor, but, needless to say, he appropriated it—in short, gave serious trouble all round, dissolute and loose with cash and with women.

"Dr. Tylecote suggested he should walk the wards of the Stafford Infirmary. He went there as a pupil, but at

---

[7] One of the main streets in central Liverpool and part of the central shopping district.

[8] A slightly different story is told in the *The Illustrated Life and Career of William Palmer* from Peschel Press. At first, workers in the post office were suspected of stealing, but after test mailings had cleared them, an inspector focused on Palmer. He was seen picking up the letters and, as he was walking back to the office, opening them and pocketing the money.

the end of a few weeks in Stafford it was decided he should go to St. Bartholomew's Hospital in London.

"The dissipations of London were too much for him, and his prospects of getting qualified appeared so remote that his family arranged with Dr. Stedall, a crammer, to specially coach him, promising a fee of one hundred pounds if successful. He qualified in August 1846, M.R.C.S. (Eng.),9 but as the fee did not reach Dr. Stedall's hands, he went to law and obtained it. An account of this trial appeared in a London paper, which Dr. Bamford brought in to show me."

Mr. Timmis gave me more details, but these give a good account of Palmer's life up to his obtaining his surgical qualification of M.R.C.S. (Eng.) in 1846.

In the same year Dr. Pritchard, the notorious Glasgow Poisoner, obtained the M.R.C.S. (Eng.). Each of these doctors poisoned his mother-in-law and his wife, each using antimony followed by a vegetable poison, strychnine being used by Palmer and aconite by Pritchard in 1865, and both had illicit relations with a favourite maidservant at the house.

Dr. Pritchard rather modelled his crimes, as we see, on those of his forerunner [Palmer] ten years before. But there is in Pritchard a curious lack, or incoherence, of motive which makes his crimes harder to understand, as they were not, like Palmer's murders, for money.10

---

9 Member of the Royal College of Surgeons of England. The group was founded in the 14th century to encourage research and regulate surgeons and dentists. The (Eng.) refers to the particular group the surgeon belongs to. There are also groups in Edinburgh, Glasgow, Ireland, Australia, and Canada.

10 "Pritchard's motives remain obscure," wrote Richard Altic in *Victorian Studies in Scarlet*. "He stood to win a two-thirds life-interest in a sum of £2,500 if his wife predeceased him: an insufficient amount, one would think, to justify a murder. Or did he wish to free himself to marry a servant girl he had seduced some time ago? As for his mother-in-law, did he find it necessary to kill her because, having come to Glasgow to nurse her daughter and being a person capable of suspicion, she stood in the way of his perfecting his plan?"

Among murderers, Edward Pritchard (1825-1865) stands out. He was vain and self-centered to an extraordinary degree. The former naval surgeon's lectures on his experiences in the South Seas were models of exaggeration. He claimed a friendship with the Italian patriot Garibaldi by displaying a cane with a fake inscription. His

These two men, with Lamson and Smethurst (British qualifications), and Neil Cream (Montreal M.D., 1876), Crippen (New York, 1875), Professor Webster (MD Harvard, 1825), holding American qualifications, go to make up an infamous band of doctors[11] who were tried for murder and all hanged, except Smethurst; and later on there was another doctor, who

---

vanity led him to grow a beard exuberant by Victorian standards and to hand out souvenir photos of himself. His fellow physicians disliked him and his quack remedies but stayed silent o protect their reputations while he was poisoning his wife and mother-in-law. No wonder Sherlock Holmes placed him with Palmer at the heads of their profession.

[11] The doctors on Fletcher's list included:

* George Henry Lamson (1852-1882) was hanged for murdering his 18-year-old brother-in-law with a slice of Dundee cake containing aconite. He had been taught as a medical student that the poison from the monkshood plant was undetectable. However, mice fed the contents of the victim's stomach showed symptoms of aconite poisoning and that was enough for the jury.

* Thomas Smethurst was nearly hanged for the death of his wife, Isabella. His 1859 trial was a mirror image of Palmer's. Alfred Swain Taylor testified that he had found arsenic in one of Smethurst's bottles, but had to recant his testimony once he learned that his sample had been contaminated. Medical experts debated whether Isabella had died from poison or from vomiting and diarrhea caused by her pregnancy. Smethurst had been found guilty, but the public uproar over the conviction was so intense that the Home Secretary consulted with the queen's former obstetrician and Sir Benjamin Brodie (who testified as an expert witness in the Palmer trial). They concluded that there was no "absolute evidence of guilt," and Smethurst was pardoned. We still don't know for sure if he got away with murder.

* Thomas Neil Cream (1850-1892) poisoned five woman in the U.S. and England and possibly more. He was captured after attempting to frame two doctors for the killings.

* Hawley Crippen (1862-1910) was hanged for murdering his wife. He fled England in the company of his mistress, who dressed as a boy to escape scrutiny. But the captain became suspicious of the couple and used the newly installed wireless radio to alert the authorities and they were arrested upon their arrival in Canada. It was the first time a radio was used to capture a suspect.

* Harvard professor John White Webster (1793-1850) was executed for the murder of George Parkman, a wealthy Bostonian to whom he owed money. A jury concluded that Parkman had been killed at Webster's lab at Harvard Medical College, his body dismembered and burned.

was also a rank hypocrite, Philip Cross, a doctor practising near Cork, who was hanged in 1888 for the murder of his wife.

He was sixty-two years of age, and, having undue intimacy with a beautiful governess, Miss Skinner, aged twenty-one, poisoned his wife in a clumsy manner with arsenic, and buried her on the second day at 6 a.m., then married Effie Skinner on the fifteenth day, entering in his Diary:

June 2.—"Mary L. Cross departed this life. May she go to heaven is my prayer. Buried on the 4th."

Compare this with his forerunner, Dr. Pritchard, who entered: "Mary Jane, my beloved, passed away"; and with the supreme hypocrite Palmer, who writes: "My poor dear Annie expired at ten minutes past one," and a week later enters: "*At Church—Sacrament.*"

CHAPTER IV

Palmer's courtship and marriage—Copy of certificate—Settles in Rugeley—Kills his mother-in-law—Dissolute life—Kills Leonard Bladen—The four youngest children died a few weeks old, 1851-54—Suspicion in five other deaths discussed.

DURING THE LATTER PART of Palmer's medical-student days he met a Miss Thornton, probably at Heywood, where she was at a "finishing school" (as it was called in those days), and Palmer was with Dr. Tylecote in the same village. She was about eighteen or nineteen years old and a ward in Chancery. Her father, an old retired officer, Colonel Brookes, had come to live in Stafford on leaving the Army in 1820 with a small fortune.

In a year or two Colonel Brookes made his pretty housemaid, Mary Thornton, his mistress, but from her general want of education and plebeian origin and a vile temper and manners, he refused to marry her.

A daughter, Anne, was born 1827, and was recognised by Colonel Brookes as his child; he had her well educated and, as he thought, well provided for in his will.

In two or three years' time her mother's temper became very violent. She took to drink and was unfaithful, and very soon ill-treated and frequently struck old Colonel Brookes. Finally he shot himself in 1834, as his four brothers also did, leaving about £8,000 to his daughter, and £12,000 to her mother, his mistress. But owing to some flaw in the will, the property was thrown into Chancery, and only about a quarter came to the mother and daughter, and Anne Thornton became a ward in Chancery.[1]

Her guardians were Charles Dawson, a rich chemist of Stafford, and old Dr. Knight, a physician, also in Stafford. Dr. Knight was a cousin of the Dr. Tylecote with whom Palmer was working.

When Anne Thornton left her "finishing school," she went to reside with her senior guardian (Mr. Dawson) who had a capital house at Abbots Bromley, about seven miles from Stafford.

---

[1] A court responsible for ruling on equity cases, including wills, trusts, land law and guardianships.

Here Palmer followed her; and Mr. Dawson, seeing what probably was the beginning of a love-affair, warned his ward against Palmer, and she refused his offer of marriage in 1845. But Palmer, seeing a pretty, fascinating young lady of nineteen and supposed to be wealthy, persevered till, in October 1847, she married him at Abbots Bromley, in a very fine old church, and a copy of the marriage certificate is given on p. 48.

In the certificate it will be noticed that his brother George signs as a witness, and it states Anne Thornton was illegitimate, aged twenty.

In the marriage register, Palmer signed his name "Wm.," as he always wrote it, but the Vicar made him write it in full and the correction is made to "William" in the register.

During the twelve months he was walking St. Bartholomew's Hospital in London as a medical student, he and Anne Thornton corresponded, and after he qualified M.R.C.S. in August 1846, they began to look around for a house, and finally settled to live in Rugeley—a fatal mistake—taking a small house opposite the Talbot Arms, and came there after the wedding tour in October 1847, putting up a brass plate, which remained eight years on the railings till the fateful December of 1855, when Palmer was conveyed to Stafford Prison, and it was sold with his belongings.

On the occasion of one of my visits to Rugeley, about 1905, the landlady of the Talbot Arms produced this plate, very carefully wrapped up, and showed it to me, adding that she had been offered five pounds for it a few months previously, and now was regretting she had not closed with the offer. On my next visit she asked me how she could best dispose of it, and I suggested Madame Tussaud's, where it could be placed in front of that dock in the Chamber of Horrors where Palmer stands, the central figure of many villains, in his well-earned chief place.[2]

Having settled there in the autumn of 1847, all went well for a year or two. Palmer's medical skill and abilities were believed in by some, and several friends and relatives always called him in.

A former partner of mine was with the aged Dr. Bamford in Rugeley a few years later, and he told me that Palmer

---

[2] An attraction at Madame Tussauds in London featuring waxworks of notorious murderers and infamous historical figures. Palmer's effigy was a fixture in the museum for 127 years.

undoubtedly had abilities, but in his time there (1854-55) his character was very bad and dissolute, and he had given up practice for the Turf, keeping a large racing establishment at Hednesford, a few miles off, having as many as fifteen horses in training there.

Within a year or less of his marriage, Palmer commenced borrowing money from his mother-in-law, Miss Thornton (called for politeness Mrs. Thornton), the Colonel having been dead a dozen years.

Mrs. Thornton loathed the man, but she sent him various cheques for twenty or fifty pounds occasionally, she told her friends, for fear he should wreak his vengeance on her daughter.

Palmer, thinking a large sum of £12,000 would come to his wife on the death of her mother, tried to persuade her to come and stay with them. After demurring for some time, she consented, remarking to a neighbour, "I know I shan't live long"; and in a fortnight she was dead. Why she went to stay there, no one can tell.

She arrived at Palmer's house on Saturday, January 6, 1849, for her visit, and was taken ill with violent headaches and sickness early in the following week, and as she did not improve, old Dr. Bamford was called in on January 10.

He was a good-natured medical practitioner of the old school of doctors, with a good practice, and a reputation in the neighbor-hood for uprightness and a kind heart. He suggested effervescing mixtures,[3] and as she still did not improve, he suggested Mrs. Palmer's guardian, old Dr. Knight of Stafford, should be called in for consultation.

But the patient and her daughter, Mrs. Palmer, suggested a delay of a few days till January 14 (so Palmer subsequently told Dr. Knight), and on Thursday, January 18, 1849, she died, Dr. Bamford's certificate of death stating "apoplexy"—the same disease for which he certified Cook's death several years later.

The charwoman who came in to help to look after her—for Mrs. Palmer had been only recently confined—described her wandering delirium, and how Palmer would bring up all her foods and medicines.

The last few days of her life she was always drowsy, and did not know where she was except once, when Palmer, in the soothing

---

[3] A bubbling or foaming mixture. From the Latin *ex-* plus *fervescere* for "to begin to boil."

1847. MARRIAGE SOLEMNIZED IN THE PARISH OF ABBOTS BROMLEY

IN THE COUNTY OF STAFFORD

No.	When Married.	Name and Surname.	Age.	Condition.	Rank or Profession.	Residence at time of Marriage.	Father's Name and Surname.	Rank or Profession of Father.
102	October 7th	William Palmer	23	Bachelor	Surgeon	Rugeley	Joseph Palmer	Timber Merchant
		Ann Thornton	20	Spinster	—	Abbotts Bromley	Natural daughter of Ann Thornton	

Married in the Parish Church of S. Nicolas according to the rites and ceremonies of the Church of England by License by me,

J.M. LOWE, Vicar.

This marriage was solemnized between us	⁂	[Wᵐ (erased)] William Palmer Ann Thornton	⁂	in the Presence of us	⁂	George Palmer Mary Knight

I hereby certify that the above is a true copy of the Marriage Register of the Parish aforesaid. Extracted this 30th day of June, 1908.

STUART BERKELEY, Vicar.

voice he could so well assume, tried to rouse her to drink some medicine. She gave a shriek and said, "Take that awful devil away!" She died the next day, and the tombstone in Rugeley Churchyard, close to the Palmer's family vault, tells us:

"Mary Thornton, late of Stafford, died January 18th, 1849, aged fifty."

But Palmer was bitterly disappointed at the money. Mrs. Thornton died three months after the birth of her grandson, her daughter's first-born, William Brookes Palmer. Palmer, making haste to get her money, had not been satisfied with the golden-egg allowance paid quarterly to his wife by the trustees, but thought he had better kill the golden goose and get rich quickly, but failed miserably.

Whatever money he may have got by his mother-in-law's death was soon swallowed up, for before he had been married two years he had commenced a career of horse-racing and gambling, soon associating with low characters so easily found there, black-legs[4] and gamblers.

In 1850 we find him strongly suspected of killing Leonard Bladen, who was collector for Charrington's Brewery. Bladen was at Chester Races with Palmer, and won considerable sums, mostly in bets paid him on the course. Palmer was indebted to him for about £600, so he invited Bladen to come and stay a few days with him at Rugeley and he would settle the debt.

Bladen came, having in his money-belt about £500, which he showed his friends when at Ashby the day after his arrival at Rugeley.

He wrote to his wife that he would not be home for three or four days, and added: "But with what I have in 'ready' and what Palmer will pay me, I shall come with a thousand pounds."

He had a brother, Henry, a shoemaker living at Ashby where he had been brought up until he went to London, and the day after his arrival at Rugeley he drove over with Jere Smith to see his brother at Ashby and ordered some boots, which Henry was to bring over to Rugeley, but he heard of his brother's death before the order was completed.

A friend going through Rugeley, seeing how very ill Bladen was, went immediately to tell Mrs. Bladen. She hurried down

---

[4] A dandy, professional gambler, or racecourse swindler, identified by their black boots.

there, but only arrived an hour before his death.

Palmer hurried the funeral on, and before the widow left she expressed great surprise that so little money was found upon her husband and his betting-book was lost.

Palmer said he was sorry to press her, but that Bladen owed him £60. She expressed great surprise, and produced the letter saying Palmer was going to pay him £600 at Rugeley.

For the sake of Mrs. Annie Palmer, who had been most kind to her in her trouble, she left the house without further fuss. But in a fortnight's time the brother at Ashby was so suspicious that he wanted her to go with him to the Magistrates or Coroner, to have an enquiry; but as it would be very costly—for exhumation, etc.—and they were very poor, they let the matter drop.[5] The brother had a long interview with Palmer, who said it was right to make all enquiries and was sorry he could not help him more, as he had to leave for London that night. But Bladen subsequently found out he had never left the town.

Before I pass on to the recognised murder of his wife and brother, I may as well mention the premature deaths of his four little children, each within few weeks of birth.

The Register of Burials in the vestry gives the following:

Elizabeth Palmer, aged 10 weeks, buried January 8, 1851.
Henry Palmer, aged one month, buried January 8, 1852.
Frank Palmer, infant, buried December 21, 1852.
John Palmer, 3 days, buried January 30, 1854.

All died from convulsions of some sort or another, and his family nurse commented loudly on the death of two, dying after his paying them a visit; and a handy woman who came in to help in the house remarked that it was sad the babies died so suddenly, exactly like two illegitimate children who died after a visit to him.

It was supposed his method was to dust some poison on his finger, smear it over with sugar, and let the baby suck his finger—almost too horrid to believe in so coldblooded a method.

---

[5] Until the late-19th century, the public and not the police was primarily responsible for prosecuting suspects. The victim would bring the suspect to the attention of the parish constable or magistrate. The magistrate would hold a trial, in the case of minor matters, or refer the case to the quarter sessions or the twice-yearly Assize Courts.

Dr. Palmer's House (1855)

But he had often commented how expensive a family growing up would be. He thought it was too great a luxury to pay for legitimate and illegitimate children, so he quietly removed them from his path, as he had no friends or relations to adopt any of them. His poor wife exclaiming with fear when she lay dying, "I do hope Willie [her only living child] is safe"— and correcting herself said, "I meant, I hope he is well."

And when her fourth baby died she said to Palmer's sister, "What will the people say? My mother died here, Mr. Bladen also, and now all these children!"

Yes, what did the neighbours say? But think what they might, and suspect, and hint, yet no proof was at hand for any enquiry, till sensible Mr. Stevens came down, as we shall see, and, brushing aside all hints, was determined to probe to the bottom the cause of his stepson's death and robbery, and the more he enquired into matters, the more deeply he was convinced there had been a foul, treacherous deed committed.

The actual number of victims can never be known. Even when Bladen was killed (*vide* p. 49), one of his very early victims, a friend of mine was at a rabbit shooting party when the news was brought that Bladen was dead. One of the party blurted out, "He has been poisoned I am sure," and suspicion did point, as we saw, to Palmer. But for five years more he continued on his career. As Mrs. Tennyson Jesse says, "It reflects great credit on the manners and personality of Palmer that, in spite of all rumours, he remained unmolested for so long." But rumour seventy years ago did not spread so quickly as now, and though George Herring, the London Turf commissioner, strongly suspected him, yet if Mr. Stevens had not come along—an almost stranger—and probed deeply and more deeply still, owing to his suspicions and detestation of Palmer personally, the career of this Prince of Poisoners might have continued with further victims.

One of the earliest accusations against him was that at the age of eighteen, when a pupil at Stafford Infirmary, he made a bet—and won—that a man named Abbey could drink off two tumblers of neat brandy. Abbey succeeded, and died within a couple of hours. Abbey's wife was described as a buxom lass and had been an out-patient to the Stafford Infirmary where Palmer was studying. The authorities at the hospital passed a strong order that Palmer should never be allowed to go into the dispensary, as he was found in there dabbling with drugs and various poisons, when only in his teens.

In addition to the murders of which there is little doubt—his wife and brother and those I have already entered into—Palmer has been accused of several others.

I have mentioned that four of his children died before they were three months old, each from convulsions, the same sort of death as one or two of his illegitimate children met with, notably Eliza Tharm's baby, born in his house nine months exactly from the date of his wife's death. It was put out to nurse, and when five months old was brought for him to see how it was getting on—and it died in convulsions on the way back to its nursing mother, only two or three weeks before the local Coroner's jury returned a verdict of "wilful murder" for killing Cook.

Two or three supposed murders by Palmer I have investigated as far as possible, but cannot feel satisfied murder was proved.

Joseph Bentley, an uncle, is said to have died after a drinking bout with Palmer as to which of them could swallow the most brandy at one sitting.

Bly—a young racing friend fond of the Turf and a fast life—was owed by Palmer £700, and when pressing Palmer for it, was taken ill, and after Palmer had doctored him for three days he died, and as usual Bamford gave the certificate, this time "*English cholera.*"

But I cannot find any clear proof of either Abbey, Bly, or Bentley. There were suspicions, and rumour seems to have handed on these cases from one generation to another.

Palmer was not a man able to drink much, nor was he fond of alcohol. One account says he was never seen drunk but once—the night of the post-mortem on Cook; and Mr. Timmis, his quondam[6] friend, told me he *could* not drink at all to excess.

When Bladen died, Mrs. Anne Palmer was terrified and exclaimed, "My mother died under our roof last year, and now this man who had come to be paid a large sum. *What will people say?*" Yes, what were they already saying and more than hinting with no uncertain voice? Whether hints reached Palmer's ears or not, he continued on his career.

---

[6] Former. From the Latin word for "formerly."

CHAPTER V

Early practice—Gambling and dissolute life—Moneylenders—He forges his mother's name on bills—Insures his wife's life in April 1854—Poisons her in September—Exhumation fifteen months later—Inquest and verdict.

PALMER BEGAN HIS CAREER as a Rugeley doctor with many things in his favour. He made a comfortable small practice quickly, he had a wife devoted to him who was much beloved and respected in the neighbourhood. This helped in the early days of the rising doctor. She had a certain safe income, and was helped financially by her mother as long as she lived. But Palmer poisoned both for the sake of acquiring all that remained of Colonel Brookes's money.

His avarice and lustful passions, with love of gambling and the Turf, soon overwhelmed him financially and socially. An illegitimate child of one of his maid-servants [Eliza Tharm], born eighteen months after he had brought his bride home, died suspiciously after a visit to his surgery for him to see how it was progressing. I showed in the last chapter how his second, third, fourth, and fifth babies at home all died under three months of age, bringing deep grief and untold horror, mixed with suspicions, to his young wife's heart. But all the children were too expensive to maintain, whether legitimate or babies of servants and other women he had seduced.

The last of these was born in his own house nine month after his wife's death—six months before he was taken to prison.

Their first-born baby, a son, was worshipped by his anxious mother, who expressed fears for his safety if he were out of her sight for long.

As he could not afford the expense of a wife and her children (five) in the state of his finances, and when £13,000 would be netted by the death of his wife, there was no doubt what her fate was to be, especially with a pretty housemaid living in the house who was his mistress, certainly within the week which his wife died, if not before.

In 1853-54 he was associating with the lowest characters, men and women, and was heavily in debt to moneylenders for bills, which he had circulated, and had raised money to the amount of several thousands, all of which bore his mother's signature, as accepted by her, whose name he had forged on all. She was a wealthy lady, about sixty years of age, worth over £30,000.

Palmer soon found himself very deeply in debt to the moneylenders, who, without any mercy, exacted their monthly interest of 60 per cent. They now threatened to sue his mother on the forged bills, which would bring him to penal servitude.[1] So, seeing there was no chance of ever getting clear, he decided to kill his wife, but before doing so to insure her life heavily.

Over £30,000 was applied for in various first-rate offices, such as the Gresham, Prince of Wales, the Scottish Equitable, the Atlas, Norwich Union, and The Sun. But after much correspondence and quibbling about terms, he finally secured £13,000 with the Prince of Wales Office, who subcontracted £3,000 with the Scottish Equitable and The Sun £3,000.

But he nearly succeeded for £12,000 more with the Solicitors and General Office, but at the last moment they could not sub-let enough to other offices to come to terms with Palmer.

Seven hundred and sixty pounds was the first year's premium paid to the Prince of Wales Office—almost 6 per cent.—for a young woman only twenty-seven years old.

One of the doctors who examined her was Dr. Knight, a physician of great repute in Stafford, a relative, and one of her trustees as a ward in Chancery and trustee of the marriage settlement—a man "somewhat advanced in years." He and two other medical men passed her as a good life, and the first premium of £760 was duly paid, a large commission being

---

[1] The Penal Servitude Act of 1853 reduced the number of hanging offenses and substituted penal servitude (hard labour in a British jail) for transportation to Australia under certain circumstances. A review of the Old Bailey records for 1856 shows a variety of punishments for forgery depending upon the severity of the offense and the age of the criminal. For example, Edward Agar was sentenced to transportation for life for uttering a £700 note, while James Railton, with 10 indictments against him, was transported for 15 years. For Palmer, a conviction of forging bills for thousands of pounds probably would have earned him a one-way ticket to Australia for life, assuming the suspicious deaths were never investigated.

deducted by Jere Smith, a solicitor in Rugeley, and boon companion of Palmer.

If we pause for one moment to look at this matter, surely nowadays all must be astonished. Here is a doctor, with a very small practice, living in a house rented at £25 a year. His character, all round, not of the best—a sporting surgeon always away at races, and owning a dozen or more racehorses. His last four children have died under three months of age; if they died "fairly," then Mrs. Palmer cannot be a very strong woman; and here is her husband trying to insure her life for £25,000, and the premium at the rate finally accepted, would have been over £1,400 a year, far more than he was worth, though finally he paid £760 for £13,000. He gave as a reason for heavy insurance that her income left to her by Colonel Brookes, her putative father, would cease at her death.

Within a few months of paying the first and only premium she died, in September 1854, at the early age of twenty-seven, the cause of death said to be a sort of English cholera. Her death occurred within a few days of a visit to relations in Liverpool, and the details of her illness are given (p. 62) at the inquest.

Half of Rugeley attended her funeral when she was buried in the Palmer family vault (only a few feet from her mother's grave). She was much loved in the place, and all felt real sympathy for Dr. Palmer, who seemed so unfortunate.

She was born under a cloud, for Colonel Brookes, as we saw, would not marry Miss Thornton, her mother, and she was deprived of a mother's care for many years of her youth, for she was brought up by her guardian and four out of her five children died under three months of age, her mother died in her house within a fortnight of coming to spend her first visit with her. All this had tended to implant deep lines of sorrow in her countenance, and there was no longer the happy smile, showing contentment at home, which was there in her first two years of married life.

Though her husband apparently was kind and lavished presents on her, yet the neighbours knew he was associating with low-class men and women—in reality neglecting his wife for the Turf, loose women, and heavy gambling.

But Palmer was an arrant hypocrite and a psalm-singing humbug, and he goes to her funeral apparently overcome by his grief, sobbing loudly through the service, and when the coffin was being placed in the vault he cried aloud, "Take me, O God, take me with my darling treasure."

And he enters in his Diary on the day of her death: "My darling Annie was called to-day by her God to the home of bliss so well deserved." And on the day of the funeral he enters: "Saw the last of my dear wife for ever. How desolate life is!"

Yet within a week he is clamouring for the £13,000 insurance money, and within a day or so is consoling himself in the arms of his pretty housemaid Eliza Tharm, who lived with him as his mistress till he was carried off to jail fifteen months later, and who gave birth to a child in his house on June 26, 1855, following his wife's death on September 29, 1854.

When Palmer applied for the £13,000 insurance money, the Prince of Wales Office was advised not to pay it over without a rigid enquiry. But as three doctors testified to the cause of death, and signed the certificates for the Office, they felt they must pay it at once. And pay they did within six weeks of the death, and the cheque for £13,000 was sent to Palmer; but it only helped him a little in his desperate money troubles over forged bills and the serious difficulties he was in. It was all swallowed up by the moneylenders Pratt and Padwick, who were showing no mercy, exacting their pound of flesh with the usual stone-hearted severity of the blood-sucking human vampires.

Before going on with Palmer's immediate career, it seems a better and simpler plan next to take here the inquest on Mrs. Anne Palmer, though held fifteen months later.

After the verdict of "wilful murder" had been returned against Palmer on December 15, 1855, for killing his friend John P. Cook, the Home Secretary, Sir George Grey, ordered the body of Mrs. Anne Palmer, his wife, who had been buried fifteen months, and the body of his brother Walter, who had been dead nearly five months, to be exhumed, and a coroner's inquest to be held in each case.

So the old family vault near the northeast corner of the church was, on December 22, 1855, again disturbed, where seven bodies were resting (Palmer's *father*, *wife*, and *brother*, and four infants), and the coffins containing the bodies of Mrs. Anne Palmer and Walter Palmer were carefully taken out and carried across the road to the Talbot INN, a corner house, now a private residence occupied by Mr. Osmond (not to be confounded with the Talbot ARMS, the hotel in the centre of the town, where Cook had recently died). And at this small Talbot Inn there were present Dr. Monckton, and Dr. Bamford from Rugeley, the Coroner, and twenty-three local jurymen to view the bodies.

The coffins were opened in the presence of the jury in the commercial-room—in fact, the only room in the house large enough to contain thirty people with the two coffins.

Mrs. Anne Palmer's coffin was first opened—a strong oak coffin—and as it had been buried fifteen months, the gaseous exudations had been able to escape through the fibre of the wood, and the corpse was comparatively dry and the smell endurable. But in the case of Walter Palmer, who had been buried in a lead coffin, on removing the outer wood coffin a hole was bored in the lid of the lead coffin in which his body had been encased, and at once most sickening and noxious effluvia escaped, which permeated the entire building and affected people at the other end of the inn, and produced a most terrible and sickening effect on all who were in the room where the coffin was.

So great was the upset, one of the jury told me forty years afterwards, that fifteen were seized there and then with vomiting, and he was himself ill for three or four days.

When the leaden lid was removed, the corpse presented a terrible sight, the face and cheeks terribly swollen and the limbs much distended—in short, a mass of corruption, dropsy, and gangrene.

Dr. Monckton must have had an almost impossible task to make the post-mortem examination of Walter Palmer's body, but not much difficulty with Mrs. Anne Palmer, and the stomach with intestines easily removed, and a few other organs, all of which were sent to Professor Taylor at Guy's Hospital for analysis.

The jury made their formal "view" of the bodies. The two inquests were adjourned promptly, to the relief of the sick jury and Coroner. They next met on Wednesday, January 9, 1856, first to enquire into Mrs. Anne Palmer's death; but Dr. Taylor was not quite ready with the result of his analysis, so the inquest was adjourned to Friday the 11th, and after a long day adjourned again to Saturday the 12th, when a verdict of "wilful murder" was returned against William Palmer. And on Monday, January 14, the inquest on Walter Palmer was commenced and adjourned to the 15th, and again adjourned for eight days to Wednesday the 23rd for Dr. Taylor's evidence, when a verdict also of "wilful murder" was returned.

It was known that there could be no satisfactory result obtained by exhuming Mrs. Thornton's body, who had been buried exactly seven years, from January 1849, and William

RUGELEY PARISH CHURCH, EAST END.

THE PALMER FAMILY VAULT

Bladen, almost six years (May 1850). And the authorities, as well as all sensible people, agreed that if the evidence in these three cases was not enough, i.e. Cook, Mrs. A. Palmer, and Walter Palmer, it would be no more use piling Pelion on Ossa[2] to add to the number. But I may as well add here that the Grand Jury at Stafford Assizes, finding a true bill in the cases of Mrs. Palmer and John P. Cook against Palmer, threw out the bill in the case of Walter Palmer, as the evidence of the cause of death of the latter could not be satisfactorily ascertained from the state of the body at the post-mortem examination, and the doctors who had attended Walter Palmer did not seem willing, from the doubtful post-mortem results, to alter their opinion of the cause of death from "apoplexy." Though Professor Taylor was inclined to think prussic acid the cause, yet he finally agreed with the six doctors (p. 71), and they said "apoplexy."

But the local jury unanimously found "wilful murder."

I have found some difficulty in obtaining an accurate account of these two inquests, but by the kindness of Mr. Isaac Bradley, the Coroner for Birmingham, I have seen extracts from the *Observer* and *Birmingham Journal* of that time, and a few local brief reports.

At this inquest on Mrs. Anne Palmer the witnesses were:

Ann Rowley, who was a sort of handy nurse and char-woman, and helped to nurse and be generally useful. She spoke about Palmer always administering the medicine to his wife; during the last two days of her life he gave effervescing mixtures, always promising her it would relieve the sickness AFTER Dr. Knight's visit.

Mrs. Bradshaw, another handy woman, was with her the last week of her life, and was struck with the constant vomiting and her inability to take nourishment beyond a little liquid. She also spoke of the apparently good and amiable terms Dr. and Mrs. Palmer were on. She helped to lay out the body after death.

Eliza Tharm, a good-looking domestic servant, about twenty years of age. She had lived over two years in Palmer's house and was living there till he was taken to prison. She said that Mrs. Palmer had to go to bed directly she returned from Liverpool on Wednesday, September 20, 1854, and never got

---

[2] Two mountains in central Greece. In Greek mythology, when the giants Otus and Ephialtes attacked Mount Olympus to capture the goddesses Artemis and Hera for their wives. To reach the summit, they piled Mount Pelion upon Mount Ossa, but failed anyway. So piling Pelion on Ossa means to make a difficult task harder to achieve.

up again. She helped to wait on her, and testified to Palmer's apparent devotion to his wife.

In answer to a question by the Crown Solicitor, pressed by the jury, she said Palmer had attempted to take liberties with her in his wife's lifetime. There is, of course, no doubt that from the time of his wife's death she was his mistress, and was confined, exactly nine months after Mrs. Palmer's death, of a little boy on June 26 following (Mrs. Palmer died September 29). What became of that baby, history recounts the old, old story. I have tried in vain to ascertain the exact facts; the last I heard was it had been put out to nurse, and died in convulsions a few days before Palmer was arrested.

Eliza Tharm remained on in Palmer's house, and when he was arrested for the murder of Cook, before going to jail he threw his arms round her neck and gave her a fifty-pound note which had been found by Bates in the drawer, when Palmer wanted to send ten pounds to bribe the Coroner, after the second adjournment of the inquest on Cook.

Sarah Palmer, sister of William, spoke of the visit on Monday, September 18, 1854, with Mrs. Anne Palmer to Liverpool, and going to a concert on Tuesday, at which Mrs. Palmer was supposed to have caught a chill! So, not feeling well, they both returned to Rugeley on Wednesday the 20th, when sickness set in severely. Miss Sarah Palmer said: "I called to see her on Saturday the 23rd, and she told me how very ill she felt and I was not to trouble to call on Sunday as my mother was not well. But I did call, after attending chapel in the morning and evening, and called again on Thursday the 28th, but she was asleep, so I did not see her. She died on Friday, so I had not seen her for six days before her death." She was buried on Tuesday, October 3 (confirmed by burial register).

George Palmer, brother of William, saw Mrs. Anne Palmer as she returned on Wednesday, September 20, from Liverpool, and walked home with her from his mother's house. He added to his evidence that Mr. Hawkins (chemist) was at his brother's sale last week and took away some books (which were afterwards produced at the trial), and said he was convinced Mr. Hawkins would return a verdict of "guilty" against William, whatever the evidence might be—a curious step for a solicitor to take, airing his personal feelings against one of the jury.

Mrs. Bradshaw, recalled, stated that Dr. Palmer was most attentive to his wife, and when Dr. Bamford suggested Dr.

Knight should be called in, he immediately wired to Stafford for him. "She was very sick and vomited her food, but I tasted most of it before it went upstairs, for I prepared it."

Here a coarse joke was made by one of the jury: "Did you taste the pills?" and another juryman replied: "We can answer for it she never did, as she is here to-day"—Curious jury behaviour in the middle of an inquest before their verdict.

Dr. Bamford stated he was sent for on Sunday, September 24, and finding her worse on Monday, suggested a consultation with Dr. Knight, who came the same day.

Dr. Knight said he saw her on Monday afternoon, September 25. "The previous history of her illness and her present symptoms Palmer told me, and answered most questions at her bedside, instead of letting her tell me her pains. She was very ill, and, chiefly due to the version given of her dangerous and previous condition, I thought it might be English cholera. I ordered her not to take a single thing in fluid or solid for three or four hours. I went out, and to pass the time I called on Dr. Bamford and other friends, and when I returned I thought her a little better. When I left I told Dr. Palmer to let me hear how she progressed and I would come again at any time. But I heard no more from the Tuesday till her death on Friday the 29th. I was one of her guardians under Colonel Brookes's will, and as regards her money she had received over £3,000 legacy and an annuity of £200 a year. I had examined her in the spring of 1854 for life insurance, and passed her as a 'first-class life.'"

Inquest adjourned till Saturday, January 12, and on this day *Professor Taylor* said he found antimony in all the organs of the body, and finding some in the stomach as well as in the liver and kidneys, was satisfied that it had been given within a few hours of death, as well as in doses extending over some days in the form of tartar emetic. There was no trace of any disease, so that death was caused "by *antimony* and no other cause."

Dr. Rees, of Guy's Hospital, confirmed this.

Dr. Knight was recalled, and said that "after hearing the evidence to-day, I am inclined to take back my certificate and agree with Professor Taylor that death was due to antimony, which had been administered before Dr. Bamford or I saw her, and was continued after our visits."

The jury consulted for twenty minutes.

Verdict: guilty of wilful murder against William Palmer for poisoning his wife.

CHAPTER VI

Moneylenders' threats of exposure—Walter Palmer's life and habits—
Dr. Palmer tries to insure him for £84,000—Effects a policy for
£14,000—Walter's illness and death—Inquest five months later—
Verdict.

WE MUST NOW FOLLOW PALMER'S CAREER, for the £13,000 paid by
the Insurance Offices on the death in September 1854 of Mrs.
Anne Palmer, we have seen, did not suffice for many weeks,
and was nearly all absorbed by the moneylenders, chiefly Pratt
and Padwick.

In January 1855 we find Palmer again raising money on
bills at 60 per cent., the interest now to be paid monthly
instead of quarterly as previously. All was raised on forged
acceptances supposed to be signed by Palmer's mother, who
was in total ignorance of all these transactions.

There are ugly remarks and suggestions in Pratt's letters to
Palmer: "Your mother must understand the bill must be met
and there will be no more renewals"; "I wrote to her twice
lately, but she failed to answer my urgent letters," and
suchlike.

There is no doubt Cheshire, the postmaster—a great friend
and racing companion of Palmer—not only intercepted all the
letters to her and gave them to Palmer, but also stopped a
letter with instructions to the solicitor in Rugeley to issue writs
against her. And he got one year's imprisonment for tampering
with letters, and came from prison to give evidence.

Once, in desperation, Pratt went down to Rugeley to see
Palmer's mother and to arrange terms for repayment, but
Palmer met him and told him his mother was so seriously ill
she could not attend to any business, and the journey was
fruitless; but I certainly think Pratt knew or strongly
suspected there was forgery, especially when out of six
supposed signatures to the acceptance, it was pointed out to
him there were three distinctly different handwritings, ALL
supposed to be written by Mrs. Palmer, senior.

Early in 1855, afraid to raise any more on his mother's
forged acceptances, Palmer was now sorely pressed how to
raise money for insistent clamouring creditors, especially the
interest on bills held by Pratt. So he decided to heavily insure

his brother Walter's life and to poison him, first getting the policy assigned to himself, for a loan of £400 lent to his brother Walter.

Walter, a heavy, coarse-featured, simple-hearted sot, whose one fault all his life had been love of too much drink (as he called it, "mixing the spirits"), married a wife with £500 a year settled on herself. She was fond of the man, but his bankruptcies, his attacks of delirium tremens,[1] compelled her to leave him when she gave up all hope of any reformation.

Walter had been a corn-merchant, but was always a lazy, indolent drunkard who, neglecting his business, had been made bankrupt in 1849. He went to live for a few years in the Isle of Man, but his drinking habits brought on an attack of delirium tremens, and he was again made bankrupt. He returned to Liverpool—for one reason, to be nearer his widowed mother at Rugeley with her £70,000, and near his eldest brother Joseph, who was living in Liverpool, a respectable citizen and a timber-merchant.

Joseph had married a Miss Milcrest, one of the three daughters of a shipbuilder, and was prosperous in business. Walter persuaded a younger Miss Milcrest to marry him, much against the advice of her sister and her husband, his brother Joseph.

She had an assured income of £500 a year, but from the date of their marriage Walter never contributed one penny to her support, and after his second attack of delirium tremens she was compelled to separate from him, much to her sorrow, for she seems to have had some affection for him, in spite of his dissolute life.

Walter soon returned to Rugeley, his old neighbourhood and after staying a few months with his mother, finally settled down in a small house in Stafford, where he was within a few miles of his brother William Palmer, his evil genius.

Walter now indulged more freely than ever in drink, chiefly gin; and on such a life his brother William tried to obtain an insurance for £84,000, applying to six offices through Pratt, the bill discounter.

After much correspondence a policy for £14,000 was secured. The first premium of £780 was paid by Pratt in

---

[1] A psychotic condition suffered by chronic alcoholics. Its symptoms include anxiety, hallucinations, and tremors. The phrase is Latin for "trembling delirium."

January 1855, who took a commission of £120 out of the first and only premium. If the whole £82,000 had been secured, the premium at 5 per cent. would have been over £4,000.

What could the Insurance Offices be thinking of to take a life on which the *best* reports of the three doctors who examined him reported only second-rate; and one doctor called attention to the fact that Mrs. Palmer had died, heavily insured, a few months previously, after only one premium on £13,000 had been paid, and advised them to be cautious.

On January 31, 1855, Pratt wrote to Dr. Palmer that he had secured a policy for £14,000 from the Prince of Wales Office, but advised him not to press for further insurance from other offices, adding these significant words: *"What would the 'Sun' or 'the Norwich Union' say"* (these offices had just paid their shares of £13,000 on Mrs. Anne Palmer's death) *"to your* speculations if the 'Prince of Wales' or the 'Solicitors and General' offer them any of their risk on Walter's life."

How much did Pratt KNOW? we shall discuss later on in an account of the inquest; but in a few months' time Palmer tried again, and the Gresham had an offer to insure Walter for £10,000, in addition to the £14,000.

The form filled up stated Walter was "unmarried and in good health."

Enquiries were made at Rugeley, and among the replies Mr. Fowke, chemist (afterwards foreman of the Coroner's jury which enquired into Walter's death), gave a very poor report.

Finally, on July 20, 1855, the Gresham agreed to accept the life of an increased premiums, but only on the condition that they should not be called upon to pay within the next FIVE years. Dr. Palmer replied: *"That would not suit my book at all"*[2]—a curious, compromising answer, so, thinking £14,000 better than nothing, Palmer decides to add the heinous crime of fratricide to his other murders, and the first premium was paid.

Living within a few miles of his brother, he began to supply him with unlimited gin and brandy—often two or three bottles a day—placing him under the care of a bottle-holder called Walkenden (with his wife as housekeeper), telling them "Walter is to have all the drink he wishes" and asked Drs. Day and

---

[2] It would inconvenience me. A reference to betting-books in which wagers were recorded. If a man decided not to accept the bet, it wouldn't "suit his book."

Waddell to see him from time to time. The evidence at the inquest will tell us all this (p. 69) and more.

In the meantime, Walter pays a visit of three days to his wife at Liverpool—August 5, 1855—and writes on the 10th, on his return, a kind, affectionate letter to her, much better in health from his absence from his evil surroundings and unlimited drink, and complains in a postscript: "Drink is always at my elbow," and alludes in a cheerful strain to a concert to which he is expecting his sister Sarah to come over.

From the date of his return to Stafford, his brother William sees him almost daily and presses drink on him.

Then we find Palmer buying jalap and prussic acid[3] on August 14 in Wolverhampton, and at the inquest evidence is given of his mixing medicine the same afternoon in the stable at the Junction Hotel, Stafford—a curious place to select for compounding medicine. He goes to see his brother that day and the next, and on the 16th Walter dies at the age of thirty-three, and is buried in the family vault at Rugeley, his three brothers—George the solicitor, William the doctor, Thomas the clergyman—following him to the grave, where he rests for four months and is exhumed in December, by order of the Home Secretary.[4]

When the body was exhumed on December 22, 1855, it was carried from the churchyard across to the Talbot Inn together with that of Mrs. Anne Palmer (see p. 58), and the local jury, after formally viewing the body together with that of Mrs. Anne

---

[3] *Jalap* is a purgative obtained from the root of a Mexican plant. *Prussic acid*: A poisonous liquid containing hydrogen cyanide. Today, it is called hydrocyanic acid.

[4] [Fletcher's footnote] Vittie, the Undertaker at Stafford, stated: "Dr. Palmer ordered on August 16, within an hour of the death, for his brother Walter a strong oak coffin, and a lead coffin, to be sent in at once, and the funeral took place on the following Monday" (August 20).

Here it is as well to call attention to Palmer's Diary, where he enters:

"16th August, Thursday. Walter died"; and on August 20, Monday: "Went to Stafford to get certificates from Dr. Day"; and on (eleven days after death) August 27, Monday: "Went to Stafford to follow Walter to his grave at Rugeley."

The register of burials in the vestry at Rugeley confirms the undertaker's evidence: "Funeral on Monday, 20th"—the commonsense view for the middle of August—and Palmer entered the funeral incorrectly, for 27th, a week later than it occurred.

Palmer as described on p. 58, adjourned to Monday, January 14, 1856.

The jury, after formally viewing the body, adjourned to enquire into the cause of Walter Palmer's death at Stafford in the previous August. It was proved that William had been in close attendance on his sick brother for the last few days of his life, and that he had heavily insured him for £14,000, and had tried for £12,000 more—£26,000 in all.

The first witness called at the adjourned inquest was *Dr. Day*, who said: "I was called in on July 7, six weeks before the death. I was there when he died, and there was no smell of prussic acid, only of brandy, in the fluids escaping from his mouth. I certified, and still believe, that he died from apoplexy and general disease of the digestive organs brought about by excessive drinking of gin and brandy. On April 7, four months previously, Dr. Palmer had brought his brother Walter to me to be examined for life insurance. Both were then strangers to me. I recommended his life, but a few weeks later, from all I was told and saw, I told the company the life was not good.

"I saw him twice daily from August 10 till his death on the 16th. On one of these visits he said, 'Doctor, those pills you sent me yesterday were twisters.' I replied that I had not sent any. 'You must have done so, for my brother William gave them to me out of your box.' I do not make up my own medicines, Masters the chemist had made up all his medicines, so I asked Masters, and he had sent none."

There is no doubt William Palmer had commenced physicking him; but his constant vomiting probably rejected the pills and he had to resort to other means.

Dr. Day added: "I did not know any life assurance had been carried out. When I told William Palmer about the pills, he replied, 'It is one of my brother's drunken delusions; I never gave him pills.'"

Mrs. Walkenden, a sort of cook-housekeeper, said she had known Walter Palmer several months. He had delirium tremens and drank excessively; would take *3 pints* of gin during the night and often a quart in a day.

She was the wife of *Thomas Walkenden*, who was described as a valet and *"bottle-holder."* He was next called, and refused to give evidence till his expenses were paid. But a hint from the Coroner soon settled that. All along he was a most unwilling, prevaricating witness. He said in his evidence: "The last few days Walter drank about three bottles of brandy and gin in a day, and had scarcely anything to eat. His brother William told me to supply him with all he asked for."

Dr. Harland gave evidence that he had reported favourably on his life for insurance a few months before his death.

Dr. Hughes, of Stafford, examined him for insurance in December 1854, eight months before his death, and passed him, but added his previous habits had made his chance of longevity not so good as the average. He owned to an attack of delirium tremens. He also thought the cause of death was apoplexy.

Dr. Monckton made the post-mortem, after the body was exhumed on December 22, and found it much decomposed, the brain quite disorganised, so no opinion could be formed about it, nor about apoplexy, adding: "From the results of my examination, and what I have heard, I think he died from apoplexy, brought by drink. I examined him on December 2nd, 1854, for insurance, and passed him but soon altered my opinion and wrote to the Universal Insurance Company that his life had been rejected by two offices, adding, 'He drinks hard, and has had delirium tremens. His brother insured his own wife a few months before for £13,000. She died after one premium had been paid. BE CAUTIOUS,' I added in large handwriting.

"I met Walter Palmer last June, and he upbraided me for preventing his being insured. I did not know he was already passed for £14,000. Dr. Palmer wrote after Walter's death and asked me not to reply to any letters the Solicitors and General Life Office might write to me. Dr. Palmer came for the insurance certificates of death and tried to suggest some words in them."

Professor Taylor examined most carefully all the organs sent up to him by Dr. Monckton. There was no appearance of disease and no traces of any poison. Dr. Rees agrees, and we both think "he may have died from apoplexy caused by drinking heavily, but the state of the organs prevents any accurate opinion."

Evidence was given that Palmer had bought jalap and prussic acid in Wolverhampton on August 14, as I have previously related; and then the Boots[5] at the Grand Junction

---

[5] A common nickname for a hotel servant responsible for cleaning boots and running odd jobs. Not to be confused with Boots, the pharmacy chain.

Hotel, Stafford, said that "on August 14, two days before Walter Palmer died, Dr. Palmer brought two small medicine bottles to the stable-yard and left them in my care. "He came next day and asked for them, and poured from a bottle which he had left in the stables overnight, into a bottle half-full of medicine which he brought with him, and took them all away with him.

"Mr. Lloyd, the landlord, came in as he was pouring and saw it all.

"Palmer asked me, an hour after his brother's death, to send off a telegram to the Clerk of the Course at Shrewsbury: 'Please tell me who has won the Ludlow Stakes.'"

Thomas Lloyd, the landlord of the Grand Junction Hotel, testified that he came into the stable and saw the pouring from one bottle to another, and added that "Dr. Palmer wished his brother to have the best brandy, as much as he liked, that he (Dr. Palmer) would pay for it and he told me Dr. Day was attending Walter, but that he did not understand his constitution."

On August 14, 1855, Walter and Walkenden came to the Fountain Inn, Wolverhampton, on their way to the races, so the *landlady* testified, and said Walter was drunk and very ill, and had to lie down all the time he was there and was freely supplied with brandy by Walkenden on his brother's orders.

Mrs. Walter Palmer came into Court, but was so broken down that she was taken to a private room by the Coroner and Foreman and the Clerk, who subsequently read her evidence to the jury.

The jury wished to adjourn to call Mr. Pratt, the money-lending solicitor of 5 Queen Street, Mayfair, about the policies, and to recall Professor Taylor and Dr. Day; so the inquest was adjourned to Wednesday, January 23, 1856, when *Dr. Campbell*, of Stoke-on-Trent, who was Walter's doctor for a year to June 1854, told the jury of his great intemperance, and when Walter Palmer spoke of insuring his life he told him his life was too hazardous for any good office to take up. He also said after the evidence he had heard to-day he believed he had died from apoplexy.

Evidence of the proposals up to £70,000 on this life was produced, and three offices accepted him at an increased premium for £14,000. The first premium, £880, was paid by Pratt in April 1855. He was called as a witness at this inquest, and said he held the policy for £14,000, and was a loser of over £4,000 through Dr. Palmer.

After two or three questions by the Coroner and jury, Pratt broke down, screaming excitedly, "How can you ask such questions of a man with three young children and a wife who will probably be ruined by this affair."

It was considered doubtful if he would be able to give evidence at the trial at the Central Criminal Court the following May, but he rallied and appeared in the witness-box on May 20, and the cold, merciless manner in which he gave his evidence made a great impression at the trial, and in a few weeks he became raving mad and—I believe—died shortly afterwards in an asylum.

Dr. Taylor was recalled at the inquest, and said that only from the medical point of view he thought apoplexy might be the cause of death, but the condition in which he found the organs sent to him was not inconsistent with poisoning by prussic acid, although he found no trace of it.

Yet, in spite of this and the evidence of Drs. Monckton Harland, Campbell, Hughes, Day, and Waddell, the local jury returned a verdict of "wilful murder by prussic acid." Of course, at the time of these inquests Palmer was in jail waiting for his trial.

But the Grand Jury at Stafford Assizes threw out the bill against Palmer for poisoning his brother Walter.

CHAPTER VII

Character—Hypocrisy—Group of so-called friends—Resources all gone—Moneylenders' threats—Proposal on Bates's life—Visit of detectives—Cook first appears.

AND NOW, HAVING DISCUSSED THE DEATHS of Leonard Bladen, Mrs. Thornton (Palmer's mother-in-law), and his wife and brother Walter, the last of whom was poisoned in August 1855, we come to the latter part of that year, full of events most important to Palmer, bringing him—none too soon—to the gallows in June 1856, six months after his arrest. But we may as well pause here after Walter's death to calmly look at the general character of the man, now in terrible straits for money, driven to desperation.

To sum up such a character is a very hard task. I know fairly well the late Dr. Mercier, a great authority on morbid developments of the brain. He lived a year or two in Highgate, and frequently visited my senior partner. He says, of the moral imbecile:

> "However astute, clever, dexterous, intelligent his shifts and dodges and stratagems and tricks may be, he is always a failure in the long run.
> "He may succeed in his immediate object. . . . His devious path soon leads him round into disaster; and usually the disaster lies so plain before him that we wonder how a man so superficially clever should be beneath the surface such a fool. He takes the most careful measures against detection by one method, and lays himself open to certain and speedy detection by another method. He has plenty of intelligence, but little or no wisdom. He is a clever fool."

A capital description to sum up Palmer's traits of character and methods.

Palmer's victims feared and distrusted him very definitely. His mother-in-law declared it would be the end of her if she went to stay in his house; she went and it WAS the end of her. His wife, who obviously had grown to dread that anyone whom her husband treated should die, could not have felt that dread without a deadly suspicion of his guilt clutching at her heart when she was ill, yet allowed him to minister to her, though she felt worse after every cup she took from his hands.

And Cook accused him to a friend at Shrewsbury of having deliberately tried to poison him, and still he went on taking food from his hands, and comes back to Rugeley with him to be under his care in the hotel exactly opposite—and in his agony calls out for Palmer, sends for Palmer, and begs him to give him medicine and some relief from his writhing tortures.

The list of murders accredited to Palmer, according to Miss Tennyson Jesse (p. 21 footnote), sums up to fourteen or fifteen. And it was for the last of these—the murder of his friend Cook—that he was hanged. But not before rumour and dark hints of poison had been busy for a long time. But his personality helped him greatly.

He was not twenty-five when he poisoned his mother-in-law, and only thirty when he killed his last victim, Cook. The bland, smiling, youthful doctor, working at his new practice with his round cheeks and fresh complexion, prevented anybody from ever dreaming there was such a sinister figure and murderous, lustful demon hidden below those fairly good looks, with a certain amount of charm and amiability of manner, especially for a class of men (and particularly women) somewhat below him in the social scale.

His so-called pleasant expression never changed. He would remain composed and quiet even in the presence of death brought about by his own hand, when his victims were suffering a lingering death of days, as in the case of his own wife and Bladen, or being hurried into eternity with the agonies of strychnine twisting every joint of the body. Yet his countenance never changed, and he would calmly survey his handiwork.

However sudden and disconcerting his reverses might be on the Turf, he would always pay up his losses with a smile, though now and then he is found murdering his friends to avoid payment, as was the case with Bladen and Cook.

He certainly had a grievous family history, as regards his father and mother and maternal grandmother (as described on p. 38). He was heavily weighted in life's handicap (if one may use his racing simile) by his mother and her many faults, even more than by his father and his shortcomings (as told on p. 38). The curious will of his father hindered his mother from marrying again, so she consoled herself with various immoral liaisons with disreputable men, generally much younger than herself. And there is no doubt the capital house where she continued to live (exactly opposite the church) was the scene of many curious revellings and dissipations with vile debauchery.

Most people were at first favourably impressed by this apparently industrious, rising doctor, and when some gross act was shown against him, they thought it was only a chance slip of the religious, well-mannered, soft-spoken young man. But he was cold-blooded and treacherous with his relentless pursuit of women and money, though he did not APPEAR to have many vices—at any rate, not on the surface before the eyes of his neighbours.

He was an affectionate husband to the wife whom he poisoned, giving her every luxury in his power; but his sensual passions and the lust of greed were too much for him. He was a kind brother to Walter till his time came to be poisoned, owing to the terrible stress for money and for the insurance which was to clear him from the forged bills.

One of the worst and most detestable points in his character was his terrible hypocrisy. He was a most regular attendant at church, making notes in the margin of his Bible about the sermons, frequently partaking of the Sacrament and appearing to worship with great fervour and sincerity a God Whom he mocked at and whose every precept he set at scorn and defiance. For example, he partook of the Sacrament the Sunday after his wife's death, recording in his Diary the solace he had received thereby, when he had already taken his servant-girl Eliza Tharm as his mistress and was living with her in open adultery and his wife only dead a week.

It is a mystery to say whether Palmer was so profoundly and coldly detestable a hypocrite that this assumed piety was part of his relentless scheme, or whether, in that distorted egoism of the true complex criminal, he did not hope that by certain concessions of his mind to the Deity he might not keep his immortal account secure for the hereafter. In this he is more than a mystery, as he was in so many points.

But in a somewhat curious way we must give him credit for kindness, generosity, and hospitality. He was a good loser and a generous winner on all race-courses, but from associating with

THE HIGH STREET, RUGELEY.

Showing Dr. Wm. Palmer's house—and the Talbot Arms, where Cook died.

blacklegs in many deceitful sharp practices he was not allowed in the betting-ring on race-courses, nor at Tattersall's.[1] He was cunning more than clever, associating from choice with those below him in station, to whom he appeared always hail-fellow.

In his pew at church was a Bible which he would study with apparent reverence before the service commenced, and he would read all the responses in the service in a very devoted, loud, saintly voice, and was a most regular attendant at church in Rugeley, but never elsewhere. He was an indulgent husband for four or five years, as long as he was not too closely pressed or questioned about his many absences and various shortcomings.

He was indolent and had no application for work, and as soon as he took to the Turf it so totally absorbed him in mind and body that what little practice he had as a doctor soon left him.

Palmer's Diary, printed for 1855 in Ward & Lock's book[2] on the trial, is most interesting to anyone studying the case. It mentions, amongst many entries, his horrid hypocrisy, which is almost unique in the annals of murderers and almost incredible. We saw his entries at his wife's death and funeral (p. 56), and another entry reads *"At Church—Sacrament,"* now and then even quoting the text of the sermon he listened to.

And when Cook was lying dead, Palmer enters: *"At Church— Hamilton preached,"* within twenty-four hours of the next entry: "Attended a post-mortem examination on poor Cook."

And an entry on October 14: "Went with Willie to Church— Sacrament" (his little boy, not quite seven years old).

His sister Sarah, who lived at "The Yard," his mother's house opposite the church, throughout these troublous years, seemed to live a very different life, and was a regular attendant at the chapel and fond of visiting the poor. A very different character to her mother and her brother William.

After Palmer had been two or three years in practice he had a few friends very firmly attached to him, and staunch, in spite of an unpleasant rumour about his shady transactions on the

---

[1] An auction house that specializes in race horses, founded in 1766 by Richard Tattersall (1724-1795). It was located until 1865 near Hyde Park Corner, then on the edge of London. The business's willingness to transact bets attracted sporting men and gamblers from all classes. It is still in business in Newmarket, Suffolk.

[2] See *The Illustrated Times Trial of William Palmer* from the Peschel Press.

Turf which had caused his expulsion from Tattersall's and the betting-rings on race-courses, but they were scarcely the class of friends a doctor who was commencing practice for his living should have made, and his own brother George the solicitor and his brother Thomas the clergyman could not approve of his mode of living nor of his friends. We read in the trial the evidence of several so-called friends, such as Cheshire, a great friend, the easy-going, deceiving, and obliging postmaster; and Jere Smith, of whom the Attorney-General said *"he blushed for the profession who could number such a man on their Rolls"*; and Newton, drinking freely with him and supplying him with drugs, unknown to his employer, and certainly against his wish, and then turning bitterly on him in the end; Bates the groom, who, to his delight, lunched with Palmer; and George Myatt, the saddler, who went frequently to races with him, even to the last visit to Shrewsbury, and joined in the drinking party at the Raven. These and a few more such characters did their best to spread abroad all his good points—and he had a knack of impressing many in his favour with his bland, soft-soapy manners.

Such is the general outline of this man's character and friends. We will now follow him step by step to the gallows from the date of the murder of his brother Walter (August 1855). We see his many resources for obtaining money were quite exhausted. During the past four years he had obtained vast sums—the share from his father's estate; and the ready money available from his various murders, as the death of his mother-in-law, and the death of Bladen—both under his roof; and the £13,000 paid by the Insurance Office on the murder of his wife a few months before. He now feels there is no time to be lost, as I will show you by Pratt's letters, who writes on September 24, 1855:

"There are three bills of £2,000 each accepted by your Mother, Mrs. Sarah Palmer, falling due in a day or two, and as the Prince of Wales Office money on Walter's death cannot be received for three months, so it is necessary that these bills for £6,000 should be renewed; and I presume the money will be ready to meet them when they do fall due; but there will be a further charge for renewal amounting to £1,500 more than your mother has given acceptances for" —in all £7,500 due in November from one moneylender alone, and more than that from other lenders, Padwick and Wright.

Pratt writes significantly (as I think) on October 6: "I have your note—acknowledging the receipt by your Mother of the acceptance due October 2nd: '*Why not let her acknowledge it herself?*' We hear frequently that no moneylender ever had direct from Mrs. Palmer a single letter or a single receipt or ever saw her."

After two bills had been renewed, Pratt writes on October 18: "You, or your mother, should prepare for payment due in a few days. I cannot obtain delay on the same ground that I did the others, for then I could have no ground for supposing the claim (on Walter's life policy) would not be admitted."

And so the torture-screw to meet these forged bills was being painfully turned on by Pratt, and he writes severely about the bills, adding: "No writs against your mother shall be served till the morning of Saturday, November 10th, before that date you are to send up £1,200, and, of course, you and your mother are not forgetting the £1,500 due November 9th" —a total of £2,700, chiefly for interest and for postponing the forged bills.

Writs were issued on Tuesday, November 6, for £4,000, but to be held over for four days.

Owing to the various bill discounters—Padwick and Wright, as well as Pratt, holding about £16,000 of forged acceptances and £4,000 demanded by November 9, for interest, etc.— Palmer, driven to his wits' end to avoid the forger's doom of lifelong imprisonment, is distracted to find what steps he can take to *immediately* raise £5,000, and £10,000 later on. He looks around and decides to try life insurance again, which had so well answered in the case of his wife, and he is hoping it is also succeeding in the case of his brother. So now he tries to insure an under-groom, George Bates, for £25,000, who stated at the trial that he lived in a room in a cottage at 6s. 6d. a week, and received wages about 24s. a week.

He was invited to dine with Cook and Jere Smith and Saunders the trainer at Palmer's, one day in September 1855. The Judge at the trial asked him pointedly, "Did you sit down at the same table with them?" "Yes, and drank freely with them all." He called himself stable-keeper, handyman, and after a good dinner "something was said about insuring my life, either by Cook or Palmer, and they explained how useful it would be to me to be able to borrow five hundred pounds on the policy." They presently produced an application form in blank, and Bates signed it, Cook's name appearing as witness, Cheshire the postmaster and Saunders the trainer as referees.

That disgraceful lawyer, Jere Smith, Palmer's boon companion (of whom much more hereafter), was to take 5 per cent, on the first premium of £500 and was appointed agent to the Sun for this policy.

It is noteworthy that in all Palmer's dealings with life insurances the policies were on the cheapest rate with no bonus attached, and thus the lowest premium was paid.

Bates is described on the policy as a gentleman "living independent, with good property and possessing a fine cellar of wine." It would be hard to beat such a tissue of lies.

Insurance Companies, not feeling easy at the late deaths in Rugeley, sent down Field, a detective, who called first on Cheshire the postmaster, one of the referees, who told him that Bates had £400 a year private means, and was an industrious man. Then Field, looking for Bates, found him—hoeing turnips and manuring a field!!! Bates knew very little about insurance and thought it was for £4,000, of which he was to have £1,000 within a year, and confidentially asked Field if he thought that was his fair share and would he have a vote for the County, a thing of very different value to the present time.

Field and his colleague, Simpson, were naturally very astonished at the proposal for £10,000 on Bates's life, so when down at Rugeley made enquiries about Walter Palmer, his mode of life and his death. They decided in their own minds there had been foul play, so wrote and advised the Company not to pay the £14,000 due on Walter's death.

Then Field and Simpson, calling on Palmer, discussed with him Walter's death, told him over the nuts and wine that many were suspicious of foul play and there ought to be an enquiry. "By all means," said Palmer. Field replied: "The Office has decided convictions that your brother was poisoned, for the purpose of obtaining the £14,000 insurance money, and as you, Dr. Palmer, were the most interested, you would be called to give evidence, and if a claim is preferred it will at once be met with a charge of murder"; and after a further warning, he left Palmer.

If this statement is correct as to that interview, it seems to me hushing up a horrible affair, intimating, "We believe you to be the murderer, but if you make no claim on us, we shall not proceed further."

Simpson and Field say their object was to protect their offices from paying a policy illegally claimed. I think it goes very near to "compounding a felony" of a terrible nature—murder.

This is one of the occasions on which, I think, ruin staring Palmer in the face, he lost his head, for however can a man, earning a pound a week, require a policy of £25,000, of which the first year's premium was quoted at £500? And so Bates's proposal was declined, and that with unpleasant hints. So we must look on Palmer more abandoned and more desperate than ever, totally unable to meet even the £2,000 required for interest by the grasping, devouring moneylenders.

He has a large racing establishment with twelve or thirteen race-horses in training at Hednesford, a few miles from Rugeley, and with the grooms and hangers-on the expenses there are terrible, in addition to several loose women constantly draining his ready money. Yet he is always hoping some piece of luck may turn up on the race-course.

Just now he has an important race coming on at Shrewsbury on November 15, and his friend Cook a horse likely to win a race there on the 13th.

This friend, John Parsons Cook, now becomes the chief centre of the remainder of Palmer's life. He was about twenty-seven years of age, and had been on very close terms of friendship with Palmer for about two years. His stepfather thought he had greatly deteriorated since he had known Palmer. He had been staying a month with him in the spring of this year, and he thought him looking so much stronger and in good health; also Cook had confided to his stepfather, of whom he was very fond, that at the end of this year he was going to give up racing altogether, probably after the races at Shrewsbury.

John Parsons Cook was a young man who had gone the pace pretty extensively. He had been articled to a solicitor at Worthing. He dressed rather showily, with a good many rings and a conspicuous watch-chain, was a cheerful fellow enough, fond of a good drink, and always hopeful that he would regain the fortune he had lost upon the Turf. Cook had a horse, whose name was to become famous outside Sporting circles, entered for the Shrewsbury Handicap—a horse called Polestar. Cook was in luck that day, or so he thought. But, as we shall see, it proved his ruin, and it caused his being murdered by Palmer.

CHAPTER VIII

At Shrewsbury Races—Brandy tampered with—Cook very sick—
Returns with Palmer to Rugeley—The aged Dr. Bamford called in—
Elizabeth Mills very sick after broth—Palmer meets Herring in
London and collects Cook's bets—Returns late to Rugeley—Obtains
three grains strychnine from Newton—Meets Jere Smith.

COOK GOES WITH CHESHIRE AND PALMER to Shrewsbury Races on
Tuesday, November 13, where his horse Polestar is to run that
afternoon in the Shrewsbury Handicap. And he may win about
£3,000 in stakes and bets, and in a moment of great excitement
he does win. Palmer, too, had a horse, Nettle, running on
Thursday, the 15th, and may win £5,000. But he lost his race.

Here I must pause for a moment, for I believe up to this
Tuesday's race Palmer had not decided to murder Cook, but
now, knowing he is coming in to £2,000 or £3,000, determines to
poison him, obtain that sum, and so stave off Pratt's
importunities for a few weeks. And, as we shall see, he succeeded
in getting all Cook's winnings except £300, the stakes which the
Clerk of the Course delayed to send up to Tattersall's. If Cook's
horse did not win the handicap, his death would not benefit
Palmer; and till that race was won, I don't think Palmer had
decided to kill him.

If he had intended to kill him under any circumstances,
why go to Shrewsbury to commence the poisoning? It is worth
noticing that Palmer started *alone* to return to Rugeley within
an hour of Cook's horse winning the race on Tuesday. Why did
he go and leave all his friends merry-making over Cook's
victory at Shrewsbury?

At home he found two or three important letters waiting,
one from Pratt urgently demanding money with threats; and if
there had been hesitation before, this decided Cook's fate.

Palmer took back with him some antimony in the form of
tartar emetic, a white powder, colourless in water.[1] And with

---

[1] *Antimony* was used in ancient times for cosmetics. It is also
poisonous, causing symptoms similar to arsenic. It can also be used
as an emetic. *Tartar emetic* is antimony potassium tartrate, a
compound used in dyes, to treat animals, and to cause vomiting in
patients (which is what an emetic does). Tartar emetic is still used in
some countries outside Europe and the U.S. to treat alcohol abuse.

George Myatt, the saddler, he returned to Shrewsbury early on Wednesday morning. On this Wednesday evening Palmer, together with Cook, Cheshire, Myatt, Fisher, Herring, and Read, dine at the Raven Hotel. After dinner Palmer leaves the rest and goes to a sort of housemaid's pantry with glass sides at the end of the passages where a Mrs. Brookes, who had called to see him about jockeys, etc., coming up the corridor, sees him pouring some fluid (colour of water) from a small bottle into a tumbler and shaking it up, holding it to the gaslight to see if it is clear. She spoke to him. He, not at all disconcerted, replied, "I will be with you in a minute," and soon joined her.

Then he goes into the sitting-room where the half-dozen men are making merry, and brandy is brought in on a tray with tumblers. They all have glasses handed round to drink, and suddenly Cook jumps up, exclaiming, "Good God, how it burns my throat," and puts his tumbler down. Palmer took up the tumbler, drank the remainder, and handed the glass to Read, saying, "Taste it; there's nothing in it. Cook says it is drugged."

Read said, "What is the good of giving it to me when you have drunk the very dregs!"

The rest of the company thought it very odd that Palmer should drain the very dregs from Cook's glass, for no man would drain a friend's tumbler when he had complained it had been tampered with.

But it is doubtful if Palmer swallowed it. Though the guests and the juries and all who studied the matter were strongly of opinion this brandy and water which Cook swallowed had been drugged with tartar emetic, yet no attempt has ever been offered to explain HOW Cook's grog was drugged and none of the other six glasses. Fisher, in his evidence, says when he went in there were half-full glasses of "grog" in front of all the guests, including Palmer, who refused to have any more unless Cook drank up his—which he immediately did, and at once exclaimed how it burnt his throat. Some of the guests afterwards remarked that there were two jugs of water of different sizes brought in with the first tray, but nobody was clear on that point. Read said, in his evidence, a second decanter was ordered just after he got into the room; but the evidence did not clear up at all whether the smaller jug of water was used for Cook alone, or whether Palmer may have mixed the grog, as they called it, and slipped the solution of antimony into Cook's glass. This latter seems the more likely.

Another and most probable solution is that the grog was

ready mixed in the seven different tumblers before the tray was brought in, and Palmer, knowing which had been drugged, took care that Cook had the right glass. But it is certainly not clear how Cook was drugged at The Raven on this Wednesday night.

Cook, feeling very ill, went into his bedroom, taking Herring and Fisher with him. He vomited freely, and said, "I believe that damned Palmer has been dosing me." He took off his money-belt and gave all his money that he had received on the course, nearly £800, to Fisher, and said, "Take care of this for me."

They at once sent for a doctor, who prescribed for him, but being much worse about 4 a.m., they had to send again for help.

In the morning of Thursday he was a little better, and able to get up after breakfast; and walking down to the race-course, Fisher gave him back his £800, and joining up with Herring he said, "Don't you think I was drugged last night by Palmer?"

Herring returned an evasive answer, and went on to say, "If you so mistrust the man, why are you going back to Rugeley with him to-night?"

And Cook replied in sorrow, "I really must go—you don't know all!"

On this Thursday Palmer sees his horse Nettle lose a race for which he had heavily backed him, and his last hope FOR READY MONEY was dashed to the ground. He returns with Cook to Rugeley late on this Thursday evening; Cook went straight to bed at the Talbot Hotel, exactly opposite Palmer's house, and lay there till Friday afternoon when he got up and dined with Palmer, meeting Jere Smith, the solicitor.

On Saturday, Palmer went over early and ordered some coffee, which the chambermaid brought and left with Palmer in Cook's room. Cook vomited up the coffee and throughout the day was constantly sick and very ill. Palmer, in and out all day, seeing to his diet and the medicine.

On Sunday morning, Cook being no better, Palmer called in the aged Dr. Bamford, whom my former partner went to help with his practice. Dr. Bamford was now eighty years of age. With the high character he held all round the neighbourhood, he was above all suspicion at conniving at Palmer's crimes. But did no twinge of doubt ever enter his aged brain at the number of sick people his brother-surgeon in Rugeley had called him to treat and to give certificates at their death? He was an old friend of the Palmer family. He had attended Dr. William Palmer at his birth, and figures very prominently in the last six years of Palmer's life.

He was a kindly, fumbling old gentleman, ever accommodating to William Palmer, and the doddering old doctor always took his friend's word, the rising young surgeon, as to what his patients (alias his poisoned victims) were suffering from, and even prescribed whatever innocuous drugs he was asked for. This invaluable complacent medical friend made up the sedative pills for Cook on the Tuesday night, carefully writing full directions on the box as he was required to do by Dr. Palmer.

He filled up the death certificate the day before the post-mortem, putting apoplexy as the cause of death, again at Dr. Palmer's suggestion. But these pills and this death certificate were the last, the very last, of nine victims he had certified (Mrs. Thornton, Bladen, Cook, Bly, Mrs. Anne Palmer, and her four infants), not to mention any illegitimate children, of whom several died under treatment. The last was Eliza Tharm's baby in Palmer's house only a few weeks before he was arrested.

Whether Dr. Bamford was legally qualified I cannot ascertain, as there was no Medical Register kept in those days. But he was in practice before 1803, and medical men in practice before 1858 did not necessarily require any qualifications nor to pass any examinations.

Dr. Bamford was now called in to the last of the many victims he had attended for Palmer.

A remarkable thing happened on this Sunday afternoon, which told heavily against Palmer at his trial.

Jere Smith sent over from his rooms at the Albion Inn some soup to Palmer's house, which he said he thought Cook would like. Why was it not sent direct to Cook's hotel? It stood by the fire in Palmer's dining-room, and in an hour's time Palmer took it across and gave Cook a little, which brought on great sickness. The rest was sent down to be kept hot by the kitchen fire at the Talbot Hotel. As it smelt very good, the chambermaid, Elizabeth Mills, took two spoonfuls of it. In less than an hour she was taken very ill with severe vomiting and had to go to bed for the rest of the day. She gave very emphatic evidence at the trial. The remainder of this broth was taken upstairs to Cook's room. He only took one or two more spoonfuls and again commenced vomiting, passing a very wretched night.

It struck the housekeeper and maid-servants at the Talbot Hotel as peculiar that broth should be prepared at another inn in the town for a gentleman staying at their hotel, and thought there must be some reason for this "*gift*" said to come through Palmer from Jere Smith, who lived at the Albion.

DR. BAMFORD OF RUGELEY.

THE OLD POST OFFICE AS IT WAS IN 1906 AND NOW.

Why could not Jere Smith, the solicitor, send it direct to Cook at the Talbot Hotel, instead of sending it to Palmer to send across the road? And this broth was in a peculiar two-handled cup which belonged to Palmer, and the man who carried it across found it standing by Palmer's fire.

Palmer hurried across about 7 a.m. on Monday morning, and told Cook he had to go to London on business. He had written to George Herring, the commission agent[2] to meet him at 1 p.m. at some Chambers in Beaufort Buildings, off the Strand.[3] When they met, Palmer apologised for Cook not coming up, but that he was too ill, and had entrusted him with a list of bets which were to be received at Tattersall's on this Monday afternoon. He read out a list of names and the various sums due from each, making a total of nearly £2,000. Out of this Herring was to pay Pratt £450 and Padwick £350, and various sums due from Palmer to pressing creditors.

All this was faithfully carried out by Herring, and before they parted, Palmer asked him to have some brandy which stood on the table. He declined, and at his death a few years ago several writers in the paper said it was fortunate he did decline, as Palmer had probably drugged it. I certainly do not think so, for what was Palmer to gain by poisoning him? Nothing at all—and a great deal to lose by his death. Palmer, being a defaulter, was not allowed in any betting-ring, nor at Tattersall's. He had abstracted Cook's betting-book, from

---

[2] [Fletcher's footnote] George Herring was a commission agent, and held in high esteem by all who dealt with him. He prospered beyond expectation, became an intimate friend of King Edward VII, was one of the founders of the King Edward Hospital Fund, and died, unmarried, in 1906, a millionaire, leaving most of his money to hospitals and charities. His *nom de plume* was "Mr. Howard" and he was at one time commissioner for Sir Joseph Hawley, and won largely over the great races in which this owner's horses were successful. Hitherto Fisher had been Cook's usual commission agent, and was greatly surprised he did not have the commission to collect these bets at Tattersall's. Moreover Cook owed him £200, which he would have deducted from what he would be receiving for Cook and repaid himself. He never received his £200. Subsequently Herring was very angry at thus being duped by Palmer to collect Cook's money and pay Palmer's bills with it. Fisher would have known the money collected was Cook's alone, and would have also known Pratt's and Padwick's bills were Palmer's, and would not have used Cook's money to pay them.

[3] Palmer stayed at a boarding house there. The buildings were torn down to build the Savoy Theatre, which opened in 1881.

which he had made this list of bets to be collected. And if they were not collected and Pratt paid the £450 on account, the writs against his mother would be served forthwith. So I cannot believe it would be to Palmer's interest to kill Herring there and then. Herring wrote that night to Cook, telling him how far he had succeeded at Tattersall's. But this letter only reached Palmer's hands.

As soon as he had arranged all this with Herring, Palmer returned to Rugeley, reached Stafford at a quarter to nine, and drove over in a "fly"[4] from the station to Rugeley, about eight miles, and going direct to Mr. Salt's surgery obtained three grains of strychnine from Newton, the assistant.

The Crown says Palmer went on to his own surgery, made up this strychnine into two pills, took them across to the Talbot Hotel, and administered them to Cook. But Jere Smith says he met Palmer getting out of the carriage at his surgery door about 9.30, and Palmer asked how Cook was. Smith replied he had been so busy all day at Lichfield he had not been to see him. He adds in his evidence at the trial: "Then we both went straight across to see Cook, who upbraided me for never going near him all day, and added, 'As you were so late, I have taken old Bamford's pills' "; thus wanting to prove Palmer never gave him his strychnine pills that evening.

A great controversy here arises, which depends, on the part of the Defence, on the word and statement of Jere Smith, the solicitor, Palmer's boon companion.

The Defence attempted to prove an alibi entirely on Smith's evidence. He was a man of most disreputable character, living about 100 yards from Palmer's house.

He is not to be confounded with Palmer's solicitor, rejoicing in the name of John Smith, of Waterloo Street, Birmingham, generally known as "*Jack Smith of Brum,*" a lawyer with a large practice and a great reputation for making the very most of his cases, and sparing no pains, no trouble, to win against any odds. He had defended many prisoners for all sorts of offences, and restored to Society some who had better have been under lock and key.

This John Smith conducted Palmer's defence from the first inquest up to his execution.

But Jeremiah Smith (called in Palmer's Diary Jere Smith) was a man of low character and a loose companion of Palmer, already

---

[4] A light carriage used to carry passengers or deliver goods.

associated with him in many revellings and low-class jollities and some nasty shady affairs, including the insurance schemes of Palmer's victims. His relations with Palmer's mother had been most disreputable and scarcely denied by him in the witness-box. He got appointed agent to the Sun Life Insurance Office and introduced Mrs. Anne Palmer for a heavy insurance, and when the first premium of nearly £800 was paid he claimed his heavy commission.

He also recommended George Bates, the groom, for insurance up to £25,000, which Palmer was only too anxious to carry out, but, as we saw, it failed. This Jere Smith made a sad exhibition of himself at the great trial in London, for his behaviour under the merciless cross-examination he underwent at the hands of the Attorney-General must have exercised a powerful influence on the minds of the jury, as it did on every person in Court who heard it, for he admitted very reluctantly, after keen pressing, that he had witnessed the assignment of the policy for £14,000 by Walter to William Palmer, and received £5 for so doing, also that he wrote to the Sun and other offices and tried to insure Bates for £25,000.[5]

---

[5] The attorney-general's cross-examination of Jeremiah Smith's role in the insurance scheme produced moments of lawyerly evasion worthy of Bill Clinton:

Q: I ask you, sir, as an attorney and a man of business, whether you cannot tell me whether you were applied to by William Palmer to attest a proposal for an assurance for 13,000*l.* on the life of Walter Palmer?

A: I say that I do not recollect it. If I could see any document on the subject I dare say I should remember it.

Q: Do you remember getting a 5*l.* note for attesting an assign-ment by Walter Palmer to his brother of such a policy?

A: Perhaps I might. I don't recollect positively.

Q: (Handing a document to witness) Is that your signature?

A: It is very like my signature.

Q: Have you any doubt about it?

A: (After considerable hesitation) I have some doubt.

Q: Read the document, and tell me, on your solemn oath, whether it is your signature.

A: I have some doubt whether it is mine.

Q: Read the document, sir. Was it prepared in your office?

A: It was not.

Q: I will have an answer from you on your oath one way or another. Isn't that your handwriting?

A: I believe that it is not my handwriting. I think that it is a very good imitation of my handwriting.

Baron ALDERSON. — Did you ever make such an attestation?

A: I don't recollect, my Lord.

CHAPTER IX

Jere Smith fails to prove an alibi for Palmer—Cross-examined by the Attorney-General—Palmer writes from jail an outline of Jere Smith's evidence—Did Cook take Palmer's pills on the Monday night?—Why was the "fly" driver not called?—Cook's terrible attack after strychnine.

WHEN IN THE WITNESS-BOX this Jere Smith made a most sorry exhibition of himself at the hands of the Attorney-General, who, merciless in his attitude and language, found an easy prey in this man. After five minutes he shook like a leaf, trembling all over, with the perspiration running off his head, and stammered out his replies. Once he commenced an answer with:

"Mr. Attorney, I am—"

"Don't 'Mr. Attorney' me, sir. But answer honestly, if you can, my questions. Where, in the course of 1854 or 1855 were you living? In Rugeley?"—"In 1854 I think I resided partly with William Palmer; sometimes I was at his mother's."

"Did you sleep at his mother's?"—"Sometimes."

"When you slept at his mother's, where did you sleep?"—"In a room."

"Was it in hers?"—"No."

"I ask you, upon your oath, whether you were not intimate with her—you know what I mean?"—"I was not; no more intimate with her than the proper intimacy that ought to exist."

"How often were you in the habit of sleeping at her house, having your own place of residence in Rugeley?"—"Frequently I slept there; I cannot say the number of times, but frequently."

"Two or three times a week?"—"Yes, I should say I did."

"Having your own place of abode in Rugeley?"—"Yes."

"Are you a single or a married man?"—"Single."

"How long did this habit and practice of sleeping two or three times a week at Mrs. Palmer's continue?"—"Several years."

"Had you your own lodgings at Rugeley at the time?"—"Yes, my own chambers at Rugeley at the time; I had chambers in Rugeley; lodging's."

OLD MRS. PALMER'S HOUSE.

Called in 1855 "The Yard"; now "Glan Camlas."

"Your own bedroom, I suppose?"—"Yes, I had a bedroom."

"How far is your house from Mrs. Palmer's?"—" I should say it is nearly a quarter of a mile."

"Will you be so good as to explain how it happened that, having your own place of abode and your own bedroom, for several years you slept two or three times a week at Mrs. Palmer's house?"—"Sometimes some of the members of the family used to come and visit her; her sons."

"It was too far, I suppose, when you went to see the members of the family, to dine and drink tea, to return a quarter of a mile?"—"I used to stop and have a glass or two of gin and water, and play at cards."

Lord Campbell: "You went to the mother's to see them?"—"Yes."

The Attorney-General: "But you did not sleep at the mother's to see them. How was it that you did not go home?"—"I had no particular reason why I did not."

"Why did you not?"—"I used to have some gin and water and smoke, and if it was late they used to say, 'You had better stop all night.'"

"Did this go on three times a week for several years?"—"Yes; but I used to stop there frequently when there was no one there, neither the mother, nor the sons nor anyone."

This cross-examination was one of the great features of the trial, and it left Jere Smith a ruined man as far as reputation and honour are concerned if he could be held in lower estimation than he had been before held in Rugeley as one of Palmer's bosom friends.

Lord Campbell said to the jury in his summing up, "Can you believe a man who so disgraces himself in the witness-box? It is for you to say if you think Smith spoke the truth."

And the Attorney-General's remarks about him are worth quoting: "Had we known what Smith was going to prove, we should have been able to meet him with contradictory evidence. I need not say that any would have been better than the evidence of that miserable man whom we saw exhibited to-day." These remarks will come in my summary of the Attorney-General's reply. But I quote them here to show what sort of man Jere Smith was.

"Such a spectacle I never saw in my recollection in any Court of Justice. He calls himself a member of the legal profession. I blush for it to number such a man upon its Rolls.

"There was not one man who heard him to-day that is not

satisfied he came here to tell a false tale. There cannot be a man who is not convinced he had been mixed up in many a villainy with Palmer which, if not perpetrated, has been attempted, and he comes here now to save, if he can, the life of his companion and friend, the son of the woman with whom he has had that intimacy which he sought to-day in vain to disguise."

And it is on this man's evidence that they attempted to prove the alibi. He was kept back by the Defence to the very end, and called as the last witness to prove an alibi concerning Palmer's giving pills on the Monday night to Cook, and, strange as it may seem, I believe he partly spoke the truth.

Both versions may be true, and agree, for Palmer did procure the strychnine, and go to his surgery and make up two pills, and may have met Jere Smith, or Smith may have called at the surgery, then both went across and gave Cook pills—or Palmer, as I think, went alone with the strychnine pills and gave them in place of Bamford's, which would be lying there. If so, the conversation about their being late and that Cook had already taken his pills was a deliberate lie on Smith's part. I have seen and copied a letter from Palmer, WRITTEN FROM JAIL during the trial, to Jere Smith, where he tells him word for word the version he is to give in his evidence when in the witness-box, and he gave it, little thinking of that cross-examination in store for him at the hands of the Attorney-General.

Here are the letters (exactly copied), as shown to me by the Governor of Stafford Jail.

DEAR JERE, —

No man in the world ever committed a grosser case of Perjury than that vile wretch Newton—he positively swore last Friday 16 May, that he let me have 3 grs. of Strychnine the Monday night before Cook's death and that I went to Mr. Salt's Surgery for it, and got it from him at 9 o'clock.

It is a base lie, for I left London on that very night at 5 o'clock by Express and arrived at Stafford at 10 minutes to 9, brought a Fly from the Junction and arrived at Rugeley at Masters' door about 10 o'clock.

Now as there is a God in Heaven (I am sure you can't have forgotten it) you know that you were waiting for my coming and when I got out of the Fly you told me that my mother wanted to see me particularly, and after bidding Cook good night we walked together down to the YARD [Mrs. Palmer's house], and got a good brushing from the old Lady about a writ of Brown's that Arminshaw had sent for; that Arminshaw told to George and George to my mother—and if you recollect she was very cross.

We then walked back to my house and you said, "Well, let me have a glass of spirit." I went to the cupboard and there was none—you said "Never mind" and bid me good night. This must have been after 11 o'clock—now I should like to know how I could get to Mr. Salt's shop at 9 o'clock on that night. You can also prove this truth, that Cook dined with me (and you) at my house on the Friday before his death and that we had a quantity of Wine. Cook then went with you and had a glass of Brandy and Water—and that he was then the worse for liquor. You can further prove that Cook handed me some money on this day, for he told you so in my presence when he gave you the £10. He told you at the same time I had won over £1,000 on his mare at Shrewsbury and lastly you can prove that he and I betted for each other, that we had "Pyrrhine" jointly,[1] and that we had had bill transactions together. These are solemn truths and I am fully persuaded that they cannot have escaped your memory.

Therefore let it be your most bounden duty to come forward and place yourself in the witness-box and on your oath speak these great truths. Then rest assured you will lie down on a downy pillow and go to sleep happy.

Bear in mind I only want the truth. I ask for no more.

Yours faithfully,
WM. PALMER.

Newton no doubt calculated upon my coming by the luggage train,[2] but this had been discontinued more than a month—thus my reason for going to Stafford.

DEAR JERE,—

Do, for God's sake, tell the Truth—if you will only consider I am sure you will recollect meeting me at Masters' steps the night Monday the 19th of Nov. I returned from London and you told me my mother wanted to see me. I replied, "Have you

---

[1] A race horse Cook owned that Palmer was trying to acquire through Smith's perjury.

[2] [Fletcher's footnote] Luggage train mentioned in Diary, August 22.

seen Cook? and how is he?" You said, "No." I then said, "We will go upstairs and see him." We did do so. When upstairs Cook said "Dr., you are late, Mr. Bamford has sent me two pills which I have taken," and he said to you, "Damn you, Jere, how is it you have never been to see me?" You replied that you had been busy all the day settling Mr. Ingram's affairs and we then wished him good night and went to my mother's.

Yours ever faithfully,
WM. PALMER.

I have shown (on page 86) that Jere Smith says he saw Palmer getting out of the "fly" at his surgery door, when he had driven over from Stafford about 10 p.m., and was with him continuously till 11.30. That they first went up to speak to Cook, who, Smith said, upbraided them for not coming earlier, and added that he had taken the pills that Bamford had sent. But for this we have only Jere Smith's word. It was proved at the trial that Dr. Bamford had been to see Cook during the day and had left a box of pills with the chambermaid about 7 p.m. They were placed by her on the dressing-table in Cook's room, *not* within reach of his bed.

The Crown contended that he had not taken Bamford's pills, but that Palmer had used the strychnine just obtained from Newton, and made up into two pills which he gave Cook, instead of the pills from Dr. Bamford's pill-box; for if Cook had already taken Bamford's pills, Palmer must, in addition, have given his two pills which produced the strychnine tetanic symptoms. It is scarcely likely that Cook took *four* pills. If the question had depended on this Monday night alone, the Crown could not have pressed for conviction; but in addition to Newton's account of the gift of strychnine, there is no doubt that Palmer paid a visit to Cook's room about 10.30 p.m. and administered two pills to him; for Cook himself tells the chambermaid next morning: "IT WAS THE PILLS THAT PALMER GAVE ME LAST NIGHT THAT CAUSED MY AGONY."[3] And Palmer tells Dr. Bamford: "*I saw Cook about half-past ten last night.*" He

---

[3] From the testimony of Elizabeth Mills on the first day:

"He asked me if I had ever seen any one suffer such agony as he did last night? I said, no, I never had. He said he should think I should not like to see any one like it again. I said, 'What do you think was the cause of all that agony?' He said, 'The pills which Palmer gave me at half-past 10.'"

does not mention Smith being with him.[4]

After giving the pills, Palmer left and walked up to his mother's house (a five-minutes' walk) with Jere Smith, and after a rather stormy ten minutes' interview, both returned and parted at Palmer's door.

But what actually did occur in the bedroom about ten-thirty can never be known. Cook was dead, Palmer's mouth, as a prisoner, was closed; and so only Jere Smith's version is all we have available, and that is worth nothing at all. In a letter written from prison (p. 91), Palmer recapitulates to Smith the trend of events of that evening exactly as he wished Smith to relate from the witness-box—and he did so.

But it has always been a mystery to me why neither side called the driver of the "fly" from The Junction Railway Inn at Stafford who drove Palmer from Stafford Station to Rugeley (*vide* p. 86) at 9 p.m. on Monday. The Crown could have summoned him, and we should then have known at what time Palmer reached Rugeley and if any man met him as he was getting out of the "fly" at his door, and if he had stopped at the chemist's. The Defence would have scored a great point if the driver had said they only reached Rugeley by 10.10, and that a gentleman did meet Palmer when he got out of the "fly," and that they had never stopped at the chemist's. There could have been no difficulty in finding the driver, for in two days Cook was dead, and within ten days the inquest commenced, and suspicion was rife all round. Besides, The Junction was not a large inn, and the driver of the cab could have been easily found, who drove at 9 o'clock to Rugeley—not an everyday drive by a great deal. And there were only three carriages for hire at the inn. The arrival of the train was proved by railway officials [8.45]: Palmer came by it from London. There was no other way of reaching Rugeley from Stafford than by road at that time of night. And it is to me almost the greatest mystery in the conduct of the case that neither side called the cabman.

I mentioned this to Serjeant Huddleston at Worcester about twenty years after the trial, and he had forgotten the details, but was certain the Defence had interviewed the driver, but did not produce him—he could not remember why the Crown

---

[4] Fletcher has the wrong time. According to William Bamford's testimony on the sixth day: "I saw Palmer on the Tuesday morning. I was going to see Cook when he met me. I asked him if he had seen Cook the night before. He said that he saw him between 9 and 10 o'clock, and was with him for half-an-hour."

did not put him in the witness-box.

But six months had elapsed from the day of this drive over from Stafford before Newton mentioned the gift of three grains of strychnine.

The occurrences on that Monday evening cannot be pressed home for a conviction by themselves, only as an adjunct to the fatal pills on Tuesday and the death of Cook. The scientific evidence all agreed that an hour after administering the pills is the average time we can expect before they begin their work. Palmer knew enough of dispensing to make up the strychnine into pills with the hardest stuff, and thus made up, they would take some time to dissolve in the stomach.

What, then, is one to say about this Monday night? I believe Newton spoke the truth about the gift for reasons already given, and three grains were given to Palmer. But I also think it was very inferior strychnine, kept in a sort of open surgery for some time. In all probability there was no sale for such a drug. Anyhow, it did not do its work. I certainly think Palmer went up on his arrival to Cook's room with his three grains of strychnine pills, and gave them to Cook about 10.30. He tells Bamford next morning he had visited Cook about ten, and does not mention Jere Smith being with him, and I have shown that Cook remarked to the maid next morning, "The pills that Palmer gave me caused my agony."

When Palmer left Cook to walk up to his mother's on "important business," Cook was left alone, and we have no knowledge when the pills began their work. But about 11.30 he was seized with cramping spasms and calling for help. The waitress, Lavinia Barnes, went in, and found him sitting up in bed, beating the bedclothes and shrieking with the pain and the feeling of suffocation.

She sent the "Boots" across the road for Dr. Palmer, who came and tried to cheer up and reassure the sufferer, and fetched some medicine, a darkish fluid, in a glass, and Cook's teeth snapped at the glass when held to his lips, but the draught was not retained in his stomach.

Lavinia Barnes left the room about 1 a.m., leaving Palmer and Elizabeth Mills with Cook, who had begun to show signs of great improvement. She is uncertain about the time, and in cross-examination says: "It might have been a quarter past ten when Palmer first came in, and I met him on the stairs going up to Cook's room, but I think it was later."

Suppose it was half-past ten, then this fills up Palmer's

time EXACTLY as the Crown contended. Palmer arrived at Stafford at a quarter to nine, drives to Rugeley by a quarter to ten, buys the strychnine, goes home, makes up the pills, and carries them across to Cook by 10.30.

One point not alluded to at the trial is that Lavinia Barnes says, "I met *Palmer* on the stairs about ten going up to Cook's room." She does not say Jere Smith was with him. Surely she would have said in her evidence, "I met Dr. Palmer AND MR. SMITH on the stairs." But neither at the inquest nor at the trial does she ever allude to meeting Smith *with* Palmer on the stairs. Thus we have no evidence but Jere Smith's own word that he ever went up to Cook's room with Palmer. I believe Palmer went up alone, sat a short time chatting, gave him the pills about 10.30, went up to his mother's, and back home— not to bed—and was fetched by the "Boots" about a quarter to twelve.

Anyhow, the symptoms of the attack are well described by Barnes and Mills—snapping at the glass, projecting eyeballs, afraid of suffocation, twisting and jerking the whole body.

"THE PILLS THAT PALMER GAVE ME AT HALF-PAST TEN MADE ME ILL," is the remark Cook made to Mills next morning. And it is plain that this remark went a long way to convince the jury that Palmer DID administer two pills on the Monday night, and therefore he had obtained strychnine from Newton, and if so it was very strong evidence confirming his guilt.

After Palmer left him—about 10.45—Cook was left alone, and we have no accurate knowledge when the symptoms and pains of strychnine poisoning began, and the pills showed their effect. The waitress, Lavinia Barnes, is the first to go on the scene, about 11.30, and calls up Elizabeth Mills. Sarah Bond, the housekeeper, said she was fetched about a quarter to twelve, just as Palmer came in, and all gave strong evidence of the nature and symptoms of Cook's sufferings.

CHAPTER X

Palmer buys strychnine, prussic acid, and laudanum at Hawkins's shop—Much confused when Newton came in—The Judge and Attorney-General comment on Newton, who appears a shuffler—Dr. Jones arrives and meets Dr. Bamford and Palmer—They agree to give Cook some pills which Palmer fetched—And gives two pills to Cook—Who is seized in an hour with terrible convulsions and dies in fifteen minutes.

WHATEVER DOUBT WE MAY HAVE about the strychnine in the pills given on Monday night, there is no doubt about Palmer buying strychnine on Tuesday morning, and administering pills on the Tuesday night. Whether the strychnine from Newton had lost some of its strength by being kept too long in the shop, or whether Palmer had not put enough in the pills, or whether, as some contend, Palmer did not wish to kill Cook on the Monday night, but only to prepare those round him for attacks of convulsions, can never be settled; I myself think the poor strength of the drug was the cause of Cook not dying on the Monday night, for really we can scarcely understand Palmer procuring strychnine deliberately twice in twelve hours from the two local chemists.

On the Tuesday morning, November 20, after having watched Cook in the agony of strychnine tetanus at midnight, Palmer goes to another chemist, Hawkins, and asks for three strong poisons—prussic acid, Batley's solution of opium, and six grains of strychnine.

Just as the assistant, Roberts, was putting up the prussic acid, Newton came in for some calomel pills, as a customer had come in to Salt's open surgery and wanted a brand he had not in stock, so came across to his fellow-chemist for the pills, and there found Palmer buying these three poisons. Directly he came into the shop, Palmer seized him by the arm and took him out on to the pavement, telling him he had something private he wished to say to him.

Standing a couple of yards away from the chemist's door, all Palmer had to say was, to enquire when Dr. Salt was going to occupy a farm fifteen miles off he had lately bought. Chatting on this topic, he detained him there till Brassington, the cooper, came up, and, leaving him to talk to Newton, he went back into the chemist's and waited till the three packages were put up, standing in the doorway all the time and keeping an eye on Newton. He paid for his purchases and went off. Two out of the three packages were seen in a drawer in his surgery three weeks later, when the Sheriff's officer was in possession, but the six grains of strychnine were not there.

When Newton came back into the shop, he remarked, "Whatever is the matter with Palmer this morning?" Roberts replied, "Matter! Why, he has bought enough poison for the whole parish," and told Newton what he had sold to Palmer.

At the inquest, when Roberts told all about this sale of the poisons on the Tuesday morning, Newton was sent for to confirm the fact that he saw Palmer there making purchases, and about his taking him out of the shop, etc. But he was not allowed to repeat in court the conversation with Roberts, the chemist, because Palmer was not present in the shop.

Speaking as a general practitioner of over fifty years' experience, I am satisfied that Palmer never required strychnine to dispense in his practice when Cook was poisoned.

In the first place, he had given up his profession three or four years before, and if he made two separate purchases of strychnine within a few hours before Cook's death, the question arises, "*What was it purchased for?*"

Of the second purchase on the Tuesday morning of six grains of strychnine at Hawkins's shop there is no doubt, together with prussic acid and Batley's solution of opium. In all, three deadly poisons.

Roberts, who sold them, was not cross-examined about this sale.

But the gift late at night, "*about 9 o'clock,*" by Newton on Monday was rightly severely criticised by the Defence. Newton never mentioned this gift till, months after its occurrence, he told the lawyers on the very day before the trial in London, giving as an excuse he had retained the secret six months because his employer, Dr. Salt, was not on good terms with Palmer. "Then why disclose it at all?" Again, if Palmer felt on bad terms with Salt the Defence argued, why did he go to his surgery for strychnine?

He could only ask for the strychnine as a favour, for Newton's employer, Dr. Salt, could not sell drugs, and if Palmer had gone to any other chemist in Rugeley or in London on that day, he would have had to sign the poison-purchase book, and calling after 9 p.m. on a November night the seller would wonder what it would be for at this time of night by a doctor not in practice! Whereas Newton was a young, dissipated companion of Palmer's, and had often been to races, etc., with him and often dropped in on him for a drink and a chat, and did not sell the strychnine, but GAVE it.

The reason given is that Palmer passed by the shop driving on his way from Stafford. And showing what terms of friendship they were on, Newton says that on the Sunday evening after Cook died, Palmer sent for him and he found him sitting over the fire in his kitchen with brandy on the table.

During the drinking, Newton says Palmer asked him, "How much strychnine would you give a fair-sized dog to kill him?" "One grain" was the answer; and "Would you find any trace in the stomach after death?" "I think not." Then, snapping his fingers, Palmer half under his breath said, *"That's* all *right* then!"

It is rather hard to be asked to believe this—here on the eve of the post-mortem which is to take place to-morrow, Palmer sends for a half-educated chemist's assistant to enquire about strychnine, more especially from a man from whom he had obtained some on the day before Cook died. This interview, which took place in Palmer's kitchen, was never mentioned by Newton even at the inquest, nor to any official for three or four months afterwards. But if it is all a lie, what an awful one in its consequences!

Newton was, in my opinion, a most doubtful, unsatisfactory character. He seemed determined to be in the front rank of importance all along. But I cannot think he would go into the witness-box and deliberately perjure himself over the present of strychnine on the Monday night! If he so intended, he would surely have been more careful in stating his version as to the hour of this purchase, and might just as well, if telling a lie, have said about 10 p.m. instead of 9 p.m. All the difference between the impossible (for Palmer to have called) 9 p.m. and the possible about 9.30 or 10 p.m.

The Lord Chief Justice in his summing up adverts strongly to Newton's evidence:

"You are to consider what is the probability of his inventing what the Defence says is a wicked and most abominable lie. He certainly had no ill-will against the Prisoner at the Bar. He had nothing to gain by injuring him, much less by saying anything to affect his life. I see no motive that Newton could have for inventing such an awful lie to take away the life of Palmer—no inducement was held out to him; and he at last disclosed this Monday-night present of strychnine from a sense of justice. If you believe him, the evidence is very strong indeed against Palmer."

And the Attorney-General was equally emphatic over Newton's[1] evidence. In his reply he says:

"My learned friend has asked your most attentive consideration to the question of motive involved in this *whole* case. Before you convict Palmer of having taken away the life of Cook, he says it is important to see what motive he had. But does not that equally apply to Newton? Even the odious crime of murder by poison is not so horrible to contemplate as the notion of a foul judicial murder effected by false witness against a neighbour. Has Newton any motive for coming forward under the sanctity of an oath to take away the life of Palmer—for, alas! if you believe his evidence, it must take away the life of Palmer. If you believe that on the Monday night, for no other conceivable purpose except the deed of darkness he was going to perpetrate on Cook, the prisoner went to Newton and obtained from him the deadly poison, it is impossible that you can come to any other conclusion than that the prisoner is guilty and your verdict must pronounce him so."

But here I am inclined to think Newton's self-importance over-reached himself. Each time he comes before the public he adds to his previous version.

First, only mentioning he saw Palmer buy strychnine at Hawkins's.

Then three months later he tells of the conversation with Palmer about killing a dog with strychnine.

Then three months later he tells of the gift of strychnine to Palmer.

Moreover, I have seen in the letter (p. 39) addressed to the Lord Chief Justice by the Rev. T[homas] Palmer that Newton told the Attorney-General after Palmer was convicted that he

---

[1] [Fletcher's footnote] Newton was an illegitimate son of Ben Thirlby, Palmer's assistant partner, and he married a daughter of Tunnicliffe, who was on the Coroner's jury at the inquest on Cook.

had made up those strychnine pills for Palmer on the Monday night as well as supplied the drug.[2]

This astounding piece of information must soon have leaked out, as the letter is supposed to be written a week or so before the execution.

But I can scarcely believe it, for no man living who can supply strychnine dare make up three grains into two pills, when one grain is a fatal dose, and he would be an accessory before the murder.

Then Newton finds Palmer next morning buying six grains of strychnine at Hawkins's, and for six months says nothing about the overnight gift. But in his boastful swagger and ignorance Newton seems determined to be of some importance in this case.

If this gift of strychnine were true, what can we think of a man who has a chat with Palmer about the dose of strychnine required to kill a dog and what traces would be found after death—all this three days after seeing Palmer supplied with strychnine, on two separate occasions in twelve hours, and knowing the somewhat sudden death of Cook within a few hours, and the post-mortem to be made on the morrow.

Newton was a real shuffler. At the inquest on December 14 he was called to confirm Roberts's sale of strychnine that he saw Palmer buying on Tuesday, November 20, from Roberts. He never mentioned at the inquest his interview on Sunday night, November 25, in Palmer's kitchen, and the chat about the dog and strychnine, till three months later (as described on p. 100), and never till the eve of the trial in London did he mention the gift of three grains to Palmer on the Monday night.

Palmer obtains his strychnine, and that night gives Cook two pills. I must mention that on Sunday, November 18, Palmer had written to Dr. Jones, of Lutterworth, with whom Cook had his permanent residence and home, asking him to come and see his friend, who was suffering from a bilious attack. Dr. Jones was not well, and could not come on Monday, but arrived about three o'clock on the Tuesday afternoon, and went up to see Cook, and was soon joined by Palmer.

They examined the patient, and Dr. Jones said he could not see any symptoms of the bilious attack. They left together, and about seven o'clock on this Tuesday evening Dr. Bamford

---

[2] The letter, published as *A Letter to the Lord Chief Justice Campbell*, was attributed to the Rev. Thomas Palmer, William brother. Thomas Palmer later disavowed any connection with it.

came with Palmer and Jones. The three doctors examined Cook, who remarked more than once: "Look here, Palmer, I will not have any more of your d——d pills, for *those pills last night* caused all my sufferings." The doctors consulted outside the bedroom, and agreed that Dr. Bamford should make up the same morphia sleeping pills as on the Monday night. Palmer agreed to fetch them, and he went about eight o'clock, and asked Bamford to write full directions on the box, and on a slip of paper which he put round the box.

About 10.30 Palmer arrived with a box of pills in Cook's bedroom, and with Dr. Jones, who had arranged to sleep in a second bed in Cook's room. When opening the box, Palmer threw the paper across the bed to Dr. Jones, and commented on the excellent writing for a man over eighty making the point that this was Dr. Bamford's box of pills.

After much persuasion Cook took two pills, and vomited immediately. Palmer looked anxiously into the vomit to see if the pills had been rejected, but they had not, and Cook's death was sealed.

Palmer goes home, and Dr. Jones goes down to supper and returns in half an hour, and gets into bed. In a quarter of an hour he is roused by Cook screaming out, "Get up, for I am going to be ill like I was last night!"

Jones jumps up and rouses (or else the screams had) the servants. Elizabeth Mills goes across and fetches Palmer, who followed her back in two or three minutes, remarking, as he entered Cook's bedroom, "I never dressed so quickly in my life"; but she noticed nothing unusual in his dress, and it is generally supposed he had not gone to bed, but was sitting up waiting to be summoned to witness his strychnine pills destroy his victim.

But it is impossible to speak with accuracy about his dress and, unfortunately, about the scenes in that death-chamber at Cook's last moments—for one mould candle was all the light they had from the time Dr. Jones got out of bed till after the death, as the scene was too heartrending and hurried for anybody to fetch candles or a lamp, and all was over in a quarter of an hour.

As soon as Palmer arrived, Cook begged him to let him have some medicine like he had had on the previous night, and Palmer goes across home, returning with two pills and a draught, and in attempting to give Cook the pills a terrible spasm of the throat and clenching of the teeth set in. And he then gave the draught and sat by unmoved, as it appeared to Dr. Jones and the two maid-servants, and watched the agonising tortures rending the life out of Cook's body, the culmination of his cruel handiwork, perhaps even with satisfaction at its completion, but let us hope with a little sympathy at the agony of his victim, even though his hellish work was to bring him £3,000.

In two or three minutes' time Cook said, "Turn me on my side," and died directly.

The death-agonies from the time he first roused Dr. Jones only lasted a quarter of an hour, but were so intense the chambermaid said no words could possibly describe the scene.

Many authorities consider the fearful agonies from strychnine are so terrible that in some countries it is forbidden to kill any animals with such a drug, and this entirely negatives the excuse put forward by the Rev. Thos. Palmer in a letter to the Lord Chief Justice that Palmer bought the six grains of strychnine at Hawkins's shop in the morning before Cook died for the purpose of destroying dogs which may have worried his brood mares when out at grass. So small a quantity for dogs in a meadow is too feeble an excuse to require contradiction.

When Cook was lying on his side, he suddenly became very quiet, and Palmer, listening with his stethoscope, turned round and said to the bystanders, "The poor devil has gone"— a shocking remark, and upsetting both Dr. Jones and the maids at the bedside.[3]

Under any circumstances it was a most unkind, cruel remark, and more especially so when applied to one supposed to be an intimate friend and boon companion.

Within a few minutes Palmer sends for two women to lay out the dead body, and as soon as the room is clear he commences ransacking the dead man's pockets, and Elizabeth Mills, returning unexpectedly, found him feeling under the bolster and shifting the pillow.

Later on he hands over to Dr. Jones the watch and about £5 in cash which he said he found in the pockets, and Dr. Jones, the nearest friend, had better take possession of the things.

It is uncertain whether he then or previously took the betting-book.[4] It was last seen on the chimney-piece on the Tuesday morning. Cook had had it in his hands on Monday.

---

[3] In the Victorian age, speaking the devil's name with serious intent was akin to blasphemy. It must have been doubly shocking in rural areas such as Rugeley. Even worse, Palmer was using it in the middle of the night after witnessing the terrifying death of (supposedly) his close friend. It's about as close to desecrating a body as one could get without touching it.

[4] A small notebook in which gamblers recorded their wagers.

CHAPTER XI

Stevens arrives in Rugeley—Lunch at the Talbot—Lost betting-book—
Palmer travels back from London with Stevens—Post-mortem ordered
under Dr. Harland—Jar tampered with—Operators jolted and
stomach contents lost—Postboy offered a bribe—Taylor's notes in his
book.

DR. JONES LEAVES EARLY ON Wednesday morning and goes to
London to tell Mr. Stevens (Cook's stepfather) of the death of
his stepson at the age of twenty-eight. They go together to Dr.
Jones's home at Lutterworth, where Cook had made his
headquarters, and they find Cook's will.

They go together to Rugeley on Friday, arriving about
twelve. Palmer joins them as they enter the Talbot Hotel, and
obtrudes himself on to Cook's stepfather all the time he and
his son-in-law Mr. Bradford were in Rugeley.

He would persist in going upstairs with Mr. Stevens when
the latter wanted to see his stepson's body, and he threw back
the bedclothes.

Mr. Stevens was struck with the contortions of the body,
and especially the way in which the whole back was bent and
twisted, till the corpse seemed to rest on the heels and the
back of the head.

The hands and arms were twisted so much that the women
who had laid out the body had found it necessary to tie them
to the side, and the feet were so distorted, from the agony of
strychnine that the soles almost faced each other.

But above all, Mr. Stevens noticed the terrible expression of
pain still visible on the countenance.

On coming downstairs to the coffee-room Palmer in a most
objectionable manner would fasten himself on to Mr. Stevens
and his son-in-law Mr. Bradford and Dr. Jones, so that, as Mr.
Stevens afterwards remarked, he was obliged to ask him to sit
down and lunch with them in the coffee-room, for he could not
get rid of him.

But that lunch was the real commencement of Palmer's
undoing. Mr. Stevens had been at a great disadvantage all that
day, because for many months he had thoroughly detested
what he knew of Palmer and was most dissatisfied with him as

a friend and racing companion for his stepson, and his behaviour at this visit to Rugeley strengthened his dislike and raised in his mind suspicions of robbery, if not of poison, at any rate of doubtful treatment.

While lunch was being prepared, Palmer hurried out to the undertaker and ordered a strong oak coffin and shell, adding the remark, "Screw him down quick." He had seen this undertaker on the preceding day, but told him to wait for confirmation of the order till after Mr. Stevens had been.

During lunch Palmer spoke of Cook as "the poor diseased beggar" and "unfortunately my name is joined with his for a bill of £4,000," to which Stevens replied in a severe tone, "There won't be 4,000 pence in the estate, and it will have to be settled only in Chancery."

Palmer irritated Mr. Stevens so much that Dr. Jones quietly rebuked him. He saw Mr. Stevens was boiling over with rage, reaching the climax when, after lunch, Stevens rang the bell and asked the maid to go upstairs and collect all Cook's letters and papers, and especially the betting-book, and bring them down.

He asked Dr. Jones to help her to find them.

When the betting-book could not be found, Palmer remarked, "It is of no value, as when a man dies his bets die with him." Mr. Stevens replied, "I am the best judge of that, for Cook won a good sum at Shrewsbury and £800 was received on the course, which he had in his belt when he arrived here." Palmer only irritated him and his son-in-law Bradford, and finally exclaimed, "Oh, I dare say it will be found." "Sir," said Mr. Stevens, at last fairly roused, "*it shall be found.*"

This trouble about the betting-book seems to me to be the turning-point in the whole matter, for up till here, though Mr. Stevens had felt very annoyed, he now became angry and very suspicious, and he now said, "I am the best judge of its use, for my stepson won a great deal of ready money at Shrewsbury, and only this book can tell me who has paid and how much and the total remaining to be paid. The list of names and bets were in the betting-book."

Palmer did not tell him he had ALREADY robbed Cook of all his cash, the bets paid on the course (£800), and he had already appropriated on the Monday (settling day at Tattersall's) all due to Cook for bets, and he had also forged a cheque for £350 drawn on Weatherby out of the Shrewsbury Stakes, which cheque fortunately was returned two days later.

Stevens rang for the landlady and asked her to have the room carefully locked up, and said he was sorry he could not settle the date of the funeral, but he hoped to bury his stepson in the family vault near London.[1]

Palmer said that would be all right, but the body must be fastened down very soon. When Stevens asked the name of a local undertaker, Palmer said he had already ordered a shell and a strong oak coffin.

"You had no authority from me to do so," said Mr. Stevens. "Oh," said Palmer, "if you are inclined to make a fuss, I will bury him myself." But Stevens saw the undertaker and gave full instructions.

Stevens went off to London that Friday evening and saw his solicitors—told them his suspicions—and he came back the next day with an introduction to Gardner & Landor, solicitors in Rugeley, and to Dr. Harland, of Stafford. Palmer saw him at Euston and tried to get into conversation with him there, and at Wolverton, and again at Rugby in the Refreshment Room.

When Stevens got back into his carriage at Rugby, he found Palmer there—who was most keen to know what steps he was taking, and showed his restless anxiety and offered to find him a Solicitor in Rugeley, who probably would have been the dissolute Jere Smith. Then he presses on Mr. Stevens that they should drive together next day over to Hednesford to see Cook's two race-horses. But all his offers were curtly refused.

On this Saturday, November 24, Palmer had been up to London, taking £400 to Pratt, the bill discounter, who held the forged acceptances for about £20,000. This £400 had been stolen from Cook's belt in all probability, as Palmer had been obliged to borrow £25 from the local butcher only a few days before to go to Shrewsbury, and had then no ready money. He repaid this £25 the day after Cook died, and also paid three other bills, £20 to £30, in cash!!

Mr. Stevens plainly showed Palmer he did not want to converse with him, and totally ignored him when he found him in his compartment at Rugby. But walking up to the town at Rugeley, Palmer joined him, and at last Mr. Stevens sharply said, "I feel very dissatisfied about my stepson's death. If I call

---

[1] Which Stevens failed to do. Cook is buried in the churchyard in Rugeley, across the street from Mrs. Palmer's home. Moreover, according to *The Illustrated Life and Career of William Palmer* (Peschel Press, 2014), he was buried "by public subscription," for reasons unknown.

in a doctor and order a post-mortem examination, will you have any objection to answer any questions the doctor or my lawyer may put to you?" Stevens said in court, "I altered my voice purposely to a severe tone," but Palmer never faltered, and replied, "*Certainly not*: only too pleased to help all I can," without flinching beyond a spasm of the throat as he spoke, for Mr. Stevens turned and looked straight at him in a bright moonlight.

Palmer was in and out of the Talbot Arms all Sunday trying to talk with Mr. Stevens, who plainly showed he did not want to have anything to do with him. On the advice of his London solicitor, he had written to the Stafford Coroner and pressed for an inquest, writing at the same time to Dr. Harland to conduct the post-mortem examination. And on the Sunday afternoon he went over to Stafford to make all arrangements for the post-mortem with Dr. Harland, which was fixed for the next day, Monday, 10 a.m.

As regards the post-mortem, Mr. Stevens asked Dr. Harland, a consulting physician of Stafford, to carefully make it, and he certainly ought to have done so; but whether from being a consulting physician in Stafford he had chief points and care required for such a case, or for what reason we do not know, but he himself did not make any practical examination, and only took notes.

The practical part of the examination was left to two totally unsuitable men, neither of them a surgeon. One Mr. Devonshire, an unqualified assistant to Dr. Monckton in Rugeley, and the other the Mr. Newton, an assistant in an open surgery, almost a chemist's shop, where strychnine and calomel were sold over the counter (as we learnt at the trial).

Newton asked his employer, Dr. Salt, to take him to the post-mortem, and when there he helped to make the examination!!—a man who had no knowledge of anatomy or pathology or of any of the delicate points involved, and had never even SEEN a post-mortem examination.

When Dr. Harland arrived at Rugeley at 10 a.m. on Monday, November 26 (the day fixed for the post-mortem), Palmer met him walking up from the station, and remarked, "I am glad you have come; for the post-mortem examination might have been entrusted to a stranger." Dr. Harland replied, "What is the nature of this case? Tell me all about it. I hear there is a suspicion of FOUL PLAY AND POISONING!" Palmer never winced, and replied, "Oh, no such thing. The poor fellow had an epileptic seizure, and you will find an old disease of the heart and brain." Certainly he must have felt the beginning of terrible danger, and never let Dr. Harland out of his sight all that day.

They call for the aged Dr. Bamford, where they find Dr. Salt, who had just come in, bringing Newton. They all five, Dr. Harland, Bamford, Salt, Palmer, and Newton, proceed to the assembly-room at the Talbot Hotel, where the body was lying— a large room opening close to Cook's bedroom.

The rooms are the same at the present time, except that Cook's bedroom has been wisely turned into a sitting-room, No. 14.[2]

Palmer takes Newton across to his house and gives him two glasses of neat brandy to prepare and stimulate him for the ugly task before him. Dr. Harland had brought no instruments for the post-mortem examination. Palmer officiously offered to lend some, but Devonshire had brought them from Dr. Monckton.

The preparations were grossly inadequate. Only one glass jar had been provided, no scales, no measure glasses, no lens, no proper instruments, and yet poison had been suggested to Dr. Harland, and an intimation that Mr. Stevens would carry all the chief organs to Professor Taylor at Guy's Hospital for analysis, and only one jar provided!!!

There were several townsfolk present in this assembly room to watch the opening of the body, as well as Drs. Harland, Richard Freer, Bamford, Palmer, Jones, and Salt, and the two unqualified operators, Devonshire and Newton.

Why a minister of a chapel in the town? Why the landlord of the hotel (Mr. Masters), Jere Smith the shady solicitor, Cheshire the postmaster, and several other persons, as Dr. Holland says in his evidence? Why this motley crowd was permitted to attend is a mystery.

Dr. Harland took notes, but the whole affair seems to have been conducted in a loose, slovenly manner.

For example, the solitary jar was soon filled, and there was no arrangement as to what part of the body should be first opened, nor who should operate, nor who should take notes and verify details; in fact, the whole proceedings were as

---

[2] *No. 14*: Although the building, now the Shrewsbury Arms Hotel, is an historically protected building, with parts dating from the 1700s, the original rooms were dismantled during renovations in the early 20th century.

slipshod and slovenly as possible, especially when we remember a man's life was at stake for murder. When these novices who were operating reached the stomach—which of course was the chief centre of interest—after tying the two ends and holding it over the body, Mr. Devonshire cuts it open from end to end, and throws the stomach turned inside-out into the jar. Why did not Dr. Harland stop him from opening the stomach?—a most fatal, unnecessary error.

But just as he was opening it, Palmer, naturally very keen, pushed Newton on to Devonshire, and so spilt nearly all the scanty contents, estimated at three table spoonfuls.

It was obvious to the bystanders that that push was done on purpose, certainly not accidental.

Slapping Dr. Bamford on the back, Palmer jokingly remarked, "They won't hang us yet, Bamford" when he saw the stomach cut open and its contents spilt.

About 3 feet of the intestines were taken out and put in this one jar, and the stomach with them.

And not being carefully tied, their contents leaked through and mixed with the stomach walls. No organs seem to have been thought about except the inverted stomach cut open from end to end and 3 feet of the bowels—and this is all that was sent up for analysis.

Dr. Harland covers the jar with two layers of bladder, ties it up, and seals the knot. In a few minutes the jar had disappeared. When a vigorous enquiry and fuss was being raised, Palmer appeared from the farther door, where he had taken it, and was sharply ordered to bring it back; and on doing so, a clean slit was found in the covering bladders, but no one knew how it was made.

Palmer remarked, "I thought the jar would be more handy for you to take it away when you leave if I placed it by the door."

Dr. Harland again covered it and sealed the knot, and it was placed on a small table in the centre of the room, and finally taken to Professor Taylor for the contents to be analysed; but before it left Rugeley, Palmer asked Dr. Harland what he was going to do with it.

He was told he was taking it to Dr. Freer's house, and that Mr. Stevens would himself subsequently take it to Stafford, and thence to London for complete analysis of the contents.

After hearing this, Palmer goes to find the postboy James Myatt, and enquires if he is going to drive Mr. Stevens and the jar to Stafford Station.

On hearing he is to drive the cab with Mr. Stevens and the jar, Palmer offers him ten pounds to upset them and smash the jar, which is indignantly refused by the driver, Palmer adding as he left him, "A lot of fuss is being made about this affair, which is a humbugging concern"—making a confidant of a post-boy.

Serjeant Shee, for the defence at the trial, contended it was Stevens whom Palmer wished the driver to upset, for already Cook's stepfather had shown strong animus against the dissolute, gambling doctor, a supposed friend of the dead man (his wife's son).

The whole behaviour of Palmer throughout the post-mortem showed such marked uneasiness and restlessness that it roused suspicion in many minds, especially of that motley assemblage there present, and confirmed the worst in those who already suspected murder.

Before leaving this part of the case I will quote Dr. Taylor's own book, which should be carefully read by all who contend that because he did not find strychnine, therefore none had been given. His account of the one jar received, into which had been thrown higgledy-piggledy all that was sent up, is sad reading, and hard to believe, especially when it is compared with a post-mortem conducted at the present day, and doubly so where a suspicion of poison has been hinted at.

His own words are (p. 10): "In the jar was found the stomach cut open and turned inside-out, presenting over the greater part of its surface a deep reddish colour, especially towards the pyloric end. On examination by a lens, no whitish spots were seen; there was no ulceration nor any perforation. There was a feculent odour[3] observed, probably arising from the mixture in the jar."

P. 11: "The stomach had been cut open and the contents, if any, had entirely drained away from it" —a keynote to a great deal of that post-mortem.

And this is a stomach which was to be analysed for a sensitive poison, under the best circumstances always very hard to detect.

Professor Taylor and Dr. Rees were so dissatisfied with this one jar and the totally inadequate mixed contents that they

---

[3] *feculent odour.* Containing dirt, sediment or impurities. Derived from the Latin *faex* or *faec-* for "dregs."

telegraphed at once for further organs, so the corpse had to be opened again, and Dr. Monckton and Dr. Freer this time took charge of the examination and sent up the kidneys, part of the liver, the spleen, and three tablespoonfuls of blood, and what remained of the head and sliced-up brain.

Dr. Rees himself told me twenty-five years afterwards it was the most shamefully conducted post-mortem he had ever heard of, and little or nothing could be expected from their analysis.

Professor Taylor had asked for Dr. Rees to be associated with him in this examination.

As death occurred within an hour or so of taking strychnine pills, the operator's chief attention would be directed to the stomach, as the pills would not entirely have passed through, but its inner surface was lying cut open on the portion of intestines sent up.

They might have found the pill material or the strychnine itself in white flakes on the inner stomach walls; but nothing was there, no fluids, no solids, no contents in those mangled remains.

In the liver and kidneys and blood sent up at their request, two days later, they found distinct traces of antimony, a drug which had not been given by the Shrewsbury doctor nor by Dr. Bamford.

Also they found *no traces* of mercury nor of opium, both of which *had been in the pills* sent by Dr. Bamford on three successive nights.

These drugs would have been found if Dr. Bamford's pills had been swallowed by the patient less than two hours before death, especially the last pills, which Dr. Bamford sent on Tuesday night by the hand of Palmer, and it is strong evidence, if it were needed, that pills other than Bamford's were administered by Palmer on both nights.

Nobody seems to have thought of angina pectoris[4] at the post-mortem. Dr. Richardson, called for the defence, said the symptoms were very similar to it, and two or three doctors agreed as to the similarity only, the symptoms of pain. But not the terrible contortions of the body and bending of the spine and arching of the back and twisting of the feet, and contraction of the chest-walls causing suffocation.

---

[4] *angina pectoris*: Chest pain in the heart region due to an obstruction or spasm of the coronary arteries.

CHAPTER XII

Haphazard management of the enquiry—All left to Mr. Stevens, luckily a man of shrewd judgment—Dr. Harland too feeble to superintend the post-mortem examination—Various doctors at Rugeley—Cook's funeral—Body exhumed.

THE POST-MORTEM EXAMINATION ON MONDAY, November 26—if such a slipshod, careless investigation can be so called—is over; the mangled stomach mixed up with intestines all in one jar is on its way to London to be examined by Professor Taylor, and Palmer is left to his own devices and occupations at Rugeley. The Coroner, urged on by Stevens and his solicitor, summons an inquest for Thursday, November 29, and here is a fitting place to call attention to Mr. Stevens's deep concern and interest in the matter and to the all-round general aspect of affairs.

Seventy years ago there was a haphazard system of enquiry in such cases. It was a matter of the most perfect chance whether the body of a person supposed to have met with his death by unfair means was examined anatomically and chemically by men of dispassionate uprightness and of adequate, undoubted skill, or by men who possessed neither the one nor the other of these qualifications. As we have seen, the post-mortem was conducted on Cook by an undergraduate and by an unqualified chemist's assistant.

Palmer tells Dr. Harland he is very glad he has come to examine the body, and not some other doctor who might entertain ill-feelings towards him—knowing there were several such in the neighbourhood.

Perhaps also Palmer was glad to see Dr. Harland, for he guessed rightly—as the result proved—that his examination would be a negligent, haphazard, careless affair, from which the public and Cook's relatives were more likely to sustain injury and be wronged, than the accused. It might so easily have happened anywhere in those days. Let us hope it could not be possible in this twentieth century that the whole examination and enquiry should be on the lines on which this post-mortem was conducted.

The jar was taken to Professor Taylor for examination not because he was selected by the Home Office or Scotland Yard for this most responsible, delicate task, but because a private solicitor in London advised Mr. Stevens to see Mr. Warrington, Professor of Chemistry at the Apothecaries' Hall, who gave him an introduction to Professor Taylor, of Guy's Hospital, as a competent, honourable analytical chemist, well versed in the class of work likely to be required.

Mr. Stevens called on Professor Taylor on Tuesday, November 27, when he took the jar which he had brought from Rugeley the preceding night, and left it with him, together with a very few rough notes outlining the history of his stepson's death.

Fortunately Mr. Stevens was a man of rare intelligence and discretion, and the British public owe him a debt of gratitude for arresting the murderous career of Palmer.

Who can tell what other lives might not have been sacrificed had not the shrewd sense of Mr. Stevens seen deep into the meaning and significance of these death-bed symptoms and appearances, added to an innate distrust of the man as a companion for his stepson, and irritated beyond words at what he thought the theft of Cook's betting-book, and the unnatural excitement and restlessness of the man he suspected? Mr. Stevens was honoured by a most uncalled-for attack by Mr. Serjeant Shee speaking for the Defence; but public opinion of the day and ever since estimates him as a man of remarkable shrewdness and a gentleman whose whole conduct in this enquiry was distinguished by true-hearted affection for his stepson, and by the greatest consistency and prudence, together with remarkable fairness.

He let Palmer see all along how suspicious he was of him, and that he was going to leave no stone unturned to get to the bottom of his stepson's death and robbery. He was not a man to make an altogether injudicious, haphazard selection of an analytical chemist, for the analysis might have been otherwise, like the post-mortem was, third- or fourth-rate, or worse, slovenly with ignorance and carelessness, and a very neutral report would have followed the analysis. Then he felt, as Mrs. Bladen five years before had felt when she thought her husband had been murdered and robbed by Palmer, that the expense was going to be great. But here, at his own expense, Mr. Stevens employs Professor Taylor, one of the very best chemists in the land, and at his own risk he notifies the Coroner and pushes him into holding an inquest, and himself engages Dr. Harland.

The expense and risk Mr. Stevens ran were no light matter.

It ought not to have been left to him alone. Surely the Government ought to have directed the proceedings, and chosen the operators for the post-mortem and the chemist for the analysis, and undertaken all risks and all expenses at the public cost.

We must regard with respect Mr. Stevens, whose actions throughout called for most unfair criticism at the hands of the Defence: "*A meddlesome old gentleman,*" "*an interfering, irritating step-father,*" one who also had disliked Palmer as a companion for his stepson and now took every opportunity of showing it, noticeably by his behaviour after lunch on the Friday at the Talbot Arms over the lost betting-book, and over Palmer's ordering a coffin, etc., and then on the journey down from Euston on the Saturday (November 24), when he shows Palmer plainly he suspects him and asks if he will object to being questioned by the doctor who may be asked to make the post-mortem.

His behaviour towards Palmer was only natural, entertaining the suspicions he did, and which really were the foundation of the inquest and trial.

He felt so satisfied of foul play, he pushed the Coroner into holding that inquest, which, with adjournments extended from November 29 to December 15, on five different days.

He selected, on the advice of friends, Dr. Harland of Stafford, a perfect stranger to him, to make the post-mortem, or, as Dr. Harland expressed it, to *superintend* the post-mortem—a man with scarcely enough experience for such an enquiry, and certainly not strong enough to deal with such a case, nor firm enough to put his foot down as he should have done.

Before Dr. Harland arrives at the hotel he met Palmer and gave the key to his being there—"*a fussy old gentleman has asked him!!!—who was suspicious of poison!!*" Then he allows a dozen outsiders to be present at the post-mortem and leaves the work to two strangers (*vide* p. 108), neither of whom was a surgeon and one of them had never seen a post-mortem before.

He does not sternly rebuke Palmer for pushing the operators as they were opening the stomach, nor does he make the enquiries as to who could have cut the bladder over the jar, and why Palmer had removed it 24 feet away from the table to the door out of the room.

In short, Dr. Harland's examination was, as I have already said, simply a negligent one—very negligent, only supervising two incompetent men.

Then the stomach, cut from end to end, and its contents, if any (after the terrible carelessness and bungling), were submitted to Professor Taylor, not because he was selected by the Government for this most responsible, delicate duty, but because a chance friend recommended him to Stevens as a competent trustworthy analytical chemist; and so he was—his reputation was European.[1]

Luckily Mr. Stevens was just the man to see to all these matters, a man of rare intelligence and discretion, and the public owes him a deep debt of gratitude for arresting the career of William Palmer.

Before going on with the inquest, this will be a fitting place to discuss the various doctors we have so far met with, especially those who are so intimately mixed up in Cook's death, for in the middle of the last century many men practised without any legal qualifications. The Medical Registration Bill, passed two years later, allowed all doctors without legal qualifications to remain on the Register if they had been in practice ten years. But after the Bill was passed, all who wished to practice must hold a legal qualification. We find Dr. Bamford was in practice before 1803—fifty-two years before he was called in to prescribe pills for Cook. He was not the only doctor without any legal qualifications, for the various so-called doctors we come across in this case show how many practised in the middle of the last century without any legal qualifications.

At Shrewsbury a Mr. Gibson attends Cook, and all we know about him is that he is an assistant to Dr. Heathcote—he was not a qualified doctor. But he stated he thought Cook's illness was due to poison, and saw him vomit. But he never took the trouble to have the vomit examined.

In all probability if he had preserved the ejected matter for further examination, the analyst would have most likely found antimony; and if Palmer had heard the vomit had been

---

[1] Ambitious scientists could make a name for themselves by maintaining contact with their colleagues by mail or publishing their discoveries in scientific journals. A young James Moriarty, according to Sherlock Holmes, "wrote a treatise upon the binomial theorem, which has had a European vogue. On the strength of it he won the mathematical chair at one of our smaller universities, and had, to all appearances, a most brilliant career before him."

reserved for analysis, a fresh chapter would have been opened, and Palmer would have been obliged to start on fresh lines—and perchance Cook's life would have been saved.

The all-night's sickness at Shrewsbury, followed by the three days' constant sickness at Rugeley and the discovery of antimony (tartar emetic) in Cook's body after death, all indicate that he was being dosed with tartar emetic right up to the Monday, when the first dose of strychnine was given.

At Stafford there was a consulting physician, Dr. *Harland*, who superintended the post-mortem (M.D. Edin. 1827; M.R.C.S. Eng., 1815).

Dr. Knight (M.B. Cantab., 1806), aged and deaf, called in to Mrs. Anne Palmer, whose guardian he was.

Dr. Day (M.R.C.S. Eng., 1829) and Dr. Waddell (M.R.C.S., 1855), both of whom examined Walter Palmer for life insurance.

Rugeley seems to have had plenty of doctors, allowing for the population and size of the place.[2]

Dr. *Bamford*, the aged, ever-accommodating; a somewhat fumbling doctor, called in to most of Palmer's victims, chiefly for certificates.

Dr. *Freer*, with his son Dr. J. H. Freer, just finishing his medical education.

Dr. *Salt*, with Newton his assistant in an open surgery, and Dr. *Monckton*, who had as an assistant Devonshire, who, we read, was an undergraduate of the London University, though of course that gave him no right to practise, and certainly not the experience and skill required to make the examination of Cook's body.

And last, though by no means least, Dr. Palmer, who was disposing of what practice he had remaining to Ben Thirlby, a chemist, who, we read, was called in to Mrs. Anne Palmer the day before she died, and to several infants who died in convulsions attended also by Palmer.

Thirlby had been assistant to Dr. Salt, and left him to come to Palmer, and this was given by Newton, then Salt's assistant, as a reason for not telling Dr. Salt of Palmer obtaining the three grains of strychnine on the night of Monday, November 19, as the two doctors were now not on speaking terms, though their two assistants, Newton and Thirlby, were on a good footing with each other.

---

[2] Rugeley's population in 1861 was 4,362.

Out of all these men practising medicine, the men with undoubted legal qualifications were Dr. Freer, Dr. Monckton, and Dr. Salt, and Palmer. Whether Dr. Bamford had any degrees or legal qualifications, I cannot ascertain. I think we can assume Devonshire had not. And this makes the conduct of Dr. Harland of Stafford all the more reprehensible, to entrust the post-mortem examination to him, aided by Newton, who had never even seen an examination, especially after he had been told by Mr. Stevens there was a suspicion of poison.

I have commented elsewhere on the shameful way in which the examination was carried out, and only the everted, mangled stomach with 3 feet of bowel sent up in one jar to Professor Taylor. But if the post-mortem had been skilfully and properly conducted, and if strychnine had been found by Taylor, then there would have been no defence on the medical ground, as Serjeant Shee said that was the foundation of it, but not the whole of the Defence, and the Attorney-General's task would have indeed been light and easy, in place of bringing home the conviction of Palmer against long odds, mainly on the circumstantial evidence, there would not have been those long evening consultations and studying tetanus at his private residence in Hertford Street, Mayfair, and posterity would have been deprived of one of the most interesting trials of the century—always supposing the stomach uncut had been safely sent with other organs to Taylor, and that he found strychnine and did not find opium or calomel, the two drugs which Bamford had put in the pills he had sent in on both nights, for which the Crown contend Palmer substituted strychnine pills.

But if after a skilful and properly conducted post-mortem examination Taylor had not found strychnine, the case would have been exactly where it eventually was, only Taylor would not have had the shameful state of the mangled stomach submitted to him as in any degree helping to account for strychnine not being found, and the circumstantial evidence would alone have convicted Palmer.

From the Monday's post-mortem till the jury met on the following Thursday, November 29, at the Talbot Hotel, Palmer was alone. The last entry in his published Diary is on November 26: "Attended a post-mortem on poor Cook with Dr. Harland, Mr. Bamford, Newton, and a Mr. Devonshire," From entering "a Mr. Devonshire," I gather he had not long been assistant to Dr. Monckton in Rugeley.

The jury on Thursday were only detained a quarter of an

hour, the Coroner telling them they are there to enquire into what caused Cook's death; and after viewing the body the Coroner adjourned the inquest to Wednesday, December 5, according to Cheshire's evidence, and according to the personal Diary of Superintendent Hatton (Chief Constable of the County of Stafford), though one or two accounts give December 8, wrongly.

The funeral was at midday on Friday, November 30, the day following the first inquest, and largely attended by the townspeople, who were beginning to take great interest in this death of a visitor to the town, and already commenting on the fact that this was by no means the first death under Palmer's care where he gained plenty of money by the death.

First of all, his mother-in-law died under his roof, leaving several freehold houses in Stafford and £3,000, his wife's share, in cash; Bladen with his full money-belt and what Palmer owed him—in all over a thousand pounds; his young wife's death and £13,000 insurance paid; and recently at Stafford his brother Walter's death, and £15,000 insurance expected to be paid shortly. All enough to raise suspicion.

But in spite of that, Palmer himself with Jere Smith went to the funeral service, and Mr. Stevens and Mr. Bradford (Cook's brother-in-law) were there, and last, but by no means least, George Herring came down from London and, we can be sure, made strict and numerous enquiries about the betting-book and the money he had collected at Tattersall's ten days before for Cook, which he now learnt had been used for Palmer's debts, and he was very irate at the deceit Palmer had practised on him.

He was particularly anxious to hear about the degree of intimacy between Cook (for whom he had some respect and friendship) and Palmer (whom he loathed and judged capable of any crime), for he had always felt a strong suspicion of the man he now saw weeping behind Cook's bier. Herring gave his evidence at the trial in London in a pitiless, cold tone—about his transactions with Palmer on the Monday before Cook died, and the money owing to Cook which he had collected and paid towards Palmer's debts.

If Palmer felt lonely and shunned by his fellow-townsmen and former companions during the different adjournments of the inquest from November 29 to December 15, at any rate he had living with him the pretty housemaid Eliza Tharm, with their baby now five months old, which died a few days afterwards, and she had friends and relations in the place who would retail the current gossip of the town, and she told all to Palmer.

After Cook's body had been consigned to its resting-place in Rugeley Churchyard, it was not allowed to rest long, for two months later the Home Secretary, after urgent requests by Palmer's solicitors, allowed the body to be exhumed on Friday, January 25, for the purpose of examining the spinal cord, which had been totally neglected at the first post-mortem.

This examination was conducted by Drs. Monckton, Harland, and Bamford; also Dr. Oliver Pemberton and Professor Bolton from Birmingham were present, representing Palmer. The former only was called at the trial, and gave very neutral evidence, for they found nothing at this examination to advance in Palmer's favour.

The Birmingham doctors were only told late on Friday, January 25, so the body remained for the night in the old church at the back of Mrs. Palmer's garden, and there the third post-mortem examination was made on Saturday, January 26.

The doctors and undertakers as well as grave-diggers preferred the large, empty, ruined church to the close, small inn near at hand, opposite the churchyard, and at this examination on January 26 the spinal cord was particularly examined by the Birmingham doctors, and nothing fresh discovered.

They were told they might take away any portion of the body remaining, if they wished for further careful *microscopic* examination, or analysis, of which we heard so much from the chemists, for the Defence, that they could discover strychnine in 1/1000 of a grain in the tissues of the body.

But the doctors only took a piece of the spinal cord, and so the body was reinterred. Palmer tried, after his conviction, to get his solicitor to have Cook's body exhumed again and give some tissues to Professor Herapath to be examined for strychnine. But, needless to say, the Home Secretary did not permit any further exhumation seven or eight months after death, when nothing could be gained by a NEGATIVE RESULT, as the jury knew strychnine had not been found, and they convicted Palmer on the evidence of the whole case, the symptoms of the death, and his general behaviour that of a guilty man.

CHAPTER XIII

Palmer's restlessness—Loses his head very often—Sends for Cheshire to fill up cheque and attest a forged signature—Persuades him to open Taylor's letter—Inquest on December 12—Adjourned to the 14th—On the 13th Palmer writes an incriminating letter to Coroner with ten-pound note—Verdict, December 15: Guilty—Palmer a witness at civil trial.

AS STRYCHNINE SCARCELY COULD BE EXPECTED to be found after the disgraceful post-mortem examination, in the mangled remains of the stomach turned inside-out which was sent up for analysis, so Palmer's conviction rested a great deal, as I have just shown, on the "*circumstantial evidence*" all along, added to his own excited behaviour and restlessness, with his guilty, over-anxious conscience which caused him to lose his head so often, and so completely to act in a most suspicious manner as to tighten the rope which appeared likely to be placed round his neck.

I will here briefly enumerate some of the occasions on which he lost his head. Most of them have occurred in the narrative, and I shall have frequently to allude to them.

He would not have drunk the dregs of the brandy on that Wednesday evening at Shrewsbury which Cook said had been drugged (p. 83). He would not have sent over to the Talbot Hotel on two or three occasions basins of broth for Cook, one of which had been standing by his sitting-room fire for half an hour, and this broth was undoubtedly drugged with antimony, and made the chambermaid very ill after sampling only a couple of tablespoonfuls of it because it smelt so savoury (p. 85).

Then, knowing Newton's character as a real ignorant shuffler, he would scarcely in calm moments have gone to ask him for three grains of strychnine on the Monday night; and next morning he would not have become totally dumbfounded and shown his confusion when Newton found him again obtaining strychnine at Hawkins's shop (p. 100).

Then, no man in his senses would have asked Cheshire to fill up a cheque for £350 payable to Palmer himself of the Shrewsbury Stakes won by Cook, which cheque he said he was taking over for Cook to sign the evening before he died (as described on p. 122), and asked the same man to sign his name as witnessing Cook sign a document a week previously; but this Cheshire sensibly refused to do. These two documents I shall enter into fully, as very important against Palmer.

When Cook was scarcely dead, Palmer listened with his stethoscope to his heart in a very excited manner, and exclaimed, "The poor devil has gone." This was not the behaviour of a doctor or a friend in his senses at such a scene, and did not pass unnoticed by Dr. Jones nor by the chambermaids.

But after the death of Cook he gives himself away completely, and utterly lost his head worse than ever with a murderer's anxious, guilty conscience, for when Mr. Stevens came with Dr. Jones on the Friday morning after Cook's death, his restlessness led him to irritate Mr. Stevens in every detail connected with the loss of the betting-book, ordering the coffin, and treatment of the corpse (as I have given fully on p. 106).

Palmer's excited, restless interference all through the post-mortem examination and his behaviour there aroused suspicion in the minds of those present.

I have shown how he pushed the operators together just as they were opening the stomach, and spilt its contents, and then removed the jar to the door of the next room, and tried to bribe the postboy to smash it, and showed great anxiety to know where it was being taken to.

What had it all to do with him unless a guilty conscience upset him? He was passing only as a friend amongst many others of the dead man.

His persuading the postmaster Cheshire to open Professor Taylor's report to the solicitors, his discussion with Newton, a chemist's assistant (about twenty-two years of age), as to the dose of strychnine required to kill a dog, and his snapping his fingers, saying "That's all right," when he hears nothing will be found after death, and, *above all*, his gross attempts to bribe the Coroner, first on December 3, with a large hamper of game which he never paid for, and then the day before the final adjournment of the inquest to send him on December 13 a ten-pound note with the letter (see p. 124), completely settled whatever doubt his neighbours might have had to account for his "intense" eagerness and anxiety.

In addition to giving himself away so often, we shall see two very foolish steps he took in sending for Cheshire the postmaster. First, a few hours before Cook died—and this became important evidence at the trial—he asked him to write out a cheque for £350, which he would take across to the hotel for Cook to sign, on his sick-bed. Telling Cheshire that Tattersall's would recognise his (Palmer's) handwriting in the body of the cheque, and, as he was a defaulter there, the cheque would be useless, Cheshire obliges him and leaves the cheque with Palmer. It was drawn on Weatherby, Clerk at Tattersall's, for £350, part of the amount of the Shrewsbury Stakes won a week before by Cook's horse Polestar at Shrewsbury; but as the Clerk of the Course at Shrewsbury had not yet sent up to the Clerk at Tattersall's the Stakes (£385), the cheque was returned to Cook at Rugeley but did not arrive till twenty-four hours after his death. This cheque was called for by the Attorney-General, at the trial, and not produced.

But why send for Cheshire to draw this cheque, when Dr. Jones is sitting across the road with Cook, and surely he would have been the more fitting person to write it in Cook's presence and then hand it to Cook to sign?

Again, Palmer sends for his friend Cheshire on Thursday, November 22, the day after Cook had died, and asks him to witness *ex post facto*,[1] and append his signature to, a document supposed to be drawn up and signed by Cook ten days before, in which Cook acknowledged that bills to the amount of £4,000 had been negotiated by Palmer, chiefly for Cook's benefit, and that Palmer had received little or no consideration for these joint bills.

It was plain that Cook's signature was a forgery, and Cheshire demurred to sign it as witness as Cook had now been dead two days, and finally he refused, after some discussion, to witness a document he had never seen executed, so Palmer in an offhand way says, "Oh, it won't matter, as Cook's friends will never think of disputing it."

Both this paper and the cheque were called for by the Prosecution at the trial, but neither was produced—a point much against Palmer's interests, for if he had produced these documents, they would have shown, if genuine, that Cook was handing over to Palmer the £350, as the cheque was supposed to be signed by Cook, paying Palmer this large sum. And Cook's signature could easily have been proved authentic or forged.

---

[1] A Latin legal term meaning "after the fact."

Also that important document which was supposed to have been drawn up two days before they went to Shrewsbury would have proved that they were in a sort of partnership for £4,000, if there ever had been any partnership or document.

When Cheshire described at the trial in London the drawing up of that cheque on the night of November 20 (which Palmer was going to take across for Cook to sign), the Attorney-General made a distinct pause in Court and said, "I now call for that cheque to be produced." Serjeant Shee only shook his head, a painful silence reigning in Court.

Then again, when Cheshire described Palmer's placing before him two days after Cook's death that document showing the deed for £4,000, he refused, as I have shown, to subscribe his name as witness to Cook's signature, on a document supposed to have been signed by Cook ten days before and Cook now lying dead. Then the Attorney-General said, "As Palmer took that document away with him, and it was last seen in his possession, I call for it to be produced." Again Serjeant Shee had to say they did not produce it. These were perhaps the most important points raised to shatter the defence, for Serjeant Shee tried to prove Cook had VOLUNTARILY HANDED OVER to Palmer all, or most of, his Shrewsbury winnings.

In referring to the fraud and forgery which had to be introduced to show the pecuniary straits into which Palmer had fallen and the consequent motive for the murder of Cook to obtain the £3,000 from the stakes and bets, the Attorney-General was careful to warn the jury, "Though a man may be guilty of fraud and forgery, it does not follow he is guilty of murder."

Again, for the third time, Palmer sends for Cheshire on Sunday, December 2, and after a general chat over cigars and brandy he suggests to him that he should open any letters which might appear to come from Professor Taylor, who was making the analysis, to the solicitors (Landor & Gardner) in Rugeley, who were representing Mr. Stevens.

We should think the matter had to be delicately brought about in conversation, but there is no doubt Cheshire for many months had been handing over to Palmer letters of all sorts addressed to his mother, chiefly from Pratt and his fellow bill discounters. And even writs sent down by them to be served on Mrs. Palmer had never reached the solicitor's hands in Rugeley. So here the matter is quietly and quickly discussed, and though Cheshire demurred, saying he could do nothing dishonest, yet on the morning of Wednesday, December 5, he goes across to Palmer before he is up, and finding him in bed tells him Professor Taylor has written to the solicitor, Mr. Gardner, to the effect that they can find no strychnine, only antimony, as the result of their analysis. Whereat Palmer remarked, "I knew they would not, for I am perfectly innocent"; and in a minute repeated it, "I am as innocent as a baby." Innocent of what? He did not say.

There had been no charge laid against him, even if he fancied many neighbours were casting suspicious glances at him. And Cheshire, his supposed loyal friend, tells all this interview from the witness-box in London at the trial, just as another bosom friend, Newton, tells about the gift of three grains of strychnine and the conversation about poisoning a dog (*vide* p. 99).

The adjourned inquest was continued at the Town Hall on that day of disclosing Taylor's letter (December 5) and after hearing some general evidence (on December 5) for five hours, the inquest was adjourned to Wednesday, December 12, when a great deal of incriminating evidence was given, and adjourned to Friday, December 14.

Between the adjourned inquests Palmer makes one of his fatal, self-convicting blunders by sending on two occasions presents of fish and game to the Coroner: the first present from London on December 1, to his private address at Stoke-on-Trent, the second by Bates to him at Stafford. Then the day after the adjourned inquest, on December 12, Palmer makes his last vital mistake and perhaps his biggest of many, for he writes to the Coroner on December 13, and encloses a ten-pound note with this suicidal, self-convicting letter, which shows restless, eager anxiety impossible to understand if it comes from a man who was only a friend of the deceased.

Dec. 13th, 1855.

RUGELEY.

MY DEAR SIR,

I am sorry to tell you that I am still confined to bed. I don't think it was mentioned at the Inquest yesterday Dec. 12th, that Cook was taken ill on Sunday and Monday night, in the same way as he was on the Tuesday, when he died. The Chambermaid at the Crown

Hotel (Masters's) can prove this. I also believe that a man by the name of Fisher is coming down to prove he received some money at Shrewsbury. Now, here he could only pay Smith £10 out of £41 he owed him. Had you not better call Smith to prove this? And again, whatever Professor Taylor may say to-morrow, he wrote from London last Tuesday week to Gardner to say, "We (Dr. Rees and I) have this day finished our analysis, and find no traces of either strychnine, prussic acid, or opium."

What can beat this from a man like Taylor, if he says what he has already said, and Dr. Harland's evidence? Mind you I know and saw it in black and white, what Taylor said to Gardner; but this is strictly private and confidential, but it is true.

As regards his betting-book, I know nothing of it, and it is of no good to anyone. I hope the verdict to-morrow will be that he died from natural causes, and thus end it.

Ever yours,
W.P.

This letter was written a week after Palmer had been told by Cheshire he had read Taylor's letter to Gardner finding no strychnine.

It is sent to the Coroner the day before Taylor is coming down from London to give evidence—showing he had had access to Taylor's private letter, and was making use of his knowledge in this letter to the Coroner, before it was publicly known, and before the Coroner had heard of the result of the analysis.

This was sent by hand, with a ten-pound note enclosed, to the Coroner, with strict orders to the bearer (Bates) not to let anybody see him deliver it. Bates fetched the Coroner out of the smoking-room at the Dolphin Inn, Stafford, and handed him the letter in the stable yard attached—which he put unopened into his pocket.

Was there ever a more condemnatory letter presented to a jury to convince them of guilt! Here is a doctor attending a friend, and evidence at the inquest already looks black against him, yet he twice sends presents of game to the Coroner, and, whatever doubt one may have had up till now, this letter, full of anxiety, enclosing a ten-pound note, settles his fate in any unprejudiced mind.

That letter is regarded by many authorities as the most damning evidence any man could weave against himself for conviction, in which he tries to bribe the Coroner, and shows that intense anxiety to hear the results of the analysis by intercepting a letter from Professor Taylor, and nobody in his senses would have told the Coroner BEFORE they were made public by the writer at the coming inquest.

A month later the Chief Superintendent Hatton demanded this letter from the Coroner. Fortunately, by some wild chance, he had not destroyed a document so incriminating, and no credit to the Coroner, for it showed Palmer thought him open to a bribe and that he would listen to his advice how to direct the jury for a favourable verdict—"natural causes." The Coroner posted the letter to the Home Secretary, and it was produced at trial in London with most crushing, damaging effect the minds of the jury.

But before he had reached the point of attempting to bribe the Coroner as this letter shows, Palmer had already sent him, as I have shown, a splendid hamper of game to his private address, Stoke-on-Trent, and a week later orders Bates to buy game in Stafford and send to the Coroner.

From Wednesday, December 12, the inquest is adjourned to Friday, the 14th, when Professor Taylor came down from London and sat near the Coroner throughout the day, putting many questions to the witnesses, each one being crushing to Palmer's chance. One newspaper mentioned the fact that Taylor put more questions than the Coroner. And with crushing emphasis Taylor gave his own evidence, winding up with the remark, "I believe the pills administered to Cook both on the night of Monday and Tuesday contained strychnine, which killed him."

On Friday the 14th Taylor also said in his evidence he could not find any strychnine. Jere Smith hurried across to tell Palmer, who was ailing in bed. He gets up out of his sick-bed and has Cheshire and Bates with Jere Smith in to lunch while the inquest is being held not a hundred yards away. And when, later in the day, the jury, wishing to give their fellow-townsman a chance, and wanting to hear his version of many suspicious matters, send across about 4 p.m. and ask him to come as a witness to give evidence, he sends word he is ill in bed and cannot attend; but he was seen just before that at lunch with his compatriots fully dressed, after he had heard the news that no strychnine had been found.

He must have endured many mental tortures from the time Mr. Stevens first came down, and now all through these various adjournments of the inquest from November 29 to December 15. He saw his neighbours flock to the Town Hall not one hundred yards away, and heard through Jere Smith and his few friends, who told him of the witnesses and their evidence, which all combined to put him through agony of mind. And we may be sure his beloved servant Eliza Tharm retailed every item, for all her friends who could manage to squeeze in were found in the Town Hall listening to the evidence of the doctors and of the hotel servants, telling many details leading to his conviction. Yet he had to go about as usual, appearing unconcerned, and fearful to go in person and listen to the evidence and to see what his fellow-townsmen on the jury were thinking of him.

From the Friday, when Taylor gave his crushing evidence, the inquest is adjourned for the last time to the next day, Saturday, December 15, and it was nearly 11 p.m. when the jury returned a verdict of "wilful murder" against Palmer and Chief Constable Hatton went across to arrest him, and found him ill in bed, in custody of the Sheriff's officer on a forged bill of exchange. He had taken possession of him and all his belongings two days before, on the suit of Padwick.

Two police constables are left in charge of him, and he is removed late on Sunday night by road to Stafford Jail. This hour was chosen in preference to waiting for daylight on Monday, as there was a strong hostile feeling aroused in Rugeley against him. And angry crowds had been outside the house all the Sunday.

He tried to kill himself by voluntary starvation soon after he arrived in Stafford Jail. But on the third day the Governor produced the stomach pump and told him he had five or six warders within reach, and unless he drank the broth produced they would come and bind him down and he would, with the doctor, pass the tube and forcibly feed him. His bravado gave way, and he made a hearty meal and gave no further trouble in that respect.

On Sunday night, January 20, 1856, Palmer was removed to London to appear next day before Mr. Justice Erle to give evidence in the Lord Chancellor's Court, in a action brought by Padwick, the bill discounter, against Mrs. Sarah Palmer to recover £2,000, the amount of a bill of exchange dated July 3, 1854, which apparently bore Palmer's mother's acceptance.

Edwin James appeared for Padwick, Serjeant Wilkins for Mrs. Palmer the acceptor.

The bill was to recover £2,000, payable three months after date (dated July 3, 1854), drawn by William Palmer, advised to Sarah Palmer, payable at Lichfield Bank and endorsed by Palmer and Padwick. The latter put in execution a power of attorney, and it was under that power Palmer had been arrested at home on December 12, and was there under the care of the Sheriff's officer when arrested on the 15th for the murder of Cook.

In 1854 the Magistrate's clerk, Mr. Crabb, had written to Padwick that Mrs. Palmer was well worth £40,000.

At this trial before Mr. Justice Erle, Mrs. Palmer, several members of her family, including her son George Palmer the solicitor, Mr. Strawbridge the manager of the Rugeley bank, her solicitor, Mr. John Smith of Birmingham, all testified in the witness-box that the handwriting accepting the bill was not Mrs. Palmer's.

Palmer was then called to give evidence. He came in by a private door and, calmly looking round the Court, nodded to several friends, and in a quiet voice gave his evidence that he had persuaded his wife to write his mother's name and he had seen her do it.

At once a verdict was given against Padwick; and that night Palmer was taken back to Stafford Jail.

CHAPTER XIV

Excitement in England and many suspicions—The Palmer Act—Also used in other recent cases—Royalty and many notabilities present at the trial—Denman's Act—Palmer never before any Magistrates—Method of procedure—Lord Chief Justice Campbell presided at trial—Notes on Counsel engaged—Serjeant Shee.

AS SOON AS PALMER WAS SAFELY LODGED in Stafford Jail after the finding of the Coroner's jury for murdering his friend Cook, the popular clamour was at once raised loudly against him, and within a week the Home Secretary, Sir George Grey, ordered the bodies of two of his victims to be exhumed. And as we have seen in the case of his wife (pp. 61 and 69) and brother Walter, verdicts of "Wilful murder" were returned by the Coroner's juries within four or five weeks. Then many most suspicious cases were raked up; not the least were the sudden deaths of four of his children under three months of age, and his mother-in-law's death and Bladen, both under his roof; and several illegitimate children which he had been supporting had died after a visit to his surgery. And last of all, Eliza Tharm's baby, which had been born in his house in June, had lately died in convulsions.

In short, except drunkenness, there was no vice, no crime, which was not raked up against him.

Throughout England the excitement became intense; newspapers in those days commented much more freely than they are allowed now, when a prisoner is waiting for his trial. But every paper hounded him down and took up the cry against him, so we can plainly see it was impossible to collect a jury in the county of Stafford or any county in that circuit who would not be prejudiced against him, and who could come into the jury-box with minds clear to decide only on the evidence.

So an Act of Parliament was specially passed (19 Vict. c. 37), as soon as Parliament met, to allow a prisoner to have his trial take place in London if he could satisfy the authorities he could not be fairly tried in his own county, or if the Crown thought the same, they could apply. This is often quoted at the present time as "*the Palmer Act*," and made use of by either side whenever there is any doubt about a fair trial. Serjeant Shee alludes most courteously to this in the opening of his speech, and also to the fairness with which the whole proceedings were being conducted.

This Act was made use of in the Penge mystery, where the Stauntons were committed for trial for starving to death Mrs. Louis Staunton in 1877; and after the Judge had charged the Grand Jury at Maidstone Assizes and a true bill found, the popular execration and clamour was so great, the trial had to be removed, under this "Palmer Act," to the Central Criminal Court, where it was heard before Justice Hawkins, and the talent of the Bar was called in for the four prisoners, as well as by the Crown, led by the Attorney-General, Sir John Hollier, and the Solicitor-General, Sir Hardinge Giffard, helped by that terror of miscreants Harry B. Poland.[1]

Within the last few months the Act has been prominently brought forward. Miss Thurburn was sent for trial at Norwich Assizes for libel, applied to be tried under the "Palmer Act" in London, AND WAS REFUSED. The jury twice disagreed at Norwich, so when brought up for the third time, no evidence being offered, she was discharged in October 1924.[2]

Also Dr. Hadwen was sent by the Coroner's inquest and by

---

[1] In 1877, Harriet Staunton died a day after her emaciated and battered body was brought to a lodging house in Penge, a suburb of London. Her husband, Louis Staunton, his lover Alice Rhodes, his brother Patrick Staunton and his wife Elizabeth were sentenced to hang for both her death and that of her infant son, who had died days before. The nature of the medical evidence and the judge's obvious bias against the defendants led to a review by the Home Secretary. Alice Rhodes was pardoned and the rest of the sentences were communed to life imprisonment. Patrick Staunton died in prison, Elizabeth Staunton was released in 1883, and Louis Staunton was released in 1897.

[2] In 1923, Dorothy Thurburn was charged with sending letters and postcards to more than 2,000 residents of Sheringham containing libelous statements against at least 60 persons. One of the letters, addressed to a Colonel Copeman, was read in court: "To Copeman, who calls himself a solicitor. You are a silly old fool, and you will never get me. You cannot be proud of your old girl you picked up in the dark, and you are years older than her. Am writing to all. What a joke! Stanley will sit up. Stanley will have to pay me to be quiet. All will be known. How is your old girl's cheap make-up? What a joke, you silly old fool! You must live on your old girl's money, as you are too much of a fool to make any." She was tried three times, and although she was acquitted, Thurburn and her mother said they received nearly 200 abusive letters and will be forced to leave the country.

the Magistrates at Gloucester to be tried for manslaughter. The Crown thought a jury at the Assizes drawn from the city and county of Gloucester would be too favourably disposed to him, partly on the ground that he was a leading anti-vaccinationist, so they applied to have him brought under the "Palmer Act" to London; but the Court of King's Bench refused the application of the Crown, saying a jury of his own county could surely be found to give an honest verdict, and he was tried at Gloucester Assizes and acquitted.[3]

In addition to the "Palmer Act" for removal of a trial to London, as I have shown, another Act was due to this case, that no insurance can be effected by any person on another's life without proof that there is money interest in his life up to the value proposed. How could Palmer ever think of insuring Bates for £20,000 or his brother Walter proposed for £84,000 (and a policy was granted for £14,000)?—almost a temptation to murder.

And in the cases of Mrs. Anne Palmer and Walter Palmer, only the first premiums were paid before the claim on death was sent in.

It is hard for the present generation to understand the sensation the Palmer case (as it was called) created throughout England and in every class of society.

Royalty was not excluded from the wish to learn any details. The Prince Consort [Prince Albert, the husband of Queen Victoria], I was told by one of his physicians, took the keenest interest in the trial; he bought one of Palmer's horses for 280 guineas at the sale after his arrest. And at the trial itself in the Central Criminal Court, Royalty was represented by the Prince of Saxe-Weimar and the Duke of Cambridge sitting near the Judges. And then we see such names as the Duke (2nd) of Wellington, Marquis of Anglesey, and the Earl of Derby (three times Prime Minister), who was present nearly every day. Also we see the Earl of Albemarle, Earl of Dufferin, Mr. Gladstone, and his wife's brother-in-law Lord Lyttelton, Sir John Pakington (Chief Lord of the Admiralty), and many other notabilities,

---

[3] Walter Hadwen (1854-1932), an anti-vivisectionist and opponent of the germ theory of disease, was tried in 1924 for manslaughter in the death of 10-year-old Nellie Burnham. He was accused of failing to diagnose the girl's diphtheria and not visiting the girl as often as he should have. The child's mother testified that she did not call the doctor when Nellie took a turn for the worse because she expected him to visit. He was acquitted.

including Mr. Justice Stephen, who was present nearly every day. Chief Baron Pollock and several Judges came in on the Saturday to listen to the Attorney-General's speech, most famous in all the literature of trials; and last, but by no means least, a dozen of the leading physicians and surgeons from the West End watched their thirty-five Colleagues in the witness-box.

But it was not made a show trial, for fashionable and titled ladies to sit next to the Judge, as we find twenty years later, with a Judge who here appears as one of the Counsel for the Crown.

In the procedure one remarkable fact stands out which is very different at the present day—namely, that at the time of this celebrated trial, when all the witnesses at Crown had been called, Serjeant Shee made his opening speech and the only one allowed by law for the Defence.

After his witnesses had been called, he was not allowed a second speech to sum up and comment on their evidence. The Prosecution had the right to the final reply, followed by the Judge's summing up. But this was all altered by Denman's Act (1865). A second speech is now allowed the Defence, and this was brought about mainly by a speech of Serjeant Parry when defending Müller in 1864,[4] and I cannot do better than quote his words addressing the jury:

"Gentlemen, if this were a case of a ten-pound theft, if it were a case of a bill of exchange, if it were a case of goods exchanged or sold, or if it were a miserable squabble between a hackney cab and a dust-cart, I should be permitted to sum up the evidence for the Defence. But this is simply a case of life and death, and the law of England forbids that to be done. I feel very strongly on that subject, but we are in a court of Justice, not of Legislature. So I forbear to express my opinion further."

The Act known as Denman's was passed soon after Parry's speech, and in addition now for nearly a quarter of a century a prisoner may go into the witness-box and give his evidence on oath.

---

[4] Müller (1840-1864) was executed for robbing Thomas Briggs and throwing him from a North London Railway train. The murder was the first ever performed on a train, and Müller was pursued across the Atlantic to New York and arrested. The case led to the establishment of communication cords to summon the staff, and the construction of railway carriages with interior corridors. Fletcher will return to the Müller case in Chapter XX.

No edition of the trial, no books on this case, call attention to the fact that Palmer never had the chance to state his case in public nor to make any statement in any Court of Justice.

The local Coroner's inquest having found a verdict of "guilty," he was at once arrested, ill in bed, and in a couple of days was driven off to Stafford Jail. He never was taken before any Magistrate, and in those days a prisoner had no chance to go into the witness-box at his trial, nor to make any statement from the dock, when defended by Counsel.

In Mrs. Maybrick's case she was allowed, as a privilege at her own request, to say a few words to the jury before Sir Charles Russell's final speech in her defence, much against the wish of her eminent Counsel, and did her case no good.[5] But Palmer was taken to Stafford in December, and from Stafford direct to the dock, at the Central Criminal Court in May. I verified this when at Stafford Assize Court a few years ago: the Chief Constable of the county kindly looked up the records, and a copy is appended.

There was some suggestion (about three weeks after the Coroner's inquest) of having a "magisterial investigation" into the charge of murdering Cook; but when John Smith of Birmingham, the defending solicitor, heard of it, he at once wrote strongly to the Home Secretary, reminding him that Lord Campbell had expressed a strong wish that the case would not be further discussed in newspapers or elsewhere to the prisoner's prejudice, and a rehearing of the evidence before the magistrates would do this; and he would on Palmer's behalf accept any *fresh* evidence which might be forthcoming, provided he had a copy of it, so the case need not be heard before any magistrates in the case of Mrs. Palmer or Walter Palmer or Cook.

And this confirms what I have previously stated, that Palmer never had the opportunity of stating his case from any witness-box or before any public authorities or giving his own

---

[5] American Florence Maybrick (1862-1941) was convicted of murdering her older English husband, James, in 1889. His body contained a slight amount of arsenic, but not enough to kill him. Since James had been known to take arsenic as a medicine, a public outcry led to a review of the evidence. The Home Secretary concluded that she tried to poison her husband, but did not cause his death. Her sentence was commuted to life imprisonment, and she was released in 1904. She moved back to the United States, where she died in poverty.

version of many matters which looked so against him. At the present time a prisoner is always asked by the magistrate if he has anything to say before committing him for trial, and here the Coroner's jury brought in a verdict of "wilful murder," and he was at once arrested in bed at home and conveyed to Stafford Jail, where he remained till his trial, except for one brief appearance as a witness in a civil trial in London on January 20.[6]

So Palmer never HEARD a word of evidence against him till at his trial at the Old Bailey in May.

When Palmer was taken back from London after conviction, he was heavily ironed and handcuffed and one chain attached to a warder. We read of his complaining of the irons when he arrived back at Stafford Station. The treatment was very different to present days, when handcuffs only are used, and those not often.

When it was discussed at the time that he should be brought before the Rugeley Magistrates, after the Coroner's jury had found his wife had been poisoned, one account says: "If it should be necessary for Justices to hear the case, they could sit in Stafford Jail." [This was done in the case of Charlie Peace.[7]] One great reason was, the authorities were afraid of the crowd attacking him, in spite of all precautions in the county town, so great was the hatred shown. In fact, when he had to appear in January to give evidence at Westminster about the bills forged in his mother's name, the police were strengthened by soldiers riding each side of the prison van to Westminster, where he was detained till dusk after giving his evidence, before being taken to Newgate for the night and back to Stafford by a very early train.

---

[6] Padwick sued Mrs. Palmer to recover £12,000 on a loan that bore her signature. The case was thrown out after William Palmer testified that his wife forged his mother's name on the bill. The story is described in *The Life and Crimes of William Palmer* (Peschel Press, 2014).

[7] Charles Peace (1832-1879) was a thief and burglar who was executed for murdering a man whose wife he wanted for his own. While being transported from London to Sheffield for a magistrate's hearing, he tried to escape by leaping from the train. Because of his severe injuries and widespread public interest, the hearing was held in a corridor at Town Hall. His memorable name, lengthy criminal career, and charismatic personality inspired stories by Arthur Conan Doyle and Edgar Wallace, and even a comic strip — "The Astounding Adventures of Charlie Peace" — from 1964 to 1974.

At the Stafford Assizes in March 1856, presided over by Baron Bramwell and Mr. Justice Cresswell, the former addressed the Grand Jury on the three Bills against Palmer for the murder of Cook and Mrs. Anne Palmer and Walter Palmer. A True Bill was found in the first two cases, but the Bill for poisoning Walter was thrown out. The Government thought so seriously of this whole matter they ordered the Lord Chief Justice (Campbell) to preside at the trial at the Central Criminal Court, aided by two other Judges, and the chief Law Officer of the Crown (Sir Alexander Cockburn), the Attorney-General to conduct the Prosecution.

In the *Life of Lord Campbell*[8] we easily see how anxious he

---

[8] Here is what Lord Campbell wrote in his diary about the Palmer case, from his memoir *Life of John, Lord Campbell, Lord High Chancellor of Great Britain* (1881):

"June 28. Since my last notice in this Journal, the great event has been the trial of William Palmer at the Central Criminal Court for *poisoning*, which began on Wednesday May 14th and did not finish till Tuesday May 27th — the most memorable judicial proceeding for the last fifty years, enjoying the attention not only of this country but of all Europe.

"My labour and anxiety were fearful; but I have been rewarded by public approbation. The court sat eight hours a day, and when I got home, renouncing all other engagements, I employed myself till midnight in revising my notes and considering the evidence. Luckily I had a Sunday to prepare for my summing up, and to this I devoted fourteen continuous hours. The following day, after reading in court ten hours, I had only got through the proofs for the prosecution. My anxiety was over on the last day when the verdict of *Guilty* was pronounced and I had sentenced the prisoner to die, for I had no doubt of his guilt, and I was conscious that, by God's assistance, I had done my duty. Such was the expressed opinion of the public and of all the respectable part of the press. But a most ruffianlike attempt was made by the friends of the prisoner to abuse me and to obtain a pardon or reprieve, on the ground that the prisoner had not had a fair trial. Having unbounded funds at their command, they corrupted some disreputable journals to admit their *diatribes* against me, and they published a most libellous pamphlet under the title of *A Letter from the Rev. T. Palmer, the Prisoner's Brother, to Lord Chief Justice Campbell*, in which the Chief Justice was represented to be worse than his predecessor Jeffreys,* and it was asserted that there had been nothing in England like the last trial since "the Bloody Assize." However, the Home Secretary remained firm and the law took its course.

"The Rev. T. Palmer has since disclaimed the pamphlet, and it is was to preside at this trial, and two or three pages are taken up with his private remarks about it. His summing up was very thorough and complete, but lengthy and prosaic, lasting nearly two days. But all speeches were eclipsed by the Attorney-General's two speeches. His *opening* speech was clear and admirable, not missing a single point, laying plainly before the Court the case he was presenting—lasting nearly five hours. But brilliant as he had proved himself for some years, he here surpassed himself, and he delivered his reply at the close with that superb ease and convincing emphasis in which he was unrivalled amongst the orators of the century, uttering the most deadly and effective speech ever met with, speaking for nearly six hours without a single note, on the tenth day of the trial, tightening the rope round Palmer's neck in every detail, and tearing to pieces the weak defence, which had relied mainly on the medical aspect of the case, and showing completely how the crushing circumstantial details had ALL remained unanswered.

This reply is often quoted as one of the finest, most convincing speeches ever met with in any Court. Well might Palmer write on a slip of paper for his solicitor at the close of the trial, after intently listening to every word: "*It is the riding that did it!*" The evidence may have been overwhelming and strong, but it was the marshalling and arranging the facts and steering it all—by such a jockey—who did it, "steering to victory" and proving his guilt.

Miss Tennyson Jesse says it was the "*riding*" of his own passions where they chose to lead him—the "riding" that had done it all his life with the cold and calculating mind which could arrange at whatever cost for the indulgence of those passions.

Some think he alluded to the Judge as Chief Jockey and his

---

said to have been written by a blackguard barrister. I bear him no enmity, and he has done me no harm; but for the sake of example he ought to be disbarred."

* A reference to George Jeffreys (1645-1689), known as "the Hanging Judge." After the failure of Monmouth's Rebellion in 1685, he presided over the trials of captured rebels for treason that were known as "the Bloody Assize." Between 160 and 170 of the 1,381 defendants were found guilty, for which Jeffreys by law was required to sentence them to death. James II could have commuted the sentences, but declined, and they were hanged.

"riding"—his summing up—did it. Last year in the *Sunday Times* appeared a letter from the son of one of his Counsel, who said he had seen the note which Palmer tossed to his father, and he thinks it alluded not only to the Attorney-General's (Cockburn's) powerful speech, but to the Judge's hostility in his summing up. And he adds a remarkable opinion, almost unique, that if the trial had been held in Stafford, no county jury would have convicted him! The persuasive charm of Palmer secured him staunch friends who would not have convicted him, even if they had no doubt of his guilt.

This opinion is indeed very different from the reasons given all over Great Britain for the removal of his trial from the county, where so much hostility was shown. The Judge said in his summing up that the prejudice was so strong against him in the whole County of Stafford that, as we have seen, the Court of Queen's Bench at the prisoner's wish ordered the trial to be removed to London, and I should think this is the only time we read of a county jury likely to acquit him. But it was the convincing speech of the Attorney-General that helped to steer the verdict, far more than the ordinary summing up of the Judge. No summary of such a speech can convey any idea of its intrinsic value and real merit, and again I would urge those interested to read it in full in Angelo Bennett's version of the trial.[9]

The Attorney-General, Sir Alexander Cockburn, became Chief Justice of the Common Pleas four months after this trial, and died, full of years and honour, as Lord Chief Justice of England in 1880.

Of the other Counsel engaged by the Crown, first comes Edwin James, Q.C., who in private life achieved notoriety not of a praiseworthy character. He was made Recorder of Brighton, and in a few years had a large practice, but soon was overwhelmed with debts to £100,000. And as he had indulged in several very shady, dishonourable transactions, he was disbarred, and after practising in America returned here to die, very poor, in 1882, aged seventy.

Sir William Bodkin (b. 1791, d. 1874) became assistant Judge at the Middlesex Sessions and Counsel to the Treasury, and Recorder of Dover, grandfather of the present Sir

---

[9] Bennett, Angelo. *The Queen v. Palmer: Verbatim Report of the Trial of William Palmer.* London: J. Allen, 1856.

Archibald Bodkin, K.C., leading Prosecuting Counsel for the Treasury, also Recorder of Dover.

Serjeant Huddlestone had been asked to defend Palmer; he had appeared for him respecting the removal of the trial from Stafford to London, and had appeared in January 1856 for Mrs. Palmer when she appeared at the trial respecting bills forged in her name. Also he had been Counsel for Palmer's friend the postmaster Cheshire, when he was convicted of opening and reading letters for Palmer.

But, after all, his services were secured for the Prosecution, and he appeared as a junior under the Attorney-General. He became a fashionable Judge and always aimed at social distinction. Died 1890, aged seventy-five.

Kenealy appeared for the Defence, a scholar of unusual diversity of learning and gifted in many ways. His gifts were great, but, as it was remarked of him eighteen years later, they were almost allied to madness. He was M.P. for a few years after he had been struck off the Rolls for his conduct and abuse of the Judges in the Tichborne trial, and died 1880, only sixty-one years old.[10]

Sir William Grove, also for the Defence, was a man of European reputation, but more skilled in science and chemistry than in law. He was forty-five at the time of this trial, but in feeble health, so he soon gave up the Law and devoted himself to science, and died, full of honours, at the ripe age of eighty-five in 1896, after being a Judge for twenty years.

For the Defence, Serjeant Shee stands out as the Leader of a forlorn case. Serjeant Wilkins had been engaged to lead for the Defence, and had appeared for Palmer at the trial in January respecting his mother's forged bills. Wilkins had received a medical education before taking to the Law, and this would have been most helpful in this case. But three weeks before the trial he was taken ill, and there was some trouble to select an eminent barrister in his place. Sir

---

[10] A notorious case in which an Australian man claimed to be Roger Tichborne, the heir to his family's ancient title and fabulous fortune. In 1854, Tichborne was believed to have died in a shipwreck off Brazil. There were rumors a ship picked up survivors and took them to Australia, so his mother advertised extensively in the newspapers there. Twelve years later, Thomas Castro stepped forward to claim the Tichborne title. The claimant lost his case in 1871, was tried and convicted of perjury in 1874, and sentenced to 14 years in prison.

Frederick Thesiger had been asked previously to help the Defence, but very firmly declined.

Serjeant Shee was decided on, and he certainly made the very best defence possible. He alluded to Serjeant Wilkins's absence in his opening speech, and most courteously thanked the Attorney-General for the manner in which the trial was being conducted.

But one great point will stand out for ever in his speech (as I believe) almost unique. Serjeant Shee assured the jury on his conscience and honour that he personally believed in Palmer's innocence! Was he exercising a dispassionate judgment? or why did he make this most unusual statement?

Here we see a distinguished member of the Bar, the leader for the Defence, Serjeant Shee (who a few years later became a judge), assuring the jury on his personal honour he believed the prisoner to be innocent of the crime for which he was being tried, and he made this almost solemn declaration in spite of the cumulative and overwhelming power and weight of circumstantial and scientific evidence, which could not leave a shade of doubt of Palmer's guilt, and which Shee in vain endeavoured to tackle.

Shee's personal character was too well known, too honourable, for anyone to think he did not believe what he stated. The Lord Chief Justice thought very little of this belief in Palmer's innocence, telling the jury in his summing up it was a licence of Counsel, and they were not to attach any weight to this remark.

It is not often mentioned, and I think there is not much similarity, but Sir John Coleridge, at the trial of Constance Kent, pledged his word that he believed every sentence of her confession of "Wilful murder" of her young brother at Road. But in that case, the prisoner having confessed and pleaded "guilty," the jury were not called upon for a verdict.[11]

But it was remarked at the time that Coleridge's statement

---

[11] Constance Kent (1844-1944) was sentenced to hang for killing her half-brother, four-year-old Francis Kent, by slitting his throat and dumping him in a privy. The investigation at Road Hill House ran into opposition from the family who objected to a working-class detective in charge of the case and the insinuation that a family member killed the child. Five years later, she confessed to a priest that she killed Francis and she was brought to trial. Her sentence was commuted to life in prison based on her contrite behavior and her age — 16 — at the time of the murder.

was meant to express thereby his belief in the complete innocence of her father and the nurse who had been suspected at the time of the murder.

Serjeant Shee's actual words were: "I believe that truer words were never pronounced than the words he [Palmer] uttered when he pleaded 'not guilty' to this charge, I will prove to you the sincerity with which I declare my personal conviction of the prisoner's innocence by meeting the case foot to foot."

The Attorney-General replied quietly and very pointedly, "You have had from my learned friend the *unusual*, I think I may add the *unprecedented* assurance of his personal belief in his client's innocence. It would have been better if he had abstained from so strange a declaration.

"If he was sincere in that—*and I know he was*—there is no man in whom the spirit of truth and honour is more keenly alive—he said what he believed. But what would he think of me if, imitating his example, I at this moment stated to you, upon my personal word and *honour* as he did, what is my personal conviction from a conscientious consideration of the whole case?"

Shee was a (strong) Roman Catholic, a cousin of Cardinal Wiseman. He gave Palmer a Bible a few days before his execution, and sent a kind, sympathetic letter with it to Stafford Jail. He became Judge in 1863, and died in 1868 at the age of sixty-three—so was fifty-one at the time of the trial.

Of the Counsel engaged at this trial, four subsequently became judges—Cockburn, Shee, Grove, and Huddlestone, and two were debarred—Edwin James and Kenealy.

CHAPTER XV

WE MAY NOW DISPASSIONATELY LOOK at some of the more deadly convicting pieces of evidence against Palmer, which, as they were virtually unanswered, told very heavily against him.

The very first of all is his purchasing strychnine at Hawkins's shop on the morning of November 20, and Palmer never gave any reason for purchasing this deadly poison. There was no attempt to answer this, and no cross-examination of Roberts, who supplied it.

Cook died within twelve hours of the purchase, with every symptom of strychnine poisoning after taking two pills at the hand of Palmer.

The *next* most deadly evidence against Palmer is his letter to the Coroner on December 13, together with the ten-pound note after the inquest had been adjourned for the third time, showing eagerness beyond belief, and even suggesting the words of the verdict the jury should find; also his presents of game and money to the Coroner—a step, I should think, unheard of in the annals of crime.

It requires a great deal of explanation to any clear, unbiassed mind, why any friend of Cook (as Palmer professed to be) should take such keen, absorbing interest in the inquest if he had a clear conscience; but with a guilty mind, we can understand his restlessness and trying to get the Coroner to close the inquest with a verdict "death from natural causes," and so end all the enquiry and silence the townsfolk's tongue gossiping not only at the death of Cook, but also about other deaths under very suspicious circumstances.

One point, a very serious one, we can now readily discern. As Palmer had robbed his friend Cook of the £800 he had in his money-belt when he came on November 15 from Shrewsbury to Rugeley, and had also stolen his betting-book, as well as appropriated all his bets and winnings at Tattersall's collected by George Herring on Monday the 19th, so it becomes very evident Cook must never get about again to see after his own affairs, or Palmer will be convicted of a shameful robbery from his friend of all his winnings, and he could see, if once his thefts and character were called in question in a public court, it would speedily follow that his forgeries would at once be disclosed for over £20,000.

And yet this two or three thousand he was robbing from Cook would only clear off the ruinous 60 per cent. interest some weeks overdue, and was postponing for only a few weeks the moneylenders summoning his mother for the forged bills. So Cook *was doomed* TO DIE, *and that, too, at once*, and Palmer get his £3,000 ready money.

I have never seen any comments on Palmer buying the three different poisons at Hawkins's shop on the Tuesday morning, when the strychnine given on the Monday night had failed. But I have often wondered what would have happened. What would Palmer have done if Cook had persisted in his refusal to swallow these two pills on the Tuesday night?—and he very nearly did refuse. Dr. Jones told a friend some time after the trial that he and Palmer were over ten minutes persuading him. I think Palmer had not overlooked this chance, and provided against it by also buying prussic acid and strong laudanum when he bought those six grains of strychnine at Hawkins's shop. For look at this how one may, what can he require the two ADDITIONAL poisons for as well as the strychnine, which he had determined to use first if possible—and did use as a substitute for Bamford's sedative pills, with fatal effect? And thus when we try to find some explanation of the extraordinary excitement produced throughout Great Britain at the facts elicited gradually at the inquest and fully at the trial, we find one reason in the deadly insidious nature of the poison selected and the cunning substitution of strychnine pills for Bamford's sedative.

Yet his friends say he used the strychnine to destroy the dogs which worried his stud mares in his paddock. Six grains of strychnine for that purpose—almost an insult to the intelligence of the British public. And if he did kill the dogs, where were their bodies—or where was the groom who would help to lay the poison? But even if this is granted, then one asks for what purpose did he also buy prussic acid and Batley's solution of opium?—two very potent poisons for which he could have no legitimate use, and certainly no patients for whom such drugs would be useful. I think they were to fall back on in case Cook refused the strychnine pills. I may be wrong in my surmise, but I have already mentioned these two other poisons were found unopened in a drawer in his surgery three weeks after his arrest, and the third packet, the strychnine, was not there.

Anyhow, strychnine was the poison selected, the name of which was at that time hardly known to the public, and this deadly cruel poison added greatly to the excitement of the public mind, far more than if the usual antimony or laudanum or arsenic had been used, and the intense eagerness of the nation was increased by the ingenious mode of administration, *i.e.* by the substitution on two successive nights of these poisoned pills for pills prescribed by Dr. Bamford on both nights. We shall find the excitement also in the fact that the accused was himself a medical man of some respectability, and a man of education and knowledge.

People called to mind the sudden deaths which had taken place in his house during the last four years—four of his children, a racing friend while on a five-day visit, his mother-in-law after ten days under his roof, and then his wife, for whose murder by poison he was to have been immediately tried in the event of an acquittal on the charge of killing Cook, as well as the murder of his brother after heavily insuring his life.

All these facts gave an interest to these proceedings far beyond that attached to any ordinary case of poisoning.

With a prevalent conviction of Palmer's guilt, there was at the same time an almost universal feeling that his trial for the murder of Cook would end in an acquittal.

His legal advisers felt confident of a verdict in his favour! For the crime had been committed in secrecy with consummate skill and care, and, above all, the poison to which death was ascribed by the witnesses for the Crown was not found in the body of Cook, even by one of the greatest analysts living.

Strychnine as a poison was almost unknown. Only three or four previous cases were on record in Great Britain, one very doubtful, the others supposed to be accidental; this was the first case in which a person had been tried for murder in England for the use of strychnine, and as the poison was not found, the jury had to be satisfied on other than scientific or chemical grounds (such as the symptoms of the dying man, the behaviour of the prisoner before and after the death). Yet it was thought there would be a difficulty that the legal advisers of the Crown would never surmount, although aided by the advice and evidence of the highest medical authorities, such as Sir Benjamin Brodie, President of the Royal College of Surgeons, and many others whose names and reputation were at the very top of the Profession, and they all unanimously spoke with overwhelming authority against the prisoner.

But in more recent days there has been a suggestion that Palmer did not use strychnine, basing the opinion on the fact that Palmer said just before his execution, "Cook did not die from strychnine," and writers suggest brucia[1]—a similar drug, but much milder, alluded to by the Attorney-General in his reply. But VERY hard to obtain—and never prescribed. Why any writers should suggest this puzzles me, for we DO find Palmer buying strychnine twice within twenty-four hours of Cook's death, and he probably had never heard of brucia. A few contended that Palmer had discovered a way of administering strychnine so that it would not be detected! Had he? Has anybody ever found that method? Almost too absurd for refutation!

Palmer was not clever enough for that. This was a cold, merciless murder, with the agony and hellish torture of strychnine, and he sat by the bedside on two successive nights watching unmoved the death-agony of strychnine poisoning, twisting and rending every joint and muscle of Cook's body, already weakened by four days' constant vomiting after tartar emetic given by Palmer.

So we surely need scarcely trouble ourselves to heed what Palmer said on his way to the scaffold when the executioner was pinioning his arms, and the Governor asked him for the last time if he would own to his guilt. His reply was, "Cook did not die from strychnine." The Governor kindly said, "This is not the hour for argument. Did you poison Cook?" He replied, "The Lord Chief Justice summed up for strychnine poisoning alone, and I have nothing more to say."

By slow degrees we are at length reaching the trial at the Central Criminal Court, which commenced on May 14, 1856, and lasted a fortnight, certainly the greatest trial for murder in Great Britain up till that time and also up to the present day.

The Lord Mayor occupied the seat of honour. There were three judges on the Bench, the Lord Chief Justice presiding. The Crown and the prisoner were represented by the notable leaders of the Bar as given on p. 138. Noble and illustrious

---

[1] An alkaloid found in the bark of the nux vomica tree whose seeds are used to create strychnine. It is a weaker poison than strychnine, but produces the same symptoms.

visitors, including Royalty itself. The Court and precincts all densely crowded, and the very streets outside thronged early every day. A setting to a drama and tragedy which has never been equalled.

This trial is remarkable for the conflict of medical and scientific evidence, as the most eminent men amongst our physicians and analytical chemists were called on each side, and the most contradictory evidence given, both as regards the symptoms of death from tetanus following strychnine and the symptoms from idiopathic or natural tetanus, a most rare disease, and the symptoms of traumatic tetanus, and very grave differences were expressed as to the possibility of detecting strychnine.

The whole nation (in fact, much of the civilised world) was intensely excited to a degree we can hardly recognise in the present day; and we have never since seen such an amount of eloquence, learning, and skill brought to bear upon the conviction of one criminal, the evidence of whose guilt appeared to unbiassed judgments abundant and overwhelming.

The morbid excitement was perhaps due to the fearful nature of the many crimes, and to the cunning way in which the murders were committed, and the interest was increased by the extraordinary steps taken to ensure an impartial trial, such as passing an Act of Parliament, with this case specially in view, to remove the seat of trial from Stafford to London.

The Old Bailey (now demolished) and its precincts were densely thronged each day, all marking out this as the greatest criminal trial of the century.

It is very noticeable in the medical aspect of the trial how we shall see witness after witness giving evidence for the Defence in the most obvious spirit of partisanship, for on the medical (so-called) weak points the whole foundation of the Defence rested, and the circumstantial convicting evidence was almost ignored.

Here we shall see for the prisoner men of science juggling with their judgment and setting at naught their most solemn obligations, for the purpose of rescuing one of the darkest criminals who has ever polluted the English soil.

The medical evidence on the two sides was remarkable.

That for the Prosecution was noticeable for its uniformity and consistency; that for the Defence for its diversity and extraordinary inconsistency, aptly called by the Attorney-General "traffic evidence" of the most surprising nature.

The *motives* of those who came forward for the Defence to speak on the medical or scientific view of Cook's death as not being due to poisoning by strychnine were as diverse as the *opinions* themselves: *some* men from the love of theorising, *some* from love of prominence, *some* from airing their hobbies, *some* from the love of notoriety to drag themselves to the front. I have shown elsewhere how they attribute his death to epilepsy with tetanic complications to arachnitis, to angina pectoris, to latent alterations of the spinal cord, etc.

In the toxicological and professional department of chemistry we find personal rivalry played an important, undoubted share, as we shall see in Professor Herapath's evidence (p. 181); nobody has ever disputed the fact that the post-mortem, left to an unqualified medical assistant to carry out, aided by a dispenser who had never even seen a post-mortem, was bungled in so shameful a manner. Palmer was present, helping, looking on, chatting and pushing the operators, that no adequate result could be obtained from the mangled, inverted, empty stomach sent to Professor Taylor, whilst the spinal cord, the centre of the seat of poison by strychnine and also of tetanus, was virtually never even looked at, much less carefully taken out and sent up to be scientifically examined.

Dr. Harland's examination of Cook's body, or rather his supervision of his ignorant workers, as I have shown, was merely a negligent one of superintending a careless, shamefully conducted post-mortem examination, one from which the public were more likely to sustain injury than the accused.

But fortunately, with Mr. Stevens discreet and far seeing, and Professor Taylor, a skilful man of outspoken, careful opinions, the accused was finally convicted.

Professor Taylor was not selected by the Government for this responsible, delicate investigation; but he was chosen because by chance a solicitor on the morrow of Cook's death happened to recommend him to Mr. Stevens as a competent trustworthy man. Yet he might have been a third-rate analyst, and only first-rate in that friend's eyes. But by the veriest good fortune, Mr. Stevens was a man of rare intelligence and discretion, and not one likely to make an injudicious selection of an analyst because he was recommended by a friend, nor of a lawyer to whom much was to be entrusted and much expected, so Professor Taylor and Mr. Gardner were chosen by Mr. Stevens, and turned out to be all one could wish for.

CHAPTER XVI

The trial—Four divisions of evidence—Chief circumstances—Events on each day of the trial—Chief witnesses: Mills, Dr. Jones and Newton, Cheshire, Pratt, local doctors—Palmer quickly dressed—Carelessness at post-mortem.

PALMER WAS BROUGHT FROM STAFFORD a week previous to the trial, so as to ensure getting him up to London in safety and enable him to interview his legal advisers.

At 10 a.m. on Wednesday, May 14, 1856, he appeared in the dock, and the trial at once commenced.

I do not wish to weary my readers with a verbatim report of the trial, which can be read in an edition by Ward & Lock,[1] published in 1856, with many illustrations, 184 pages of close type, also in a very excellent verbatim account (of Angelo Bennett), published by Allen in 1856, closely printed 326 pages, and a somewhat abbreviated copy of 260 pages, larger type, in the "Notable Trial" Series, published 1912.

But the last named did not give in the first edition the magnificent opening speech of four or five hours by the Attorney-General, and omits some evidence altogether and abbreviates much. The second edition, improved greatly, has been under the care of Eric Watson.

The opening speech arranged the mass of evidence very cleverly and clearly, and was listened to most attentively by the jury, and the many facts and intricate details were skilfully marshalled, and all that he described was confirmed by the witnesses. The evidence at the trial seems to resolve itself under four headings, and it will simplify matters and be less tedious to my readers if I summarise the evidence under each heading separately, and give an outline of Serjeant Shee's speech for the Defence, and an outline (very brief, I fear) of the Attorney-General's reply for the Crown, winding up with the Lord Chief Justice's summing up.

The headings under which I will group the evidence are:

A. Pecuniary straits to which Palmer was reduced in the autumn of 1855.

---

[1] See *The Illustrated Times Report of the Trial of William Palmer* (Peschel Press, 2014).

B. *Circumstantial evidence*—subdivided under twelve headings.

C. Medical evidence for the Crown, after some remarks on strychnine poisons.

D. Medical evidence for the Defence.

Taking them in order:

A. The terrible pecuniary straits to which Palmer was reduced under the moneylenders' hands (Pratt, Padwick, and Wright) in the autumn of 1855, and the necessity to find several thousand pounds *at once* to pay up only the monthly interest flow several months in arrear, and to pay the daily expenses of a large racing stud (fourteen race-horses, stablemen, jockeys, and touts, etc.), all had to be met, every nerve strained, every resource tried, to avoid arrest, which would at once disclose the forgery of his mother's name to the bills held for over £20,000 by Pratt and Padwick, entailing probably transportation for life if once exposure should be made, and his mother sued for the bills.

So ready money must be found and Cook must be poisoned in order that Palmer can appropriate all his ready money, cash winnings, stakes, and bets, won at Shrewsbury. And this infamous plan succeeded as far as the money was concerned, for all Cook's winnings found their way into Palmer's hands, by theft and forgeries carried out with cunning. But at last it raised suspicion in the minds of many, notably Mr. Stevens, George Herring, Fisher, and even Pratt and Padwick, the two bill discounters who had lent the money.

When once suspicion was fairly aroused, one noticed the circumstantial evidence, as regards the steps taken for the actual murder, drugging Cook at Shrewsbury with antimony to give an appearance of illness for two or three days, and then poisoning him with strychnine. The two purchases of strychnine, appropriation of his bets, all details were thoroughly suspicious, and finally administering pills on two successive evenings containing the strychnine bought by Palmer. Moreover, the medical evidence for the Prosecution showed Cook's symptoms could not be attributed to any natural disease ever heard of, and the symptoms agreed in every detail with known deaths from strychnine. And this poisoning was done with an eye to get about £3,000 ready money to help Palmer out of the pecuniary quagmire of debts to moneylending harpies, and to avoid exposure of forgeries for over £20,000, due chiefly to Pratt, who proved at the trial he had had dealings with Palmer for over two years, and had advanced loans of some thousands secured on bills of exchange, IN ALL cases accepted by Mrs. Palmer, which bills in 1854 had reached over £12,000, but the insurance money from murdering his wife had nearly wiped that out, even though 60 per cent. per annum was the lowest interest charged. But in the next year he again got into terrible debt, and to summarise briefly, Palmer owed him in July 1855, £15,000 at 60 per cent. per annum, or, as it was now paid, 5 per cent. monthly (£750)—all borrowed on his mother's forged acceptances.

As Palmer lost heavily on the Derby and several races that summer of 1855, and there was a final crash at Shrewsbury in the autumn, Pratt wrote to him that he could wait no longer, and this decided Cook's fate.

Palmer owed about £25,000 (half to Pratt), including four months' overdue interest—a sum so totally impossible for the ordinary man to grasp that we are almost bound to believe that Pratt, if not Padwick and Wright, must have long since known there was forgery of his mother's name and deliberate robbery going on. More especially so, as not one of that trio HAD EVER RECEIVED A LINE from Mrs. Sarah Palmer whose acceptances were on ALL THE BILLS. And if the signatures were looked at carefully, two, if not three, TOTALLY DIFFERENT handwritings of "Sarah Palmer" could be easily discerned.

Pratt in the end of the summer of 1855 threatened Mrs. Palmer with legal proceedings, but his letters to her were all handed over to Palmer by Cheshire, the easy, complacent postmaster and so his mother *never heard* anything about the bills supposed to be signed and accepted by her for over £20,000 till after his arrest.

Pratt also went down in the spring to see Mrs. Palmer, but on his arrival Palmer told him his mother was too ill for any interview. The total amount in September 1855 owed to Pratt was £12,500, to Padwick £2,000, and over £10,000 to Wright of Birmingham, nearly £25,000 in all. The last named held a bill of sale on all Palmer's possessions—wine, furniture, stables, with fourteen race-horses. And later on, early in December, finding matters which were being divulged at the inquest looked very suspicious, Wright immediately put in an execution for over £10,000, for which he had been pressing since October, and the Sheriff's officer took possession on December 12, and was in charge when the police came to arrest Palmer, on the night of December 15, after the verdict of "wilful murder" had been returned at the inquest.

With this terrible accumulation of debts in the moneylender's hands, well over £25,000, and interest payable monthly (£1,250), we can see Palmer's case is hopeless; and if once his mother is summoned, nothing but penal servitude is in front of him for forgery.

The life-insurance method is played out, Bates's proposal rejected, the office refusing to pay the £14,000 due on Walter's death; so now, as a last resource, he determined to kill Cook for the sake of his two or three thousand pounds ready money won at Shrewsbury, and thus pay off the monthly interest overdue, and so stave off for a very few weeks the certain evil day which, though postponed, must soon fall with crushing effect.

The witnesses who proved all these debts are chiefly Pratt and Padwick. Their part of the evidence in the trial was kept very distinct from the circumstantial evidence of the murder of Cook. They proved the desperate straits Palmer was in for ready money, as I have here shown, and that he was willing to resort to any crime, theft, forgery, and murder to obtain money.

And this brings us to Section B, the circumstantial evidence (three-quarters of the whole trial), which chiefly was the means of convicting Palmer. Out of fifty-four witnesses called by the Crown, seventeen spoke on the medical aspect of the case; and of the thirty-seven others, thirty-one testified to the circumstantial evidence.

In the Syllabus of Lectures I gave twenty years ago, I stated Palmer was hanged on the unrefuted circumstantial evidence, and I divided this under twelve headings, as follows:

1. The straits for money, which I have thoroughly entered into in the last few pages: £2,000 for interest alone, being overdue, had to be paid by the middle of November to avoid exposure of the forged acceptances. This was proved by Pratt and Padwick, the moneylenders, as shown in the last few pages.

Then Strawbridge, the Rugeley Bank Manager, proved Palmer's balance was under £9 on November 3, and nothing paid to credit from that date.

2. His being detected at Shrewsbury tampering with Cook's brandy, proved by Mrs. Brookes, Dr. Gibson, Messrs. Fisher and Read (on p. 81).

3. His assiduous attention to Cook when lying ill at the Talbot Arms, Rugeley, taking across the road to him broth and coffee, all of which made him very sick and desperately low and ill, and more easily dispatched by the poison selected.

4. His obtaining, through a forged letter from Cook to George Herring, all Cook's bets at Tattersall's and appropriating them, and paying the bill discounters, Pratt and Padwick, sums on account (p. 85) out of Cook's winnings.

5. Cook had £800 in his money-belt, which he entrusted to Fisher at the Raven Hotel, Shrewsbury on the evening of Wednesday, November 14, and received it back next morning. He went that day to Rugeley with Palmer, who robbed him of the whole, and became suddenly extra flush with ready money, paying Pratt £600, bill for Hay £50, spirits and wine £60, repaying a loan to the butcher of £50—all within two days of his return from Shrewsbury. And only £5 was found in Cook's pockets at his death four days later.

6. Cook's betting-book was seen in his bedroom on Sunday morning, the day before Palmer took a list of bets due to Cook, for Herring to collect. And the book was never seen again, in spite of every search, and over its loss Mr. Stevens showed plainly his distrust of Palmer (*vide* p. 106).

7. Obtaining two separate lots of strychnine from the local chemists in Rugeley. The most damnatory pieces of evidence against him (as fully described, pp. 93 and 94). Certainly only circumstantial evidence, as it might have been for private use in destroying dogs, etc. But the jury and all sensible people were satisfied this strychnine was not bought for any purpose except for killing Cook, and no explanation was ever given in Court why he bought nine grains of such a deadly, cruel poison, nor for what purpose it was used.

8. He ordered a shell and a coffin without instructions from Mr. Stevens or any relation of Cook's, and ordered the undertaker to "box him up quick"—very anxious to get the body out of the way, to be buried as soon as possible. But in any case, as he remarked to Mr. Stevens, he ought to be fastened down at once.

9. His behaviour at the post-mortem I have fully shown (on p. 109) to be almost incredible. Restless to a marked degree, interfering in every detail, walking about the room all the time of the examination, bumping up against the operators just as they came to the most important part of the examination. And when the stomach was opened (as it never ought to have been

till it was in the hands of the analyst), deliberately pushing Newton against Devonshire and causing all the contents to be spilt.

Then removal of the jar (as described, p. 110), and a slit found in the cover when he returned the jar to Dr. Harland.

10. Offering a bribe to the postboy to smash the jar (described on p. 110).

11. His dealings all along with Cheshire, the postmaster and especially asking him to open Professor Taylor's letter to the Rugeley solicitor (for which Cheshire received a year's hard labour at Stafford Assizes), and getting him to fill up a cheque, etc., and wishing him to attest Cook's supposed signature to a document, etc. (p. 122).

12. And no excuse can account for the terrible evidence against him in bribing the Coroner, a step, I believe, unheard-of in England before then, and not repeated since (p. 125).

I have entered fully into the details under these twelve headings in the course of the narrative, and so, with all this evidence against him—called "circumstantial"—when added together and produced with crushing effect by the Attorney-General, *he had no chance.* It is rarely known that an eye-witness is found who has seen a murder committed, and so it must be by the accumulation of many items of circumstantial evidence added together that a prisoner is convicted, and few cases are on record where the accumulation is so great and convincing and crushing as in this case.

I have now discussed—

A. The pecuniary straits.

B. The circumstantial evidence.

But before I attempt C, the Crown medical evidence, I will first give the events on each of the twelve days of the trial, and then the witnesses.

The 1st *day.*—The opening splendid speech of the Attorney-General, who marshalled and arranged his facts very cleverly and claimed the ears and full attention of the jury, speaking for four or five hours, followed by two or three witnesses the same afternoon.

2nd and 3rd *day.*—General circumstantial evidence.

4th day.—Medical evidence.

5th day was almost all occupied by Professor Taylor, F.R.S., the great analytical chemist, the *deus ex machina* as some newspapers called him, and his four hours' cross-examinatiOn by Serjeant Shee, that eminent Counsel's finest effort in the whole trial, not even excepting his eight hours' speech, for, as I have related, on Taylor's evidence at the Rugeley inquest, when he exclaimed in a firm, confident voice Cook died from strychnine administered in pills on the Monday and Tuesday night, showed what an important witness he was.

6th day was taken up with general evidence, chiefly the bill discounters.

7th day.—Serjeant Shee's eight hours' speech for the Defence.

8th and 9th days and half the 10th.—Witnesses, chiefly medical, for the defence.

10th day (latter half).—The masterly reply of the Attorney-General, not ending till late on Saturday, May 24.

11th and 12th days.—The Lord Chief Justice's summing up, ending 2.30 Tuesday. Verdict, "guilty."

Now I will briefly give the witnesses in the order in which they were called and the substance of what they had to say, and then give the medical witnesses for the Crown and those for the Defence, the former all agreeing death was from strychnine, the latter mentioning half a dozen diseases it might have been.

The first witness called was *Fisher*, then *Jones* the accountant (NOT Dr. Jones, the old friend of Lutterworth), *Read*, and *Dr. Gibson*, all speaking of the Shrewsbury events at the races, chiefly the tampering with Cook's brandy, and Cook handing his winnings (£800) to Fisher, telling him he believed Palmer had drugged him.

Elizabeth Mills was the next witness called, a very important witness who was in the witness-box the latter half of Wednesday and up to lunch time on Thursday, and came out of her ordeal remarkably well—three hours' cross-examination at the hands of Serjeant Shee.

She was chambermaid at the Talbot Arms, and told the Court she had known Cook well for six months before his death, and he always seemed in good health. He had paid one long visit of three months in the spring of that year. She remembered his arrival with Palmer from Shrewsbury on Thursday, November 15, looking very ill, and he went at once to bed, asking for an extra piece of candle to read by. (We see later on the lighting of the bedroom was very poor.) She spoke confidently to his having coffee next morning for breakfast, for he always had taken tea. She gave the coffee into Palmer's hands, and in a quarter of an hour she found it all vomited in the pail. This was supposed to be the first dose of antimony given by Palmer at Rugeley. Coffee disguises the taste and appearance of tartar emetic far better than tea.

She spoke of toast and water, and broth, being given by Palmer, and noticed the fact that Cook's illness was always much worse, or, as she said, was "*confined to vomiting*," after taking food.

Then she clearly related how she took two tablespoonfuls of broth sent over by Palmer on Sunday midday because it smelt so savoury, and she began in ten or fifteen minutes to be sick and vomited all the afternoon, and had to go to bed for several hours. She told the Court how much better Cook was the latter part of Monday (the day Palmer met George Herring in London), and clearly remembered the disputed pill-box arriving from Dr. Bamford at 8 p.m., which she placed on the dressing-table, not near Cook's bed.

Then came her graphic description of Cook's symptoms on that night. She was roused at a quarter to twelve by the screams from Cook's room, and hurrying down, found him sitting up in bed beating the bedclothes with his hands and arms, which were very stiff. "His screams were intense. When I asked him to try and lie down, he said he would be suffocated if he did. There was much jerking and jumping of his whole body, especially of his head and neck, which he begged me to rub, and I noticed his hands were clenched and his arms very stiff. He was conscious all through the attack (and also the next night up to his death). When I gave him a spoonful of toast and water his jaws snapped and held the spoon firmly fixed in his mouth between his teeth for a few seconds, and he snapped at the glass in which Palmer gave him the medicine he had fetched. The convulsion would leave him for a few minutes and then return suddenly, twisting and racking his whole body. He called out '*murder*' several times, and between the attacks said he was sorry he gave way so much to the '*hellish tortures*,' as he called them."

She gave very clear evidence about Cook's symptoms, especially the stiffness of the hands and arms, rigidity of the body, and the *eyeballs projecting* out of their sockets, and the twitching and jerkings of the whole frame.

In cross-examination she was pressed by Shee and asked if she had noticed the colour of his face and if congested, and she replied carefully, "I could not see that, for there was only one mould candle in the bedroom, and the same next night when he died." It is hard to understand a good-sized bedroom (two good beds in it) and no gas, no lamps, and nobody fetched extra candles to see better the terrible scenes.

She stayed in his room till 3 a.m., and "when I left Palmer was asleep in an easy-chair at the bedside. Next morning I went in about six, and Cook told me Palmer had left about five. He asked me if I had ever seen such agony as he endured a few hours before. I said I never had, and went on to ask him what he thought caused the agony, and he replied in that sentence I have often quoted. 'THE PILLS THAT PALMER GAVE ME AT HALF-PAST TEN WERE THE CAUSE OF MY SUFFERINGS.'"

Surely this settles the point that Palmer had given him some pills on the Monday night, as I have clearly shown (on p. 93).

Mills continued: "On the Tuesday night about a quarter to twelve Cook's bell was violently rung, and when I went up, Cook was sitting up in bed yelling with pain, worse if possible than the preceding night. Dr. Jones was supporting him, and he begged me to fetch Palmer, and I ran across. Palmer appeared at his bedroom window directly I rang his bell, and came across, remarking as he entered the bedroom, 'I never dressed so quickly before in my life.' He appeared to me fully and properly dressed, and certainly had not had time to dress after I rang his bell."

It is always thought that Palmer had never gone to bed, but was sitting up waiting to be called, ready dressed for going out, on this November night.

"The symptoms were much the same as on the night before, only more severe. And in ten minutes after Palmer came, Cook died. I was standing in the doorway as he died. I had seen Cook's betting-book on his table that day, but never saw it again."

The cross-examination was chiefly to "credit": hints that she had been prompted by Mr. Stevens, by Superintendent Hatton, and by others, as to what she was to testify and especially about using the words twitchings, jerkings, convulsions, etc.—not her own words but suggested by others, which she indignantly denied.

Then as to what situations she had been in, and about the man Dutton she was engaged to. But her evidence was not shaken at all, and was very important. Sir Benjamin Brodie paid her the compliment of saying she had given her evidence clearly and well.

She married Dutton a year later and lived in Rugeley as caretaker to the Institute, and died about thirty years ago.

The Defence tried to make a great deal out of some minor differences between Elizabeth Mills's evidence at the inquest and what she said at the Old Bailey, hinting that Mr. Stevens and others might have prompted her, and that she had read in the papers about twitchings and jerkings, etc.

But the discrepancy in her evidence is due to the slovenly, ignorant manner in which the inquest was conducted, rather than to any intention on the part of the witness to tamper with the truth, and this slovenliness came out in a very marked manner when Dr. Jones was giving his evidence. As we shall see, the Attorney-General had the original depositions put in, and it was found the clerk had erased many words of importance, not knowing their meaning and had substituted simpler words—"*tetintis*," "*tethanus*," "compression" all half erased, and "convulsions" finally entered both in Dr. Jones's and Elizabeth Mills's evidence.

I have given her evidence more fully than the rest, and I need not repeat the giving broth and coffee by Palmer and the death-bed agony, all testified to and confirmed by Lavinia Barnes (chambermaid) and Mrs. Bond (housekeeper).

Lavinia Barnes settled the question of the broth which had made Mills so sick on the Sunday, for she saw it, and noticed it was in a two-handled cup with a lid on, and they had no such cups in the hotel. Moreover, she herself sent back the cup empty next morning to Palmer's house.

The Defence had hinted perhaps the broth had been made in the hotel, and also that Elizabeth Mills might have been sick on some other afternoon. Lavinia Barnes confirmed Mills's sickness and testified to the symptoms of the death-bed scene, emphatically stating Cook's eyes were "*wild looking and standing a great way out of his head*," and she noticed on the Tuesday night that Palmer was fully dressed in his usual way. She also spoke to the undertaker's men coming on the Wednesday (which must have been on Palmer's order), but not bringing the coffin till *after* Mr. Stevens's visit on the Friday (as described on p. 106). She also, at Mr. Stevens's request, went to look for the betting-book with Dr. Jones, who remarked to her, "Palmer knows where the book is."

The door of the room where Cook's body lay was locked, but the key seems to have been given indiscriminately to the charwoman, to the barber, to the undertaker's men, and several times to Palmer, and Serjeant Shee, in his defence, said very likely some of the former might have taken the betting-book. But it certainly would be of no use to any of them—but of course of great consequence to Palmer.

Dr. Jones, with whom Cook had made his home and headquarters for three or four years at Lutterworth, described his arrival at Rugeley on the Tuesday afternoon and the administering two pills brought by Palmer about ten that night, the onset of the attack 1¼ hours later, and the symptoms and death-bed: all over in fifteen or twenty minutes from the time Cook roused him up. He said Cook told him early in the evening the pills that Palmer gave him last night made him so ill and caused all his sufferings. He described the symptoms of the last fifteen minutes very carefully, and when cross-examined about the eyeballs and the congested face, he replied quietly, "The room was so dark, only one candle, I could not observe the countenance nor the eyeballs."

He next described his visit with Mr. Stevens on the Friday and the lunch at the Talbot Arms Hotel (all told in the narrative on p. 105). But he also added that on the night Cook died he looked for the betting-book and asked Palmer if he knew where it was, and he replied it would not be of any use to anybody.

Then he spoke strongly on the slipshod manner in which the inquest on Cook was conducted, the Coroner failing to put questions of consequence and the Clerk taking down answers he did not understand.

He was followed by *Dr. Henry Savage*, Cook's London doctor, who spoke to the good health Cook was in when he saw him ten days before he was taken ill at Shrewsbury. He had seen him several times during the last year and found him on each occasion in capital condition. This evidence was to disprove the rumour that as he was so delicate, a cold had brought on the convulsions in which he died.

Charles Newton—an important witness—followed. When he was called there was an excited murmur throughout the Court, as only during the last twenty-four hours had the public learnt that he had come forward, scarcely two days before, to state Palmer had been supplied by him with strychnine (three grains) late on the Monday night, the first night of the two tetanic seizures before Cook died. Newton was about twenty-two years old, and his evidence was the cause of some disputes between the Judges and Counsel. He was dispenser to Dr. Salt in the town, and supplied Palmer with three grains of strychnine on the night of Monday, November 19, which the Crown contend Palmer made up into two pills and gave to Cook that night.

The Defence disputed this chiefly on the grounds that Newton never mentioned supplying strychnine till the eve of the trial (two days before). He gave as his reason for his silence that he was assistant to Dr. Salt, who had fallen out with Palmer because Ben Thirlby, a chemist in Rugeley, had left Dr. Salt's employment, and had gone to help Palmer with such practice as he had remaining.

The Defence questioned if Palmer would have gone to Salt's surgery for the strychnine, where he might have come across Dr. Salt. But he took the chance to obtain it from his boon companion Newton, and got it without seeing Dr. Salt.

In his summing up the Lord Chief Justice remarked to the jury that there was no contradiction, no alteration of anything Newton had previously said, but the jury were to consider the probability of his inventing such a wicked and most abominable lie. He had no ill-will towards the prisoner, nothing to gain by saying anything to affect his life, he had no motive for inventing such a lie as obtaining this strychnine. No inducement had been held out to him, and "if you believe him, certainly the evidence against the prisoner is much strengthened, and a FEARFUL CASE is made out against him."

The Attorney-General, in commenting on Newton's disputed evidence, said: "What conceivable motive can this young man have in making this statement? Before we can charge a man with having taken away the life of another by deliberate malice, it is important to see if there were motives which could cause him to commit so foul a deed as murder. And that question of motive does not apply to Newton, for though the hideous crime of taking life by poison is not so horrible to contemplate as JUDICIAL murder effected by false witness against a neighbour, can we suppose Newton has the shadow of a motive for coming forward to take away the life of the prisoner—for, alas! if you believe his evidence, it must take away the life of Palmer! If you believe that on this Monday night the prisoner obtained from Newton the deadly poison whereby Cook's life was to be destroyed, it is impossible that you can come to any other conclusion than that the prisoner is guilty, and your verdict must pronounce him so. [This is given more fully in the Attorney-General's reply (p. 188).]

"And all my learned friend can say is you are not to believe his evidence because he is wrong by some half-hour of the clock, and because he never revealed this till ten days ago, six months after its occurrence, and because Dr. Salt and Palmer were on bad terms with each other."

Newton also testified to seeing Palmer buying strychnine next morning in Hawkins's shop, and also to an important chat in Palmer's kitchen on the following Sunday night about what strychnine would be found after death in a dog poisoned with it (all fully related on p. 101). Here again the Defence plainly doubted his word. Was it likely that Palmer would take the opinion of a young assistant who had twice seen him supplied during the past week with such a deadly drug? He was an illegitimate son of Ben Thirlby, Palmer's assistant, and died at the age of thirty.

Roberts, who sold six grains of strychnine to Palmer, came next, and was not cross-examined.

Mr. Stevens followed and was three hours in the witness-box, but all his evidence is given in the narrative.

Captain Hatton produced the incriminating letter from Palmer to the Coroner (given in full on p. 124).

George Herring (known on the Turf as "Mr. Howard") told the Court, in what was described as "*merciless tones*," of his collecting Cook's winnings at Tattersall's. He was the one who urged Mr. Stevens on to the investigation of Cook's death, and was angry at being taken in by Palmer in collecting Cook's money at Tattersall's and using it to discharge Palmer's debts.

James Myatt, the post-boy, spoke to Palmer's offer of ten pounds to upset Stevens and the jar containing the remains of Cook's stomach.

Samuel Cheshire[2] spoke to opening Professor Taylor's letter

---

[2] Cheshire was brought up before the Rugeley Bench on Thursday, January 10, 1856, and on Friday, January 11, and finally tried at Stafford before Justice Bramwell, defended by Huddlestone (who afterwards appeared for the Crown in Palmer's trial). He was sentenced to one year's imprisonment and was brought from the jail to give evidence at the Central Criminal Court, and coming from jail he had to walk through the dock to the witness-box, passing Palmer, and back by the same way. In an hour's time he was recalled to answer two questions, but as it was only a matter of two to three minutes, he stood to reply in the dock, close to Palmer, with a warder between them.

and telling the contents to Palmer, for which he was sentenced to one year's imprisonment. He told of Palmer's asking him three days after Cook's death to attest Cook's signature to a document drawn up six days before, and to Palmer asking him to fill up the body of a cheque (all related on p. 123).

Thomas Pratt, a solicitor and moneylender, of Queen Street, Mayfair, said he had been lending money to Palmer from 1853, chiefly on bills purporting to be accepted by Sarah Palmer, the mother of the prisoner.

These transactions were continued up to the time of Palmer's arrest, and he owed him and his clients about £8,000. He had never seen Mrs. Palmer, nor ever had a single letter from her. The interest charged was generally 60 per cent., and payable quarterly, or on some bills monthly.

Mrs. Tennyson Jesse says of him (p. 21 footnote): "One of the most repulsive characters in the trial was Pratt. In an account published soon after the trial he is described as a sinister figure, tall and big, trying to be fashionable in his style of dress, enormous brown whiskers almost meeting at the chin, the face that of a small boy, the low, weak voice of a retiring female."

George Bates, Palmer's groom, whose life he tried to insure for £20,000, and who took the incriminating letter with a ten-pound note to the Coroner just before the last day of the inquest, gave very damaging evidence.

Then came the local doctors:

Bamford, the aged practitioner, well past his fourscore years, who had attended all Palmer's victims who had died in Rugeley and given certificates for each (p. 85).

Dr. Monckton, who made the second examination of Cook's body, and the post-mortem on Mrs. Anne Palmer and Walter Palmer.

Devonshire, the undergraduate, who made the post-mortem on Cook.

Dr. Harland of Stafford, who superintended the post-mortem on Cook, and his evidence confirmed the general opinion that he was unsuitable and too feeble to superintend so important an examination. He was followed by an array of skilled doctors, whose evidence is discussed in another chapter.

CHAPTER XVII

Both sides agree Cook died from tetanic convulsions—But differ as to the cause—The two attacks point entirely to strychnine—Antimony was found in the system—Crown called seventeen doctors, many at the very top of the profession, as Brodie, Christison, and Taylor—All agreed on strychnine—Four cases produced of deaths known to be due to strychnine.

I MUST TRY TO EXPLAIN THE DIFFERENCE between the Prosecution and the Defence as to the cause of Cook's death, before I enter upon the evidence of the doctors called for the Crown and for the prisoner.

I must impress on my readers again that the verdict did not rest on the finding or not finding strychnine in the body. If it had been found (as in the recent case of the Frenchman Vacquier at Byfleet[1]), there would have been no defence. But the cumulative and overwhelming weight of circumstantial evidence and the terrible symptoms preceding the death (all so well and accurately related by Dr. Jones and the chambermaid) could not leave the shadow of a doubt of Palmer's guilt in the mind of anyone capable of exercising a judgment free from the influence of prejudice and interest in his welfare, and added to all this, the behaviour of Palmer before and after the murder, when he fairly lost his head, as I have frequently mentioned.

Both sides agree that Cook died a terrible death, suffering from convulsions of a cruel form which twisted and racked his whole frame till the body itself was so bowed and bent from his agony that it rested on the back of the head and the heels, the whole spine being arched and twisted in the death-struggle.

Tetanus is the name given to this form of convulsions, and

---

[1] Jean-Pierre Vaquier (1879-1924) was hanged in Britain of killing his mistress' husband using strychnine. Mable Jones had met Vaquier in Biarritz, France, while recovering from a breakdown. He followed her to Byfleet, a suburb of Woking in Surrey, and took rooms in a pub Jones ran with her husband, Alfred. One morning, Alfred came downstairs, drank his usual glass of Bromo-Seltzer for his hangover and died. Strychnine was found in both Alfred and the bottle. Vaquier was seen buying strychnine and signing the poison book with a false name.

is divided into three groups, from one of which Cook died.

1st, *idiopathic*, or spontaneous, coming on from an unknown cause like a chill or derangement of the stomach—a very rare disease in England, and no doctor was found who could speak to a death in England from that cause.

2nd, *traumatic tetanus*, due to some external wound or open sores, known as *"lockjaw"* in England. But the course of this disease is very different from what Cook died from. In lockjaw there is the history and signs of a wound, and the illness commences with a general feeling of malaise—headache and general constitutional disturbances—followed in *a day or two* by stiffness of the jaws, noticeable in the few cases I have seen by an alteration of the speech from the spasm and stiffness of the jaws, and a sort of fixed "grin" on the countenance, followed in a day or so by spasms and convulsions of the whole of the muscles of the body, and ending finally, as Palmer wrote in one of his books, by a fixing of the muscles of respiration, and the sufferer generally dies from terrible suffocation.[2]

The doctors agreed at the trial that from the commencement of lockjaw (traumatic tetanus) until death a few days elapse, never less than two days, often three or four, and here from the first onset when Cook woke up Dr. Jones only fifteen or at the most twenty minutes elapsed before he died.

He had no fixing of the jaws, his eyeballs stared prominently out of their sockets, his teeth snapped at the glass when Palmer offered him some medicine, his fingers tightly clenched and remained so after death.

There was a great deal of jerking and twitching of the head and limbs. The whole body stretched out was much bent and stiff, the feet were arched inwards, and the whole frame was terribly convulsed.

He was *conscious to the last*. The convulsions shook his whole frame and returned every two or three minutes. In a somewhat milder form he had suffered on the preceding night from similar convulsions, also after swallowing pills administered by Palmer. There was no alteration to be noted in his speech, for his voice was clear to the end, when he said,

---

[2] On the first page of his copy of *Manual for Students Preparing for Examination at Apothecaries' Hall,* Palmer wrote "Strychnine kills by causing tetanic fixing of the respiratory muscles."

"Turn me over on to my side," a minute or two before he died. And not any fixing of the jaws and no fixed "grin" on the countenance.

It is almost an insult to the Medical Profession to ask them to believe Cook died from lockjaw—traumatic tetanus. But, as we shall see in the next chapter, the doctors called for the Defence tried to account for the convulsions by some half-dozen different diseases, but all agree it was not lockjaw (traumatic tetanus) due to any "wound or sore." So there remains as classified in 1856 only—

3rd, *tetanus due to strychnine,* so called (erroneously) at this trial. But strychnine cannot produce tetanus, though it causes terrible convulsions somewhat RESEMBLING tetanus, but the seizures differ in important respects from real tetanus. This latter is a specific disease caused by a bacillus discovered about forty years after this trial.

The first symptom of strychnine poisoning is a peculiar sensation described by some as a fearful suffocation, soon followed by jerkings and twitchings with convulsive bending of the whole body, generally commencing twenty minutes to an hour after taking the poison.

The jaws are only affected for a few seconds or minutes during the paroxysm, then there are clear intermissions, often for some minutes, between the attacks of convulsive spasms. And if the sufferer is going to improve, the intermissions grow longer and longer between the convulsive attacks, which grow shorter.

The mind and voice are clear to the end—not the voice of lockjaw, forced out from fixed jaws and lips. The voice in Cook's case was very clear, asking for Palmer to be sent for, asking for medicine, and to have his neck rubbed, and finally "turn me over on my side," and instantly then died.

A peculiarity which always attracts the non-professional eye is that the head always is jerked violently backwards in its spasms, and the neck is rigid all the time, with the muscles of neck and jaws standing out prominently.

The body is contracted and convulsed, and after a few minutes becomes curved or arched, or, as Dr. Jones noticed in Cook's case, if he placed it on its back it would rest only on the heels and back of the head, so much so that the hollow of the back was 6 or 8 inches from the bed. The face is congested, partly from the terrible strain of the whole body, the countenance expressing great anxiety of a terrible nature.

The eyeballs became staring and very prominent; as Mills said, Cook's appeared as if they would come out of their sockets. The pain is intense from the contractions of all the muscles of the body; and then, the muscles of the chest contracting violently, the patient dies from suffocation, as recorded by Palmer in his notebook on Poisons.

If the strychnine is administered in the form of a pill, the onset is much longer than if given in solution, and still longer if food is in the stomach, as was the case with Cook.

Keeping in mind the symptoms of tetanus due to a wound and the symptoms due to strychnine, we can more easily look at the medical evidence, so all-important in this trial.

C. That for the Crown is to show Cook's symptoms and death were due to strychnine and to nothing else, and there was also found antimony in his remains, which had never been prescribed by any of his doctors.

Seventeen witnesses were called to speak to this medical aspect, the chief of whom was *Sir Benjamin Brodie*,[3] and his evidence and manner of delivery stand out conspicuous in this trial. He was held in the highest estimation throughout England; his name was a household word for integrity and honour. And as President of the Royal College of Surgeons he ranked top of the profession, and gave in a "quiet, clear voice" his opinion that, after hearing all the symptoms of Cook's last illness and death, he had not the least doubt that he died from strychnine and that it was given both on the Monday and Tuesday evenings, adding, "There is no NATURAL disease which can account for the death"; and emphatically raising his voice said, "I HAD BETTER SAY AT ONCE THAT I HAVE NEVER SEEN A CASE IN WHICH THE SYMPTOMS I HAVE HEARD DESCRIBED AROSE FROM DISEASE, AND THIS DEATH DID NOT ARISE FROM EITHER IDIOPATHIC OR TRAUMATIC TETANUS. THE COURSE THIS ILLNESS RAN, THE HISTORY, AND THE SYMPTOMS ARE TOTALLY DIFFERENT FROM ANY NATURAL DISEASE, AND INDICATE DECIDEDLY DEATH FROM STRYCHNINE."

In cross-examination, which was very short after such crushing statements, he said he thought the evidence of Dr. Jones and the chambermaids was very clear and had been fairly given, and he added, "My opinion is he died from

---

[3] [Fletcher's footnote] Sir Benjamin Brodie reached the highest honour in his profession: Serjeant-Surgeon to King William IV, Surgeon to Queen Victoria, President of the General Medical Council, President and Fellow of the Royal Society.

strychnine poisoning."

Samuel Solly, who was President of the Royal College of Surgeons a few years later and Senior Surgeon at St. Thomas's Hospital, gave strong evidence about tetanus, and stated that this death was certainly not able to be classed under any form of illness.

He was a man with a large practice and had seen many cases of traumatic tetanus, and later on, during the time I was his dresser[4] in 1870, two cases of tetanus from wounds—lockjaw—were admitted to his ward, and I took the opportunity to ask him about this trial, in which he had taken such keen interest fourteen years previously, and had given firm, unshakable evidence.

Mr. Curling, Senior Surgeon at the London Hospital, and *Dr. Robert Todd,* Physician and Lecturer at King's College Hospital, a great authority and writer on tetanus, would not apply the word "tetanus" to any case of poisoning, as the symptoms are so totally distinct. And from the evidence they had heard in this case, they were satisfied it was not tetanus (lockjaw) in any form.

The *Attorney-General* asked Dr. Curling: "Assuming tetanus to be synonymous with convulsive or spasmodic action of the muscles, was there in that sense tetanus on the Monday night?" The reply was: "No doubt there was a spasmodic action of the muscles, but certainly not "to idiopathic or traumatic tetanus," and he adds in his evidence: "Some poisons will produce symptoms like tetanus, and the *chief of these poisons is strychnine."*

The Crown urged that this latter form of (SO-CALLED) tetanus killed Cook. All the doctors for the Crown agreed Cook did not die from any natural disease!! and that his symptoms all pointed to death from strychnine; and some added that the non-finding of strychnine after death did not alter their well-considered opinion, as they agreed the shameful way the post-mortem had been conducted and the condition in which the mangled stomach had been sent to Professor Taylor almost certainly prevented him from finding it, and three doctors said that in animals to whom a fatal dose of strychnine had been administered, no trace of it was found after death in 25 per cent., even after a careful post-mortem examination.

---

[4] A surgeon-in-training who treats patients under supervision. It is a step above being a pupil or apprentice.

Dr. Todd and all the surgeons who were asked the question were very emphatic that death did not—could not possibly—occur from apoplexy, epilepsy, angina pectoris, nor any of the various ailments brought forward by the surgeons called for the Defence. The Crown doctors ALL agreed he died from strychnine, and that no natural disease could account for his symptoms.

The judge left the question to the jury, directing that they should be satisfied that his symptoms were consistent with death from strychnine and inconsistent with death from natural causes, and that strychnine was administered by Palmer.

This I have gone into more fully later (p. 197), together with Serjeant Shee's interruption at the close of the Judge's summing up.

The Crown called *Professor Taylor*, and he gave a full account of the state of the stomach when sent to him for analysis. He had been present at a great deal of the inquest (two full days), and suggested many questions to the Coroner to put to some of the witnesses who spoke to the symptoms of Cook's death-bed. He was in the witness-box nearly the whole of the fifth day and underwent a most searching cross-examination at the hands of Serjeant Shee, for he was the chief scientific witness called by the Crown. But his evidence remained unshaken and uncontradicted. A great deal was made of the fact that he had written a long letter to the papers whilst Palmer was waiting for his trial, and had been interviewed by the editor of an illustrated paper which published a long article with illustrations after the interview.

This rightly called forth a rebuke from the Judge, and at the present time we can scarcely understand the chief Crown professional witness writing to the papers in any strain, much less in the language Taylor used.

To confirm Professor Taylor and to considerably strengthen their case, when Taylor at length left the witness-box, he was followed by *Professor Christison*, one of the very few *Fellows* of the Royal College of Physicians. He had published a standard work on Poisons, and had given much attention to strychnine, commencing his studies in Paris in 1820, where this poison had been first discovered only two years before. A greater authority on such a matter could not be found in Europe, and he gave evidence as to strychnine in general, the time it takes to act, and the symptoms arising from it. His exact words were almost fatal to Palmer's chance:

"AFTER HEARING ALL THE SYMPTOMS EXHIBITED BY THE DECEASED, THE RESULT OF MY EXPERIENCE INDUCES ME TO COME TO THE CONCLUSION THEY WERE ONLY ATTRIBUTABLE TO STRYCHNINE. THERE IS NO NATURAL DISEASE THAT I AM ACQUAINTED WITH TO WHICH THOSE SYMPTOMS COULD BE REFERRED.

"IF THE QUANTITY OF STRYCHNINE ADMINISTERED IS SMALL, I SHOULD NOT EXPECT TO FIND ANY TRACE IN THE BODY AFTER DEATH. THE STOMACH OF COOK WAS SENT IN A VERY UNSATISFACTORY STATE FOR EXAMINATION."

Next to Sir Benjamin Brodie, one must place Christison as a man of wide-spread fame, recognised on all hands as a most careful, conscientious witness, and he gave skilled evidence about the drug strychnine which the Defence could not shake.

These three witnesses considerably shattered all chances from the medical aspect of the case which Palmer's Counsel thought he possessed—three men of European reputation and skill, far above any suspicion of unfair bias for or against the prisoner.

After the evidence relating directly to the poisoning of Cook and the evidence of the skilled medical witnesses, the Attorney-General called evidence of four cases of undisputed accidental deaths from strychnine in the human frame, all—or nearly all—that were known at that time in Great Britain, and the doctors in attendance on those patients were called, showing how exactly their symptoms and sufferings corresponded in every detail with Cook's symptoms and death, and showed that the length of time after taking the poison before the symptom set in, and before death occurred, together with all the particulars, were exactly the same, and nothing called for the Defence could upset these proved, unquestioned strychnine deaths.

The first, a young woman in Glasgow Infirmary, took three-quarters of a grain of strychnine in two pills and died in an hour and a quarter from the time of taking the pills, with every symptom exactly the same as Cook's.

The two doctors, a nurse, and the dispenser were all called, and proved the case.

The next was a lady at Romsey, who took some medicine wrongly made up by the chemist, who had put by mistake three grains of strychnine to each dose of medicine. She died in an hour and a quarter from the time of drinking the fatal dose. The symptoms were again *exactly* those of Cook, even to the expression "Turn me on my side"; and she died directly after they had turned her over, just as Cook died. The chemist, from remorse at his fearful carelessness poisoned himself.[5]

Two other cases of undoubted poisoning by strychnine were brought forward. One recovered, one died, the latter attended by Mr. Morley of Leeds, who helped Mr. Nunneley of Leeds with more than half his experiments with strychnine and Mr. Nunneley was the chief and important witness called here for the Defence.

During 1924 a Frenchman, Vacquier, was hanged for killing with strychnine, at Byfleet, the husband of Mrs. Jones, a woman with whom he had been on very intimate terms, and the chief evidence against him was that he also had twice purchased strychnine, signing the poison book under a false name, stating that he required it in connection with his wireless apparatus, shortly before Mr. Jones's death. The poison was given in a liquid state, and the symptoms commenced within a quarter of an hour of taking the salts dissolved in water, in which salts strychnine had been placed.

The account of the convulsions, the bending and twisting of the body, the sitting up for fear of suffocation, and the death from asphyxia are all exactly similar to Cook's death. But here the post-mortem was carefully conducted; the analysis, revealing over half a grain of strychnine in the body, proved he died from strychnine, and Vacquier was hanged.

---

[5] The story can be found in *The Illustrated Times Trial of William Palmer* (Peschel Press, 2014). In the Glasgow Infirmary case, see the testimony on the trial's fourth day of Henry Lee, Dr. Henry Corbett, Dr. J. Patterson and Mary Kelley. In the case of Mrs. Sarjantson Smyth at Romsey, see the testimony on the same day of Caroline Hickson, Francis Taylor, and Charles Broxholme.

CHAPTER XVIII

Shee's Defence on medical grounds—It was to Palmer's interest Cook should live—He died from some natural disease—But his doctors suggested six or seven causes—Shee passed over the death-bed characteristic symptoms, and ignored almost all the circumstantial evidence—Scarcely alluded to the £20,000 forged bills—Herapath in witness-box—Traffic evidence.

WE NOW COME TO THE DEFENCE, and it must have been a very hard task to handle and upset such overwhelming evidence as the Crown had laid before the Court.

At the time of Palmer's trial the Counsel for the Defence was not allowed a second speech unless the Crown called rebutting evidence to contradict that called on behalf of the prisoner. But at the present time, and for over fifty years, as soon as the case for the Prosecution is closed, the Counsel for the prisoner opens his defence and gives an outline of what his witnesses are going to prove. At the close of their evidence he is allowed now to address the jury again, summing up their evidence; and after this speech the Counsel for the Prosecution has the right to reply on the whole case, as fully explained previously.

After Serjeant Shee had made his speech and called his witnesses (who occupied two and a half days), he asked permission to sum up their evidence, to address again the jury, on the ground that the Crown had given him that right by their method of getting at the contents of some cheques and about the policy on Walter Palmer's life and the proposals to various Insurance offices.

But the three judges were unanimous in refusing his application.

THE DEFENCE

No witnesses were called to contradict Palmer's restlessness and anxiety and remarkable behaviour when he so often seemed to lose his head before and after Cook's death, and very few (none of any consequence) to upset or contradict the general convicting evidence of facts—the *circumstantial* evidence—so that Palmer's whole chance rested on upsetting the medical evidence, and this rested mainly on the fact of no poison found in the body after death, and secondly that Cook's symptoms were not necessarily those of strychnine poisoning. They might be due to other causes or to some diseases, even though they certainly did resemble strychnine tetanus, so called at this trial.

But what disease? Here the Defence over-reached itself, overshot the mark. Almost each of their various doctors summoned gave a different disease, reminding one of a celebrated Barrister's remark a few years before this case. He had been defending a prisoner for murder and procured his acquittal on the ground of an alibi. A friend congratulated him, adding, "I think your alibi was very weak." The Counsel replied, "Perhaps it was; but it was the best of the four the prisoner offered me." So here the jury had a variety of very different diseases from any of which the Defence contended Cook might have died. He certainly could not have died from them all, though one witness—Letheby—had the candour to admit "Cook's death is irreconcilable with everything and every disease with which I am acquainted"—an opinion more honest than most of those called on the medical side for the prisoner, for his Defence relied on the medical scientific differences as to the cause of death.

Serjeant Shee occupied the whole of the seventh day with a masterly speech of eight hours' duration, and, feeling he had a desperate case, made the very best defence possible, though when calmly looked at and weighed in the balance against the Crown evidence, the substance in reality amounted to very little.

In the first place he set out to prove that Cook's death was the worst possible thing to happen to Palmer, quoting one example to prove this, that on the night before he died Cook gave Palmer that cheque on Weatherby, the Jockey Club secretary, for £350 out of the stakes won at Shrewsbury. This cheque Palmer had got Cheshire to fill up in the evening, saying he would take it over for Cook to sign (as fully described on p. 123). We must remember the Attorney-General called for this cheque to be produced during Cheshire's evidence, but Serjeant Shee only shook his head and did not produce it, and laboured to prove their intimate pecuniary relationship, quoting after that cheque several instances about partnership in two race-horses which were mortgaged to Padwick.

From this Shee went on to say they would rely chiefly on the medico-scientific evidence, almost totally ignoring the terrible circumstantial evidence which, I contend, chiefly convicted Palmer.

Under the medical evidence he contended, firstly, were the symptoms such as could ONLY be produced by strychnine? or could they not have been caused by some recognised disease, or by "*ordinary tetanus*," whatever that might mean, certainly not traumatic tetanus, and he could not produce any evidence of idiopathic tetanus.

Then he laboured the point that if strychnine had been given, could it not have been discovered by so eminent an analyst as Professor Taylor? And as he could not find any, was that not proof none had been given? He ignored the facts proved by some of his own witnesses and by the Crown medical and analytical evidence, that in cases where they had themselves administered strychnine to dogs, it had not been detected after death.

He was silent as to Taylor's diminished chance of finding it owing to the mangled stomach sent up to him. He totally omitted to mention the undisputed, unchallenged fact that Palmer had bought six grains of strychnine twelve hours previous to Cook's death. This terrible evidence he never even alluded to, but he had some grounds for disputing and challenging the gift of three grains by Newton on the previous night.

Moreover, he could not handle, nor did he allude to, the awful death-bed scene, when Cook, in his agony of pain and his whole body racked with torture, called aloud for help, and in a paroxysm of suffocation died within a quarter of an hour of his first seizure, after taking two pills from Palmer's hands in Dr. Jones's presence. Shee would have been compelled to own, as nearly all the doctors on both sides agreed, they were symptoms EXACTLY SIMILAR to those of strychnine poisoning, if not caused by it, and could be laid, the Crown contended, to no other cause. Though his doctors suggested half a dozen other causes or diseases which might have killed him, no unanimity existed amongst the twelve doctors called for the Defence, whilst all the doctors called by the Crown were unanimous in ascribing the death to strychnine.

The fact that Serjeant Shee passed over in ominous silence the purchase of six grains of strychnine, and the attempts to bribe the Coroner, and many similar terrible facts, did not escape the attention of the jury, and certainly did not escape the remarks of the Attorney-General.

Serjeant Shee called nobody to disprove the £20,000 debts and the crushing weight of overdue interest at 60 per cent. on forged bills. He tried in vain to account for Palmer's remarkable restlessness and general behaviour, whereas, as I have shown, Palmer lost his head so strangely, nearly all of which had to go unchallenged, except here and there a few points were contradicted or explained contrary to common sense—such as the offer to the post-boy (p. 110) to upset and break the jar. Shee said it was Mr. Stevens he wished to be upset, and the removal of the jar after the post-mortem (p. 109) was to prevent anybody tampering with it!!! And the lost betting-book, he said, might have been stolen by the barber or the undertaker's men!

Thus Shee had to rely on what he called the doubtful medical aspect of the case, and he started with the theory "no poison found in the body, therefore no murder." And he promised to call medical men of the highest standing who would attribute the death to other causes, to some natural disease, and they certainly did so. But the first six doctors called for the Defence gave half a dozen different causes of death, from any one of which they said Cook might have died, though here they disclosed a weak spot in their armour, for the doctors called for the Defence could not agree amongst themselves from what disease he did die: (1) *excessive debility* and fast living, culminating in the excitement of mind and body at Shrewsbury; (2) granules on the spinal cord; (3) epilepsy; (4) apoplexy, actually given on the certificate by the aged and feeble, complacent Dr. Bamford, which alone must convince us that he knew very little of his profession, whether qualified or not. One hinted at (5) *hysteria*, another at (6) epilepsy with tetanic complication; (7) latent alteration in the spinal cord (not easily detected); and at the very last, (8) *angina pectoris*, which one of the leading physicians remarked was the best medical suggestion for the Defence, if they really had any at all; and all the doctors should have agreed to stick to it, as so little was known about it seventy years ago.

The first witness called was *Mr. Nunneley*, a surgeon, with a large practice at Leeds, who had had great experience. He mentioned a variety of causes which might have killed Cook, finally saying convulsions in a weak man caused by undue excitement. His cross-examination by the Attorney-General will fully repay the trouble taken to read it in full in any account of the trial, and he certainly left the witness-box a sad man, and upsetting many hopes for the Defence. But every symptom, every reason, he gave for doubting the Prosecution, was ruthlessly torn to shreds in cross-examination.

He was followed by the second witness for the Defence, who fared even worse at the hands of the Attorney-General, *Professor Herapath*, of the Bristol School of Medicine, one of the greatest analytical chemists of the day, and his grandson told me fourteen years afterwards that there was some jealousy and ill-feeling between him and Professor Taylor, so that he perhaps took this opportunity to express his opinion in court which he had so often expressed privately, that Taylor was by no means the most skilful analyst in England.

But he took a step fraught with great risk as well as danger to his own reputation, he gave his opinion in Court that there could not have been strychnine in Cook's stomach, as it was not found by analysis, for he could detect $1/20000$ of one grain.

The Attorney-General said he had very few questions to ask him. "Did you not say at the Mayor's banquet in Bristol that there was no doubt Cook had died from strychnine, but Taylor did not know how to find it?" A terrible poser for the great and chief witness for the Defence, on whom such great reliance had been placed. At first he shuffled and partially denied this. His very attitude and confusion led on to worse and worse, and he had to own, to the cross-fire of the Attorney-General, that he had expressed frequently privately and once before the Mayor that he had said Cook had died from strychnine, but tried to explain that he spoke then as a private citizen, judging only from the printed evidence at the inquest, and was entitled to express to friends his own opinion.

So it came to this: that to-day he said strychnine could not have been there, but a few weeks ago he expressed his private opinion that Cook had died from the poison.

The Attorney-General, in his reply, commented strongly on Professor Herapath: "He was not content to come forward for the purposes of justice, to state that which he knew as a matter of science, but he has been mixing himself up as a thorough-going partisan, advising my learned Friend, suggesting question upon question, and that on behalf of a man whom he has so often asserted was a poisoner by strychnine. It does make one look at the credit of those witnesses with great suspicion. For the partiality and partisanship of such a witness is so acutely evident. I reverence a man who, from a sense of justice and love of truth, comes forward in favour of a man against whom the world is running in a torrent of prejudice; he will stand up honestly and say what he thinks is the truth. But I abhor and denounce the *traffic* in testimony to which some men of science have condescended to lend themselves."

Herapath was followed by *Rogers*, a Professor of Chemistry in London, but his was very neutral evidence.

And then the Medical Officer of Health to the City of London, *Dr. Letheby*, who gave various reasons why Cook did not die from strychnine—the length of time after the pills before the symptoms began, his consciousness to the end, and he could not have rung the bell the Monday night, and could not have had his neck rubbed, etc. etc. But he had the open honesty to say he did not know what DISEASE Cook could have died from.

Professor Partridge, a surgeon of repute to King's College Hospital, spoke about the granules of the spinal cord, and thought they might have caused death; but he had never seen any such case, and could only suggest this, for he could not give any opinion as to the cause of Cook's death.

Dr. Macdonald, a general practitioner, said he thought Cook died from epileptic convulsions with tetanic complications.

The Attorney-General asked the two chief doctors called for the Defence a very hard question.

After reading to them in Court Cook's dying symptoms, he asked Mr. Nunneley, "Can you show any one point in which the symptoms in Cook's case differ from those of strychnine tetanus?" To the second doctor: "I ask you to distinguish in any one particular between Cook's symptoms and those of strychnine tetanus." And in both cases a negative reply was given, after shuffling and prevaricating answers had been tried in vain with such a cross-examiner as Attorney-General Cockburn.

CHAPTER XIX

The Attorney-General's reply, much abbreviated.

SIR ALEXANDER COCKBURN, the Attorney-General, had the whole management of the case for the Crown from the earliest days.

He was shown the evidence from the Coroner's three inquests directly after a verdict of "wilful murder" had been returned on the last, early in February, and had to decide on which he would first proceed. There is no doubt the evidence on Mrs. Anne Palmer would have presented a very simple, clear case with no complications. The evidence in the case of Walter Palmer was much open to criticism—in fact, the Grand Jury at Stafford, later on, threw out the bill for the murder of Walter Palmer.

Cook's case was full of interesting complications, such as strychnine being almost unknown as a poison. And there was none found in the body. Then there was the serious bungling at the post-mortem, and though Cook's terrible sufferings on the Monday and Tuesday evenings were the same, yet at that time and for six months there was no evidence of Palmer possessing the drug, except his purchase on the second day at Hawkins's shop. Still, the Attorney-General thought he could prove his guilt.

And he thought he would be opposed by Serjeant Wilkins— well skilled in medical knowledge, as he had been educated for a doctor till he was twenty-five years old. So, after due consideration, Cockburn decided to proceed on Cook's case first, and if he should be acquitted, then on Mrs. Palmer's. He relied mainly on the circumstantial evidence and Palmer's general behaviour.

For several weeks he worked at his private residence in Hertford Street, Mayfair, at medical studies with special reference to convulsions, tetanus, strychnine poison, and was helped by a physician of eminence, and in his own library at home he mastered all the necessary details, and came into Court as fully equipped with medical detail as any of the professional witnesses who were summoned.

His masterly conduct of the case, and his two speeches—

his opening and his reply at the close—are aptly described as unrivalled specimens of forensic eloquence and ability (especially his clear, convincing reply at the close) and are amongst the traditions of the legal profession.

I am sorry space forbids me giving in full his two speeches and the one of Shee's, which was a good speech for the Defence, the best that could be made out of so hopeless a case. The Lord Chief Justice Campbell's summing up was nothing out of the common—it was clear, and perhaps somewhat against the prisoner; but Cockburn's clear, convincing reply on the whole case on the Saturday afternoon has never been excelled—and sealed Palmer's fate.

He almost passed over in silence a point which Serjeant Shee had much laboured for the Defence, for one-third of his whole speech had been taken up to try to prove that Palmer had no motive to kill Cook, in fact, he continued, "it could not be to his interest that Cook should die," ignoring the simple fact that he came to Rugeley under Palmer's care with £800 in cash, none of which was found after his death, and nearly £2,000 had been collected at Tattersall's—all used to discharge some of the more pressing of Palmer's debts unknown to Cook. And if he should get about again the detection of this shameful robbery must be followed by terrible exposure of forgery and thefts, so Palmer killed him to save himself. He obtained the list of bets and the names of those who had to pay from the stolen betting-book.

The Attorney-General went on to say:

"If I prove beyond the reach of reasonable doubt that Cook died from strychnine administered by Palmer, the question of motive becomes a matter of secondary consideration. There is no doubt that Palmer was in the direst embarrassment with ruin and imprisonment for forgery staring him in the face, and nothing could avert that ruin save money which must be obtained AT ONCE, for his purpose to pacify Pratt for a few weeks.

"He owed £20,000 on bills which were all forgeries. Pratt demanded something towards the interest £800 was sent up in four instalments. But on November 13 he wrote a threatening letter that he could wait no longer. On that very day Cook's horse won at Shrewsbury, and he was entitled to a large sum of money, which at once afforded temptation to his murderer, who ultimately got it all.

"Thus winning this race was the cause of Cook's death.

"Palmer had no source to which he could turn for money. He could not again forge his mother's name; the life-assurance method was played out; and he could feel Pratt must be partly satisfied or there would be a prosecution and terrible disclosures, the very first of which would show forgery of his mother's name; and then the further disclosures would open the floodgates of systematic robbery and forgery on every bill held by the bill discounters, and nothing but transportation in front of him. We all know when the usurer's interest is safe and regularly paid, all is well; but as soon as it is overdue and security looks doubtful, one may as well ask mercy of a rabid tiger or ask pity of stones as hope to find bowels of compassion in a Pratt or a Padwick. My learned friend says Cook was his best friend, and as long as he was kept alive he could resort to such a friend for assistance! What! in what way!! Was Cook to offer or give acceptances to Pratt? who certainly would not take them—for Cook had already assigned to Pratt all the property he possessed, and all he now had to live on was his winnings at Shrewsbury, and he could not deprive himself of those to enable Palmer to meet Pratt's insatiable demands. As long as Cook held his Shrewsbury winnings, he was safe financially for the coming winter."

The Attorney-General said in opening his speech:

"The whole case resolved itself into two main questions. Did Cook die a natural death? or was he taken off by strychnine? If so, did Palmer administer it?

"The case for the Crown is that, having been first practised on by antimony, he was then killed by strychnine administered by Palmer in pills.

"The witnesses for the Prosecution one and all have told us that he died from tetanus due to strychnine. I assert, deliberately that no case of a human subject, or animal, has been brought under your notice in which the symptoms have been so marked by strychnine as they are in this case. The doctor who was present at the death tells us that every muscle in the body was terribly convulsed and Cook expressed the most intense dread of suffocation. Well, then, if it is a case of tetanus, as to which I will not further waste your time, was it a case of tetanus from strychnine? Tetanus may proceed from natural causes as well as from poison but NATURAL tetanus, lockjaw, is always a case not of hours but of several days. This is testified to by the evidence of the highest doctors, chief amongst whom is Sir Benjamin Brodie—though the symptoms are slightly similar, the results and length of time are very different.

"Traumatic tetanus is always brought on by a wound or a sore, and lockjaw is an early symptom. In Cook's case there was no sign of a wound nor any locking of the jaws.

"I called before you an eminent physician who had had Cook for two years under his care, till within a week or two of his death, and found him in a good state of health. No wound, no sore was found on him, and his illness on the Monday and on the Tuesday evenings was only a matter from first to last of twenty minutes, not of hours and days, so we can dismiss traumatic tetanus at once, as a supposed cause; but it is only a pretence which has not a shadow of a foundation, and which I should be shrinking from my duty if I did not denounce it as unworthy of your attention.

"The first and perhaps the chief witness my learned friend called was Mr. Nunneley of Leeds, who said it was a case of general convulsions which assumed a tetanic character. But I bade him pause and tell us if he had ever seen such a case which did not end in total unconsciousness. No, he never had. But he had read of a case in Dr. Copland's book. Why was Dr. Copland not called? though I threw out a challenge to see him. Why? Because it is easier and better in such a case to call together from the east and the west practitioners of more or less obscurity, instead of bringing to bear upon their case the light of science which is treasured up in the brains of the eminent doctors with whom (including Dr. Copland) this great city abounds. The Defence then called Mr. Partridge, an eminent surgeon who spoke to the granules causing inflammation of the spinal cord which may have occasioned death. I asked him the symptoms and in what respect they would differ from Cook's symptoms, and there were such a case, how would they differ from strychnine symptoms? And would he pledge his opinion, in the face of the medical profession and this Court, that this was a case of inflammation of the spinal cord? He honestly admitted he could not!

"Look at the doctor brought all the way from Scotland to suggest another disease—epilepsy with tetanic convulsions. He owned he had never seen such a case, especially as there never was any loss of consciousness, but finally told us he did not know to WHAT ELSE to ascribe Cook's death! And I must remind you of that special evidence—most speculative—to which their doctors resorted."

Finally, summing up the doctors called for the Defence, he said:

"I can assert there is not a single case to which they have spoken or of which they have read, in which there were the formidable symptoms so decisive of strychnine which produced Cook's death-bed agonies.

"But I contend—and on this the whole matter of strychnine rests—that the fact of strychnine not being found does certainly not afford negative conclusive proof that death was not caused by strychnine. I have no positive proof; but, on the other hand, the Defence is in the same predicament—he cannot say he has negative proof conclusive of the fact that this death did not take place from strychnine. And I go on to say the *symptoms are only reconcilable with strychnine.*

"Yet you will see the evidence does not end there. I wish it did. I must now draw your attention to a part of the case which has not been met, nor grappled with, by my learned friend. We have here a death of which the dread manifestations bore upon their face the character of strychnine poisoning. Was the prisoner at the bar possessed of that poison? Did he obtain it upon the eve of the death into which we are enquiring? These are matters of fearful moment. They are matters with which it behoved my learned friend, indeed, to have grappled with all the vigour of which he was capable and with all the means that his case afforded. But I grieve to say that this part of the case is left untouched as regards the Defence. Did the prisoner at the bar obtain possession of strychnia on the Monday night? Did he get it again upon the Tuesday morning? The fact of his having got it the Monday night rests, it is true, upon the evidence of an individual whose statement, as I said to you at the outset, and as I repeat now, requires at your hands the most careful and anxious attention before you adopt it easily. . . . It is for you to say whether you are satisfied with his explanation. It is unquestionably true that it detracts from the otherwise perfect credibility which would attach to his statement. But then, gentlemen, on the other hand, there is a consideration which I cannot fail to press upon you. What possible conceivable motive can this young man have, except a sense of truth, for coming forward to make this statement? My learned friend, with justice and with propriety, has asked for your most attentive consideration to the question of motives involved in this case. Before you can charge a man with having taken away the life of another by forethought and deliberate malice, it does become important to see whether there were motives that could operate upon him to do so foul a deed. That does not apply to this witness, for, even though the hideous crime of taking life by poison is not perhaps so horrible to contemplate as the notion of judicial murder effected by false witness against a man's neighbour, can you suppose that this young man can have the remotest shadow of a motive for coming forward upon this occasion, under the solemn sanction of an oath, in a Court of Justice like this, to take away the life—for, alas! if you believe his evidence, *it must take away the life*—of the prisoner at the bar? If you believe that on the night of Monday, for no other conceivable or assignable purpose except the deed of darkness which was to be done that night upon the person of Mr. Cook, the prisoner at the bar went to Newton and obtained from him that fatal and deadly instrument whereby life was to bc destroyed, it is impossible that you can come to any other conclusion than that the prisoner is guilty, and that your verdict must pronounce him so.

"My learned friend has produced here to-day a witness of whom all I can say is this, that I implore you for the sake of justice not to allow the prisoner to be prejudiced by the evidence of that most discreditable and unworthy witness who has been called to-day on his behalf. I say that not to one word which that man has uttered will you attach the slightest value.

"This witness pretends he saw him alight from the carriage and that he went to Cook and stayed a certain time with him, so as to cover the whole evening. I ask you not to believe a single word, and I do so because in my heart I do not believe one word of it.

"It is a remarkable fact that my learned friend did not open with a single word of the testimony he was going to call. He said he hoped and thought he should be able to cover the whole of the period at Rugeley! Did he tell you what Jeremiah Smith was going to prove?

"I need not say that any evidence would have been better than the evidence of that miserable man whom we saw exhibited to-day. Such a spectacle I never saw in my recollection in a Court of Justice. He calls himself a member of the legal profession. I blush for it to number such a man upon its roll. There was not one that heard him to-day that was not satisfied that that man came here to tell a false tale. There cannot be a man who is not convinced that he has been mixed up in many a villainy which, if not perpetrated, had been attempted to be perpetrated in that quarter, and he comes now to save, if he can, the life of his companion and his friend—the son of the woman with whom he has had that intimacy which he sought to-day in vain to disguise. I say, when you look at the whole of those circumstances, balance the evidence on both sides, and look at the question of whether Newton can by any possibility have any motive for coming here to give evidence which must be fatal to a man, who, if that evidence be not true, he must believe to be an innocent man—when you see that he can have no motive for such a purpose—to suppose that he would do so without a motive is to suppose human nature in its worst and most repulsive form to be one hundred times more wicked and perverse than my experience ever yet has found it—I cannot but submit to you that you ought to believe Newton's evidence, and I cannot but submit to you deferentially, but at the same time firmly and emphatically, that if you do believe that evidence it is conclusive of the case.

"Then on the morrow of that day we find Palmer purchasing six grains of strychnine at Hawkins's shop, when Newton came in, and the whole transaction showed he did not want Newton to know what he was buying. But the Defence has not accounted for that strychnine nor was it found in his house.

"If it was for the purpose of professional use for the benefit of some patient for whom small doses of strychnia might have been advantageous, where is the patient and why is he not produced? My learned friend did even advert to the question of the second purchase of strychnia in the whole of his powerful observations. He passed it over in mysterious but significant silence. Account for that six grains of strychnia, the purchase of which it is an undoubted and indisputable fact. Throw doubt if you please—I blame you not for it—upon the story of the purchase on the previous night; but on the Tuesday it is unquestionably true that six grains of strychnia were purchased. Purchased for whom? purchased for what? If for any patient, who is that patient? Produce him. If for any other purpose, at least let us have it explained. Has there been the slightest shadow of an attempt at explanation? Alas! I grieve to say, none at all. Something was said, in the outset of this case, about some dogs that had been troublesome in the paddocks where the mares and foals were, but that proved to have been in September. If there had been any recurrence of such a thing, where are the grooms who had the care and charge of those mares and foals, and why are they not here to state the fact? If this poison was used for the purpose of destroying dogs, someone must have assisted Mr. Palmer in the attempt which he resorted to for that purpose. Where are those persons? Why are they not called? But, not only are they not called, they are not even named. My learned friend does not venture to breathe even a suggestion of anything of the kind. I ask, gentlemen, what conclusion can be drawn from these things, except one, and one alone? Death!! death with all the symptoms of strychnia—death in all the convulsive agonies and throes which that fatal poison produces in the frame of man—death with all the appearances which follow upon death; and mark how that death has come to pass: all these things, in the minds of those who can discuss and consider them with calm, dispassionate attention, who do not mix themselves up as advocates, partisans, or witnesses, leading to but one conclusion. And then the fact of the strychnia being purchased by the prisoner on the morning of the fatal day, if not obtained by him, as was sworn to, on the night before, is left wholly unanswered and wholly unmet, without the shadow of a defence. Alas! gentlemen is it possible that we can come to any other than one painful and dread conclusion? I protest I can suggest you none.

"Then, gentlemen, it is said that there are two other circumstances in the case which make strongly in favour of the prisoner, and negative the presumption of a guilty intention, and those are the fact that he called in two medical men. Here again I admit that this is a matter to which all due consideration ought to be given. He called in Dr. Bamford on the Saturday, and he wrote to Mr. Jones on the Sunday and desired his presence to attend his sick friend. It is perfectly true that he did. It is perfectly true as medical men they would be likely to know the symptoms of poisoning by strychnia, and they would be likely to suspect that death had ensued from it; and yet even here it strikes me that there is a singular inconsistency in the Defence. See the strange contradiction in which the witnesses called for the Defence involve my learned friend who puts them forward, if all those symptoms were not the symptoms of strychnia. If they are referable to all the multiform variety of disease to which those witnesses have spoken, why, then, should Mr. Palmer have the credit of having selected medical men who would be likely to know from those symptoms that they were symptoms of strychnia?

"The prisoner at the bar selected his men well, for what has come to pass shows how wisely he judged of what was likely to take place. This death occurred in the presence of Mr. Jones, with all those fearful symptoms which you have heard described; yet Mr. Jones suspected nothing; and if Mr. Stevens had not exhibited that sagacity and firmness which he did manifest in the after-parts of this transaction, and if Mr. Palmer had succeeded in getting that body hastily introduced into the strong oak coffin that he had had made for it, the body would have been consigned to the grave, and nobody would have been aught the wiser. The presence of Mr. Jones, and the presence of Dr. Bamford, would not have led to detection, would not have frustrated the designs with which I shall presently contend before you this death was brought about. And so, hoping to put off suspicion, he took care that medical men should be present at the time of death.

"Nor is there anything to show that the prisoner had the most distant notion that Mr. Jones intended to sleep in Cook's room that night; and if he had not, the man would have been found dead in the morning alone; he would alone have gone through his mortal struggle and intense and fearful agony; he would have died there alone and unbefriended; he would have been found dead the next morning; the old man would have said it was apoplexy, and the young man would have put it down to epilepsy!!

"But if you believe the evidence of Newton and the chambermaid Mills, pills were administered by Palmer on the Monday night at 10.30, and a few minutes before that time he had procured strychnine from Newton, and an hour later the terrible symptoms of strychnine set in. Can you doubt for one moment poison was given on this Monday night? Though how it came to pass he did not die I can only speculate. Whether it was to bring about by some minute dose convulsions which should not have the complete character of tetanus, but would bear a resemblance to natural convulsions which should justify his saying afterwards that the man had had a fit, and so prepare those who were to hear of it on the next night, when the death was to ensue, for the belief that it was merely a succession of the same description of fit that he had had before. That is one solution. The other may be that he attempted on that Monday night to carry out his fell purpose to its full extent, but that the poison proved inefficacious.

"We do know for certain that Palmer bought strychnine on the Tuesday, and Cook died that night suffering from the same strychnine symptoms as on Monday, but more severe and more intense.

"From this much disputed question of strychnine I pass on to an undisputed poison, antimony, found in his body after death. NOT ONE DOCTOR CALLED for the Defence made any allusion to this poison.

"On the Wednesday night, November 14, at Shrewsbury Mrs. Brooks sees Palmer pouring from a bottle to a glass [as fully told on p. 81], and later on Cook drinks his grog and suffers from severe vomiting, which lasted more or less to the Monday, when, I contend, strychnine was first administered.

"Why was antimony given? It is difficult to say with anything like precision; one can only speculate upon it. It may have been, however, to produce the appearance of natural disease, to account for the calling in of medical men, and to account for the catastrophe which was already in preparation; but it may also have had another and a different object, and it is this—if we are right as to the motives which impelled the prisoner at the bar to commit this great crime, it was (at all events in part) that he might possess himself of the money which Cook would have to realise upon the settling day at Tattersall's on Monday. If Cook went there himself, the scheme was frustrated; Mr. Cook intended to go there himself, and if he had done so the prisoner's designs would have failed of accomplishment. Therefore to make him ill at Shrewsbury—to get him in consequence to go to Rugeley, instead of going to London or anywhere else—to make him ill again and keep him ill at Rugeley, might be part of a cleverly contrived and organised scheme. It might have been with one or other of those motives, it might have been with both, that the antimony was administered, and so sickness produced; but that the sickness was produced and that the antimony was afterwards found in the body are facts *incapable of dispute*. Put them together and you have cause and effect; and if you are satisfied that antimony was introduced into the poor man's stomach for the purpose of producing vomiting, then I say there is no one who could have given it to him but the prisoner at the bar. Then how great does it render the probability that he gave it to carry out his purpose of murder, by making him ill and sick for a few days before giving the strychnine of which the deadly effects have been but too plainly made manifest!"

From this point the Attorney-General digressed to look at the conduct of the prisoner, all of which has been fully entered into in the narrative of the case, dwelling very much on the third packet of poison (the six grains of strychnine) not being found nor accounted for; then upon Palmer going to London and collecting Cook's bets for his own use—not employing Cook's agent, Fisher, but asking a comparative stranger, Herring.

Then he dwelt on the Defence not producing the cheque which Palmer said Cook gave him for £350 (the Shrewsbury Stakes), filled up by Cheshire. If it were genuine, where was it, after it had been returned from Weatherby?

Then on to the lost betting-book, of no use to anybody except the owner and Palmer to make a list of names and bets.

He was very emphatic over Palmer's behaviour at the post-mortem, and trying to bribe the post-boy and subsequently the Coroner with game and money, and that letter to him (p. 130), dwelling, as he explained to the jury, on the circumstantial evidence as a whole, winding up with a strong exhortation, briefly summing up the chief points.

"It is for you to say whether, upon a review of the whole of this evidence, you can come to any other conclusion than that of the prisoner's guilt. Look at his restless anxiety; it may possibly, it is true, be compatible with innocence, but I think, on the other hand, it must be admitted that it bears strongly the aspect of guilt; if it stood alone, I would not ask you upon that to come to a conclusion adverse to the prisoner, but it is one of a series of things small perhaps, each individually in themselves, but, taken as a whole, as I submit to you, leading irresistibly to the conclusion of the guilt of this man.

"Now, gentlemen, the whole case is before you. It will be for you to determine it. You have, on the one hand, a man overwhelmed by a pressure almost unparalleled and unexampled of pecuniary liabilities which he is utterly unable to meet, involving the penalties of the law, which must bring disaster and ruin upon him. His only mode of averting those consequences is by obtaining money; and, under those circumstances, with a bad man, a small amount, if that amount will meet the exigencies of the moment and avert the impending catastrophe and ruin, will operate with immense power. Then you find that he has access to the bedside of the man whose death we are now enquiring into; that he has the means of administering poison to him; and you find that, within eight-and-forty hours, he has twice acquired possession of the very poison, the symptoms of which are found in the death, and after the death; and then you have the death itself in its terrible and revolting circumstances, all of which are characteristic only of death by that poison and of no other.

"Gentlemen, you have, indeed, had introduced into this case one other element which I own I think would have been better omitted. You have had from my learned friend the unusual, and I think I may say unprecedented assurance of his conviction of his client's innocence. . . . I think my learned friend had better have abstained from making any observations which involved the assurance of his own conviction. I say, further, I think he ought, in justice and in consideration for you, to have abstained from reminding you or telling you that the voice of the country would not sanction the verdict which you were about to give. I say nothing of the inconsistency which is involved in such a statement, coming from one who but a short hour before had complained in eloquent terms of the universal torrent of passion and prejudice by which he said his client was oppressed and borne down. Why, gentlemen, in answer to my learned friend, I have only to say, pay no regard to the voice of the country, whether it be for condemnation or acquittal; pay no regard to anything but the internal voice of your own consciences, and the sense of that duty to God and man which you are to discharge upon this occasion. Seek no reward, except the comforting assurance, when you shall look back to the events of this day, that you have discharged to the best of your ability and to the uttermost of your power the duty that it was yours to perform. If, upon a review of this whole case, comparing the evidence upon the one side and upon the other, and weighing it in the even scales of justice, you can come to a conclusion of the prisoner's innocence, or even entertain that fair and reasonable amount of doubt of which the accused is entitled to the benefit, in God's name acquit him. But if, on the other hand, all the facts and all the evidence lead your minds, with satisfaction to yourselves, to the conclusion of the prisoner's guilt, then, but then only, I ask for a verdict of 'guilty' at your hands. For the protection of the good, and for the repression of the wicked, I ask for that verdict, by which alone, as it seems to me, the safety of society can be secured, and the demands, the imperious demands, of public justice can alone be satisfied."

CHAPTER XX

Campbell too old for such a trial—Shee's argument in the final summing-up—Jury's plan of deciding their verdict—Sentence in full—Palmer removed to Stafford chained to a warder—Palmer's reply to the Governor and to the Chaplain—Execution and burial.

LORD CHIEF JUSTICE CAMPBELL

FROM THE PUBLISHED LIFE of Lord Chief Justice Campbell as well as from newspapers of that time there is no doubt but that he wished very much to preside at this trial. He was getting on in years—seventy-six or seventy-seven—and, before it was decided under the "Palmer" Act to remove this trial to London, he had thought of retiring.

His summing up was most ordinary. He would read the evidence of a witness and then make a few commonplace remarks on it. And with important witnesses like Newton or Elizabeth Mills he would say, "If you believe them, there is a strong case against the prisoner; if you doubt any part of their evidence, you must see if it is confirmed by what others tell us."

He took the most unusual step of himself passing the sentence of death, for when more than one Judge sits at a trial, the junior Judge generally passes sentence. I need only allude to the well-known Tichborne trial, where three Judges sat—the Lord Chief Justice Cockburn, Justices Lush and Mellor (Cockburn had been the Attorney-General in prosecuting Palmer). Sentence was pronounced on the Claimant by Justice Mellor.

Also in a murder trial where two or more Judges sit, as in the trial of Franz Müller in 1864 before the Lord Chief Baron (Sir Frederick Pollock) and Mr. Baron Martin, the latter Judge passed the sentence of death, both Judges being in Court. But Campbell took throughout this trial a great deal upon himself, and as the Rev. T. Palmer says in his letter, often without consulting his colleagues. He listened most attentively and made notes throughout the opening speech of the Attorney-General, which is a perfect model of clearness and lucid arrangement of the many intricate facts, and then after his reply on the Saturday afternoon, which is aptly described as an unrivalled specimen of forensic eloquence and ability, the

Lord Chief Justice had the whole of Sunday to prepare his summing up, which reads tamely for so important an occasion and is not removed beyond the ordinary remarks of Judges.

When the Lord Chief Justice had ended his summing up with the words "May God direct you to a right finding," Serjeant Shee caused a somewhat unseemly interruption by stating the question left by his Lordship was whether "*the evidence proved that Cook's symptoms were consistent with death from strychnine.*" *This* ought to be followed by the questions "*Is it inconsistent with death from natural causes?*" and does the medical evidence *establish* the death of Cook by strychnine?

In the middle of the arguments Shee invoked the Almighty with the words, "It is my duty not to be deterred by any expression of displeasure—I am accountable to a much higher tribunal than even your Lordship's—to submit what occurs to me to be the proper question."

At the end of the argument the Judge said to the jury, just before they retired:

"The question whether the symptoms were consistent with death from strychnine was not THE question, but it was most material in finding your judgment as to whether he died from natural disease, or from poison administered by the prisoner. If the symptoms were consistent with death from strychnine, then you must consider the other evidence in the case as to whether the death was due to natural causes or whether he did not die by poison—by strychnine. And if it were, was it administered by the prisoner.

"If you so believe, then it is your duty to God and man to find a verdict of guilty."

The jury retired to their room (of which a picture is given in Ward & Lock's book, p. 179) to consider their verdict.

A letter appeared in *The Times* a few days after the trial from one of the jurymen, in which he says:

"When we reached our room, there was silence for ten or fifteen minutes. A short discussion of the facts took place, the Foreman, Mr. Mavor, intimating he did not wish any juryman to express aloud his personal opinion what the verdict should be, for fear of unduly influencing a colleague. Each man took pen and paper and wrote his decision separately and folded up the paper.

"*Guilty* was found to be the unanimous verdict. It is quite untrue that we were absent a long time for the sake of appearances—our situation was too dreadful and too solemn to admit of humbug."

And this was confirmed by what one of the jury told me twelve years later.

After an absence from 2.18 to 3.35, the jury returned into Court, the three Judges came back to their seats, and amidst breathless, painful silence a verdict of "guilty" was returned.

The Lord Chief Justice, in pronouncing sentence, told the prisoner his two "learned brothers and he himself agreed with the verdict"; and the Rev. Thomas Palmer, in the letter to the Lord Chief Justice immediately after the trial, commented on this statement that they must have agreed before the verdict, as he was certain not a word passed between the three judges after the verdict—*before* the Sentence. And he added his family felt deeply indebted to Mr. Justice Cresswell for his kindness from the Bench.

The words of the sentence were as follows. Lord Campbell said:

"William Palmer, after a long and impartial trial you have been convicted by a jury of the crime of wilful murder. In that verdict my two learned brothers, who have so anxiously watched this trial, and myself entirely Concur, and consider that verdict altogether satisfactory. The case is attended with such circumstances of aggravation that I do not dare to touch upon them. Whether it is the first and only offence of this sort which you have committed is certainly known only to God and your own conscience. It is seldom that such a familiarity with the means of death should be shown without long experience; but for this offence of which you have been found guilty your life is forfeited. You must prepare to die; and I trust that, as you can expect no mercy in this world, you will, by repentance of your crimes, seek to obtain mercy from Almighty God. The Act of Parliament under which you have been tried, and under which you have been brought to the bar of this Court at your own request, gives leave to the Court to direct that the sentence under such circumstances shall be executed either within the jurisdiction of the Central Criminal Court or in the county where the offence was committed. We think that, for the sake of example, the sentence ought to be executed in the county of Stafford. Now, I hope that this terrible example will deter others from committing such atrocious crimes, and that it will be seen that whatever art, or caution, or experience may accomplish, such an offence will be detected and punished. However destructive poisons may be, it is so ordained by Providence that there are means for the safety of His creatures, for detecting and punishing those who administer them. I again implore you to repent and prepare for the awful change that awaits you. I will not seek to harrow up your feelings by any enumeration of the circumstances of this foul murder. I will content myself now with passing the sentence of the law, which is, that you be taken hence to the jail of Newgate, and thence removed to the jail of the county of Stafford, being the county in which the offence for which you are justly convicted was committed; and that you be taken thence to a place of execution and be there hanged by the neck until you be dead; and that your body be afterwards buried within the precincts of the prison in which you shall be last confined after your conviction; and may the Lord have mercy upon your soul! Amen."

It will be noticed the Judge says:

"Such an offence will surely be detected and punished. However destructive poison may be, it is so ordained that there are means for *detecting* and punishing those who administer it.

He does not say for DETECTING THE POISON, with this case of *undetected* strychnine in front of him, as some contended his remarks implied, but detecting those who administer it.

There are allusions in this sentence of death to other victims poisoned by Palmer, and though the jury were trying him solely for the murder of Cook, yet human nature can never be totally erased, and the twelve jurymen had heard for the last six months of the various murders, and though they decided this verdict, we may be quite sure, only on the evidence for killing Cook, yet his misdeeds could not be wholly blotted out of their minds.

AFTER SENTENCE TO EXECUTION

On returning to his cell after sentence of death had been pronounced, Palmer was told to change his garments, and a convict suit was provided for him; then he was handcuffed and a chain attached to his ankles and to a warder, and a cab brought to the Governor's private door, as well as a cab into the Courtyard at Newgate, where "Black Maria" (the convicts' van) was standing, and, the crowd intently watching the cab there, Palmer was hurried into the former cab and driven rapidly across to Euston, the waiting crowds following, and yelling *"Poisoner,"* *"Murderer,"* as soon as they found out he had gone in the cab from the private door. But by aid of the police, he safely reached Euston, and was taken down to Stafford on this night of Tuesday, May 27, after a fortnight's trial, and was hanged on the high-road in front of Stafford Jail on Saturday, June 14, 1856.

A few petitions were sent to the Home Secretary, Sir George Grey, praying for a respite entirely on the grounds of strychnine not having been found in the body. But those who urged that plea could have known nothing about the shameful way in which the post-mortem had been carried out and the mangled stomach sent to Professor Taylor.

Another point urged was that we were in the height of our re-joicing with France at the close of the Crimean War, and the Prince Imperial[1] was going to be baptized on this very 14th of June—surely we would not contaminate so festal a day by the execution of a man about whose guilt there was any doubt, etc. etc. But the Home Secretary wisely turned a deaf ear to this and to similar appeals.

Just before they started for the scaffold, Palmer was asked by the Governor if he would not acknowledge the justice of his sentence. He replied, "Cook did not die from strychnine"; and when the Governor of the jail said, "This is not the time for quibbling. Did you, or did you not, kill Cook?" he answered, "The Lord Chief Justice summed up for poisoning by strychnine."

During the last few years, in magazine articles and short histories of the trial, a great deal has been made out of this reply as tending to prove—not that Palmer was innocent—but that he poisoned Cook by other means (!) or had found a method of administering strychnine in small doses so that it could not be detected, and one writer contends that he gave the small dose on the Monday night with this idea, but that it was too small. It is not generally mentioned that this was a comparatively recent poison—or drug used as poison—and the *first* case where a trial had taken place for murder by strychnine.

But why should there be any doubt after the unanimous opinion of Judges and juries? He undoubtedly bought strychnine within a few hours of Cook's death, and could not afterwards produce the packet, nor did he ever say for what purpose he

---

[1] *Prince Imperial*: Napoléon Eugène Louis Jean Joseph Bonaparte (1856-1879), the only child of France's Emperor Napoleon III and grand-nephew of Napoleon I. When Napoleon III was dethroned in 1870, the family went into exile in England. The prince trained as a soldier and volunteered to fight in the Anglo-Zulu war, where he was killed in a skirmish in 1879. His death ended hopes of restoring a Bonaparte to the throne.

bought it. Then Cook's symptoms and sudden death all pointed to strychnine, and followed on the administration of two pills on the evenings of the days on which Palmer had bought that drug.

His reply to the Governor, and a few minutes afterwards to the Chaplain, are rather in the tone of annoyance at being bothered by them just in the last few minutes of life, and he refuses to answer them further.

In those days not only were the executions carried out in public (up to 1868), but it seems as if all the preliminary proceedings were in the presence of reporters and friends, as the papers immediately published this refusal to the Governor, and *The Times* of June 16, 1856, publishes the following account from an eye-witness:

"The wretched man was pinioned, the executioner was standing by him waiting for the signal to move forward to the scaffold (which was erected on the road just outside the gates of the prison), the Chaplain in the most solemn manner exhorted him to admit the justice of his sentence. The Prisoner firmly replied it was not a just sentence. The Chaplain quickly said, '*Then your blood be upon your own head.*' To this Palmer made no reply."

The reverend gentleman had laboured strenuously to obtain a confession of guilt. He had preached a sermon so impressive and almost personal that it had fetched tears and sobs in the chapel from Palmer, but it had also driven him from again partaking in the services of the Church. But at the last awful moment, even if he did feel mortified at his failure to extract a confession, it was not in the exercise of charity and Christian forbearance that God's minister should part from the wretched, half-dazed criminal with the above denunciation.

Why, the very parting words of the Judge in passing sentence are by comparison merciful and humane, "May the Lord have mercy on your soul!"

In my opinion and that of others who have carefully studied Palmer's character, thus worrying him for a confession was the worst way to obtain it. Palmer was a stubborn, sullen man at heart, and his obstinacy was stimulated by the attacks of the Chaplain and other well-meaning persons. It would doubtless be consolatory to Judges and jury that murderers shall confess before execution. But the unwritten language of the law is, or should be, "Your guilt is proved; you have nothing to confess. The law is satisfied."

But was Palmer bound to confess? Did he increase his moral

guilt by refusing? If by his refusing to confess he did not withhold restitution to those he had injured, or if by refusing to confess to his fellow-man he did not infringe any sacred commands, he could scarcely augment his guilt. The confession of a criminal is no doubt in some cases the expression of a contrite spirit, but it does not always imply penitence. The criminal, on the other hand, who refuses to confess may be truly penitent, and his refusal may be due to his fear that a confession would injure those near and dear to him.

One can call to mind certain murders where a confession by the murderer might have caused distress to innocent parties and even actual damage to their reputation.

I have gone over this rather fully, as Palmer's remarks have caused a few—very few—to throw out some doubts as to his guilt, in consequence of his replies to the Governor and the Chaplain within a few minutes of his execution.

Moreover, as he had never confessed during the two or three weeks after his sentence, in spite of the most earnest entreaties by his brothers and others and by the Chaplain of the jail, he was scarcely likely to do so when a few minutes of life were all that remained to him.

Both Palmer and his relations spoke in high terms of the kind way in which he was treated by the Governor and all the officials in Stafford Jail during the last fortnight. He seems to have had his time much more occupied than is permitted at the present day, friends coming and going, as well as lawyers and relations. He also wrote many letters, one of which is in my possession.

On the morning of his execution, when the hangman came into his cell, he was offered some wine before he was pinioned. When it was brought and poured out quickly, he blew off some bubbles and remarked, "They always give me indigestion next morning if I drink in a hurry."

Within less than ten minutes he was dead.

In those days of public executions, the prisoner generally seems to have had some distance to travel after being pinioned—different from the present day, when a few yards, as at Pentonville and Wandsworth, is all they have to walk, and no steps to mount.[2] Palmer, after walking some distance, had

---

[2] By the time capital punishment was abolished in Great Britain in 1965, the procedure for hanging a criminal had been standardized into an efficient routine. As part of the system, the condemned inmate would be placed in a cell next to the execution chamber, separated from it by a

a very rudimentary ladder to mount on to the platform, which he crossed in full view of the public, and looking up at the rope took his position exactly underneath it.

We read *very* different versions of his reception by the public. One account says the mob screamed at him and yelled "Murderer!" "Poisoner!" with great clamour.[3] Another version tells us he was received in almost breathless silence, and the mob watched the proceedings with awe-struck solemnity. A distant connection of mine, who was nineteen or twenty years old at the time of the execution, showed me the exact spot where he stood and saw the execution, and near him there was a marked silence.

But the crowd which had been collecting since the evening before was so vast in extent that we can quite believe a few roughs near the scaffold may have yelled and shouted, but not those some distance away from the gallows. The mob stretched the whole length of the front of the jail, for the scaffold was erected in front of the central gates, close to the spot where the Governor's private house now is. I have remarked how they were bringing out the scaffold just as my father, at 11 p.m., was walking from Stafford to Stone,[4] having missed the last train. Even then, ten hours before the execution, the mob was immense, and he met hundreds hurrying along the road from Stone.

After Palmer was hanged, a step was taken which seems to us in the present century most unusual. His head was shaved and a plaster cast was taken by Mr. Bridges, of Liverpool. The cast was photographed, and one was given me by a son of the Rugeley solicitor for the Prosecution, and another was sent me by Dr. Douglas, of Lancaster, who had deeply studied the trial.

About twenty years ago I interviewed an old man who had been a warder at Stafford Jail and sat up with Palmer the last night he was alive and helped to bury him. No coffin was supplied, and unslaked lime was poured over his naked body in the grave. And so passed out of this world the notorious Prince of Poisoners.

---

false wall. Preparations for the hanging would take place out of the prisoner's sight and hearing. When the time came, the process of moving the wall, pinioning the prisoner, stepping him to the noose and effecting the drop could take as little as 20 seconds.

[3] [Fletcher's footnote] *Vide* p. 111, Ward & Lock.

[4] A market town 7 miles north of Stafford and 14 miles north of Rugeley.

PORTRAIT OF WM. PALMER.

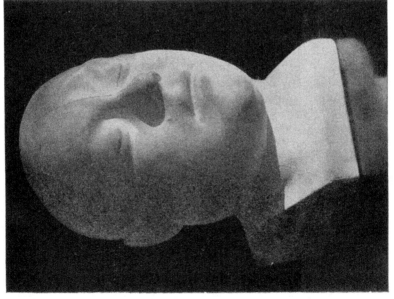

PHOTOGRAPH OF A CAST TAKEN AFTER WM. PALMER'S EXECUTION.

BIBLIOGRAPHY

The interest taken in Palmer and his murders and his life and trial is shown by the number of pamphlets, short articles, etc., published in the first few years after his execution.

In nearly every book of trials, Palmer has a conspicuous place for a few pages.

My own collection of books has all of any consequence, and I will append a list of them.

But there is no book, with the exception of the first, which gives any account of his life and career.

Life and Trial (Illustrated). Ward & Lock.
Trial (in 2 parts). Allen, from Angelo Bennett's shorthand notes.
Central Criminal Court Sessions. The whole evidence verbatim. Barnett & Buckler.
Notable Trial Series (Knott), 1st and 2nd Editions.
Trial. Lofts.
Trial (small print). Ireland.
Trial, Regina v. Palmer. Collier.
Letter to Lord Chief Justice by the Rev. Tom Palmer.
Professor Taylor on Strychnine. A full account of his connection with this case.
Murder by Poisoning. Stewart & Browne. 150 pp.
Cries of the Condemned (Unfair Trial).
Criminal Law. Justice Stephen. 3rd volume. 150 pp.
The Analysis of the Evidence. Dr. Fife.
Sketch of Wm. Palmer. Inquests on Mrs. Anne and Walter Palmer.

Also separate chapters in books on murders by Walter Wood, Miss Tennyson Jesse, Attlay, Harold Eaton, etc.

EXPANDED BIBLIOGRAPHY

Below is an expanded version of Fletcher's bibliography, in the same order. Sources that could not be traced are noted.

Anonymous, *The Illustrated Times Report of the Trial of William Palmer*. London: Ward and Lock, 1856. Republished by Peschel Press, 2014.

Bennett, Angelo. *The Queen v. Palmer: Verbatim Report of the Trial of William Palmer*. London: J. Allen, 1856.

Proceedings of the Old Bailey, "William Palmer," http://www.oldbaileyonline.org/browse.jsp?id=def1-490-18560514&div=t18560514-490, accessed Feb. 24, 2014.

Knott, George H. (ed., 1st ed.), Eric R. Watson (ed., 2nd ed.). *Trial of William Palmer* (Notable British Trial Series). Glasgow: William Hodge and Co., 1912.

Lofts, John. *A Full Report of the Trial of William Palmer*. London: John Lofts, 1856.

Anonymous. *The Yelverton Marriage Case, Thelwall v. Yelverton*. London: George Vickers, 1861.

Collier, George Frederick. *Regina v. Palmer. The Paradoxology of Poisoning; and Pudding in a Lantern*. London: C.H. Clarke, 1856.

Anonymous (falsely attrib. to Thomas Palmer). *A Letter to the Lord Chief Justice Campbell*. London: T. Taylor, 1856.

Taylor, Alfred S. *On Poisoning by Strychnia*. London: Longman, Brown, Green, Longmans and Roberts, 1856.

Browne, George Lathom and C.G. Stewart. *Reports of Trials for Murder by Poisoning*. London: Stevens and Sons, 1883.

Wakley, Thomas. *Cries of the Condemned*. London: C. Elliot, 1856.

Stephen, James Fitzjames. *A History of the Criminal Law of England, Vol. 3*. London: Macmillan and Co., 1883.

Fife, George. *Trial of William Palmer, For the Murder of John Parsons Cook: An Abstract and Analysis of the Evidence*. London: Longman & Co., undated, poss. 1856.

Sketch of Wm. Palmer. Inquests on Mrs. Anne and Walter Palmer. Not traced but for a fee articles can be found at the British Newspaper Archive (www.britishnewspaperarchive.co.uk).

Wood, Walter, ed. *Survivors' Tales of Famous Crimes*. London: Cassell and Company, 1916.

Jesse, F. Tennyson. *Murder and Its Motives*. London: Harrap, 1952.

Atlay, James Beresford. Possibly these titles: *Famous Trials of the Century, The Tichborne Case, The Tichborne Claimant, Etc.*, and *Trial of the Stauntons* in the Notable British Trials series.

Eaton, Harold. *Famous Poison Trials*. London: W. Collins Sons & Co., 1923.

Additional Sources

The editor also consulted these resources to write the footnotes and the essays.

Altic, Richard D. *Victorian Studies in Scarlet*. New York: W.W. Norton & Co., 1970.

Anonymous. *The Illustrated Life and Career of William Palmer of Rugeley*. London: Ward and Lock. 1856. Republished by Peschel Press, 2016.

Anonymous. *The Times Report of the Trial of William Palmer*. London: Ward and Lock. 1856. Republished by Peschel Press, 2014.

British History Online, http://www.british-history.ac.uk/report.aspx?compid=53407, accessed April 27, 2014.

Brown, Donald. "A Walk Through Rugeley" (pamphlet). Rugeley: Landor (Local History) Society, 2003.

Buckingham, John. *Bitter Nemesis: The Intimate History of Strychnine*. New York: CRC Press, 2008.

Dickens, Charles. "The Demeanour of Murderers." Dickens Journals Online. http://www.djo.org.uk/indexes/articles/the-demeanour-of-muderers.html, accessed June 13, 2014.

Google Earth

Henderson, Laurence, "The Hangman's Story," *Murder Ink*. New York: Workman Publishing, 1984.

The Infamous Rugeley Poisoner William Palmer. http://palmer.staffscc.net/, accessed June 13, 2014.

"Rugeley: Manors and economic history," "A History of the County of Stafford: Volume 5: East Cuttlestone hundred" (1959), http://www.british-history.ac.uk/report.aspx? compid=53407, accessed April 27, 2014.

Singletrack. "Possibly moving to Rugeley," http://singletrackworld.com/forum/topic/possibly-moving-to-rugeley, accessed April 27, 2014.

Wikipedia.

Appendix

'The Scene of a Tragedy'

Rugeley Then and Today

William Palmer's bottle of strychnine brought notoriety to Rugeley without any of the benefits. Tourists do not drop in at the former Talbot Arms for a pint. They do not visit John Parsons Cook's grave at St. Augustine's church. No actors trace Palmer's path on "murder walks" like they follow Jack the Ripper's in the East End.

There's a kernel of truth in the tale that Rugeley was so embarrassed to be associated with Palmer that the village appealed to the prime minister to be allowed to change its name. The Ripper risked all to dissect prostitutes in the East End streets. His crimes thrilled an audience who were neither poor nor prostitutes. Palmer's crimes, you might say, hit too close to home.

It didn't help Rugeley that it was not an alluring place to set a crime. It was a plain country town, and it must have been even more bleak in winter. In January, 1856, as Palmer awaited trial in jail, one anonymous reporter for *The Illustrated London News* filed this description:

"Rugeley was built to be the scene of a tragedy. There are many towns of the kind in Holland-like Staffordshire. . . . Every village made a rapid rush to be a town, and stopped half-way; and, at present, Staffordshire has only about two towns, neither of second class importance, while she is almost totally destitute of that beauty of less energetic shires. . . . Rugeley is the worst of these; for it seems to have fallen back — from the staring red brick, perfectly modern, outworks that can get nothing to do — upon the old village street, which is built of sad, sullen-looking dirty-brown stone, miserable without the once-adjoining fields, and most disheartening to the passenger from the utterly unprosperous look of the place. You enter Rugeley from the station by a road that winds between two churchyards — an old and a new one — and which seem to compete with one another in dismal suggestiveness. The people are neither country people nor townsfolk, have neither rustic ease nor civic smartness, and the gloom of failure appears to pervade talk and 'trade.'

"An inn in a town is always a representative place. In Rugeley the inns are as miserably inconvenient, insufficient, and uncomfortable, as posthouse inns in Poland. Like the other houses, they are drear, the principle inn looks like an aged gaol; and the next most melancholy building in Rugeley is that opposite — and that building is the house of William Palmer the surgeon. A deserted inn, as the Talbot Arms is, was not a healthy sight for a surgeon without practice, and heavy in debt, as Palmer was. 'The Talbot Arms,' a dilapidated sign, swings in front, and its creaking at night must have wearied William Palmer's wife when she lay dying. The motto of the Talbot—'Nihil humani alienum' [Nothing human is alien]—is emblazoned on the arms—a constant, beneficent suggestion to the eyes of Mr. Palmer, but of which he availed himself in the manner sinister."

The anonymous writer of Ward & Lock's "Illustrated Illustrated Life and Career of William Palmer" (republished by Peschel Press) strained to find something nice to say about the place. Perhaps he didn't want to hurt sales in Rugeley. Its "utterly unprosperous look" is "kept very clean, and occupied by persons extremely well to do in the world." He quotes commercial travelers whose accounts are "particularly safe" there. Its deserted streets have "a certain charm," and its inhabitants are working hard at Bladen's brass-foundry or Hatfield's manufactory. "It is a very curious little over-grown village, and too pretty to be abused." To reporters from the big city of London, Rugeley was a town to come from, not a town to grow old in.

Rugeley Then

Rugeley was a farming village, founded to exploit its fertile soil and the nearby River Trent. It surfaces in records from before William the Conqueror's time, and it might be older than that. Its name is a derivation of "ridge," and not many villages can be identified by common geographic names before you start running out.

King William acquired Rugeley in 1071 after putting down a rebellion by a local lord. The crown held onto it for a century before selling it to the Bishop of Coventry and Lichfield. To give you an idea of how close the past nestles next to the present, the agreement mentions a particular church. Mrs. Palmer's house was built next to its ruins and her children would play there. Those preserved ruins can still be seen today.

Rugeley grew slowly like many other farming villages. In 1259, it was allowed to hold a weekly market, and a three-day fair in June. This enhanced the village's status and gave the locals a break from the monotony of planting and harvesting. The area was also noted for its horses and cattle, and by Palmer's time regular markets drew buyers from as far as London.

By 1700, there was enough industry around for anyone who wanted to work to find it. There were ironworks, a brewery, brass and chemical works, hat makers, brick and lime kilns, even open-pit coal mining. But Rugeley was still a small town. With a couple hundred families, it was still possible to know everybody, if only by name.

As the Industrial Revolution geared up, the steady cycle of life in Rugeley began to change as it did everywhere. The town was already a stop on the London-Chester turnpike when the Grand Trunk Canal connected it to the Mersey River, and hence to Liverpool. The railroad arrived in 1847 allowing anyone, including Palmer, to visit London for business or pleasure and return the same day. By Palmer's time, more than 4,000 people called Rugeley home.

Rugeley underwent its share of boom and bust cycles. Manufacturing fled after World War II for more profitable locations. A deep mine opened in 1960 followed by a power station, boosting employment, which then fell in the 1990s when they closed. Supermarkets came in, forcing shops to close, which were left vacant or redeveloped into other businesses.

Rugeley Now

Today, there are more than 22,000 people living in Rugeley, many of them pensioned-off coal miners. Rugeley today is a lot like many small towns. The jobless rate is a bit higher than the national average. Housing prices are a bit cheaper. One of its attractions is Cannock Chase, an Area of Outstanding Natural Beauty (what we in the U.S. would call a national park). If you have a job and want to raise your family or be left alone, there are a lot worse places to go. Otherwise, there doesn't seem to be a lot going on.

While researching this book, I came across a forum devoted to bicycling where someone asked about moving there. The responses ranged from shrugs to outright horror. "It still haunts my dreams," said one poster without explanation, and he lived there for less than a year. "If you turn your computer off and look at the screen it is mimicking Rugeley nightlife," chimed in another. The majority opinion was "you could do better."

On the Internet, Rugeley leaves a small footprint. The top three sites from a recent search was the town's Wikipedia page, a few reviews of hotels and B&Bs on TripAdvisor, and a real estate agents' list of properties for sale. The top news story at the regional Express & Star newspaper announced that there were 6,223 lost cats and dogs in the area. An item titled "Sculptures planned to promote history of town" announced a plan to place statues in the town to celebrate the town's mining and horse fair. No mention was made of Palmer.

It's a pity. Because like it or not, Palmer will always be tied to Rugeley. And a visitor to the town can be surprised to see how much from Palmer's time can still be found.

Palmer's House

The stone building, set back slightly from the sidewalk to allow for a strip of grass, has undergone changes. An addition was made to the front after 1900, the street-facing gables were reconstructed and the house converted into the post office that Fletcher saw. Today, two businesses occupy the building. Only the rear of the house reveals the gables that were part of its original Tudor design.

The Talbot Arms

The coaching inn where Cook died is still a pub, but only the shell survives as a historically protected building. Renovations cleaned the interior of its original character. The name was too notorious for its owner, who changed it to the Shrewsbury Arms, then its present-day name of The Shrew.

Mrs. Palmer's House

In her time, it was known as "the Yard," short for timber-yard and a reminder of the source of her late husband's wealth. The correspondent for the *Illustrated Times* liked the looks of it, although he thought the "two-storeyed bow window" that faced the canal looked tawdry.

Development and road building has encroached on the grounds around the house. Although it has been converted into a business, the shape of the building has been preserved, and by going down a side street, the tawdry windows can be seen. The preserved ruins of Rugeley's first church where Mrs. Palmer's children explored still stands.

St. Augustine's Church

With the exception of a few additions, the church and graveyard looks unchanged. The grave of John Parsons Cook can still be seen under the yew trees by the entrance, although time and weather has worn the inscription on its slab. In the back, the Palmer family's crypt has nearly vanished. The slab's stone sides are gone and the wrought-iron fence, according to local lore, was removed during a World War II scrap drive. Only the stone top remains to mark the final resting place of the Palmers of William's generation.

Palmer in Popular Culture

"When a doctor goes wrong, he is the first of criminals. He has nerve and he has knowledge. Palmer and Pritchard were among the heads of their profession."
Sherlock Holmes, "The Adventure of the Speckled Band"

The year 1856 was an eventful year in British history. Three years of bloody fighting in the Crimean ended, but Britain prepared to fight in China and Persia. British Guiana issued what would become the world's most valuable postage stamp. Covent Garden Theatre burned down for the second time. Queen Victoria gave Norfolk Island in the South Pacific to the descendants of the *H.M.S. Bounty* mutiny.

But the Palmer trial interested people the most. Everything about it was big: the number of victims, the 12-day trial that drew royalty and high government officials, the newspaper coverage, the glimpses into the shady worlds of money-lending and crooked horse racing, and the rare use of a poison that was far more available than people realized.

Then, there were the elements that thrilled newspaper readers. The murderer was a doctor, a figure of trust who could give you a pill meant to kill instead of cure. Worse, he was a husband and father who could calmly poison his wife, brother, mother-in-law and five of his six infants. In an age that celebrated family and science, this was an assault on the pillars of society. Even today, Palmer's crimes can make the blood run cold.

But Palmer's story didn't end on the dock at Stafford. Hardly was his body moldering in the unmarked grave on the prison grounds than writers began rendering his life into art.

Charles Dickens

On the day Palmer was executed, Dickens published an essay about the doctor in his magazine *Household Words*. "The Demeanour of Murderers," printed in this book, was a polemic against the newspapers who admired Palmer's composure during the trial.

Ironically, Dickens' description of Palmer's "complete self-possession, of his constant coolness, of his profound composure, of his perfect equanimity," according to biographer Peter Ackroyd, "is also a description which Dickens liked to give of himself."

The Palmer case also found his way into Dickens' fiction. Inspector Bucket of "Bleak House" is based on Inspector Field, who investigated Palmer's application to insure Bates' life. Dickens scholar Philip Collins also believed that elements of Palmer's character surfaces in Slinkton, the poisoner in the short story "Hunted Down" (1859).

Wilkie Collins

The Palmer trial, with its vast cast of characters that, day by day, slowly built a picture of the man and his murders, inspired Collins to use a similar structure for "The Woman in White."

Agatha Christie

In 1915, as a volunteer at a hospital dispensary, Christie began her education in poisons in preparation for her first mystery novel. The result, "The Mysterious Affair at Styles" (republished in an annotated edition from Peschel Press) shares numerous similarities with the Palmer case:

* Both murderers use strychnine.

* Both victims die in the middle of the night.

* Doctors play a prominent role in both cases. When they are called in the middle of the night, they raise suspicions by arriving arrive fully dressed.

* A witness testifies he sold strychnine to someone who says he needs it to kill a dog.

* In the Palmer trial, a witness describing the death of Mrs. Sergison Smith says that the pharmacist who compounded the fatal dose raced to the house when he realizes his mistake. In "Styles," a chemist's assistant who sold strychnine does the same thing.

Dorothy L. Sayers

The mystery writer and creator of aristocratic amateur detective Lord Peter Wimsey used Palmer as a touchstone in her books.

* In "Unnatural Death," Lord Peter comments: "Look at the scores and scores of murders that have gone unproved and unsuspected till the fool of a murderer went too far and did

something silly which blew up the whole show. Palmer, for instance. His wife and brother and mother-in-law and various illegitimate children, all peacefully put away — till he made the mistake of polishing Cook off in that spectacular manner."

* During the exhumation scene in "The Unpleasantness at the Bellona Club," the gruesome Dr. Horner says "the jars are just behind you. Thanks. Look out! You'll have it over. Ha! ha! that was a near thing. Reminds me of Palmer, you know — and Cook's stomach — always think that a very funny story, ha, ha!"

Francis Iles and Alfred Hitchcock

Called by novelist Colin Dexter "the father of the psychological suspense novel," Anthony Berkeley Cox (1893-1971) published "Before the Fact" (1932) under his penname Francis Iles. The crime novel broke new ground by focusing not on the murder investigation, but on a lonely woman's discovery of her new husband's true character. The story of the caddish mad who blows his wife's money at the racetrack and kills his best friend neatly parallels the Palmer story. The novel was sold to Hollywood, where director Alfred Hitchcock turned it into "Suspicion" (1941), starring an actor who was the polar opposite of Palmer: Cary Grant.

Palmer In Profile

Ironically, it took nearly a century before Palmer's story began to spread through the culture. During the 1950s, the CBS radio show Crime Classics broadcast "The Hangman and William Palmer." Folkways Records in the U.S. released "The Murder Trial of William Palmer, Surgeon," a spoken-word record that used court transcripts to recreate the trial. Yorkshire Television made the TV movie "The Life and Crimes of William Palmer" (1998). Historian Lucy Worsley visited Rugeley and discussed the Palmer case in the documentary series "A Very British Murder" (2013). The next year, the story was retold with the help of material drawn from archives and newspaper of the period in Stephen Bates' "The Poisoner."

Poison Nuts and Quaker Buttons

A Brief History of Strychnine

> *"It still seems to me that my mother's death might be*
> *accounted for by natural means."*
> *"How do you make that out, Mr. Cavendish?"*
> *"My mother, at the time of her death, and for some time*
> *before it, was taking a tonic containing strychnine."*
> Agatha Christie, *The Mysterious Affair at Styles*

It starts in your mind.

Something is not right. Your heart is hammering in your chest. You fidget and find it hard to focus. You consider going for a walk to burn off the excess energy. You begin to feel nauseous.

Your mouth tastes of pennies.

The first sign that something is seriously wrong is when the muscles in your arms and legs stiffen, then jerk like you're a marionette. Close your eyes, and you see lights sparkle in the darkness. You grab your belly and heave. The spasms cause your hands and feet to draw closer to you. Your face contorts, and the pressure grows behind your eyeballs, causing them to swell.

You vomit some more. Quite a lot, actually.

If you know what to do at this point, you still have a chance of surviving. Otherwise, the time between spasms grow shorter and shorter. You're losing control of your body. If you haven't pissed yourself by now, you do. You can't taste the saliva frothing down your chin because you're suffocating. Taking a breath feels like someone is sitting on your chest.

Your body stiffens.

As the lack of oxygen sinks you into unconsciousness, your back thrusts into an arch and your head and heels stay on the floor and your arms jerk spasmodically in slower and smaller motions.

The muscles in your face settle into a teeth-baring grimace. A doctor passing by could tell you that the Joker-like expression is called the *risus sardonicus*, from the Latin for "sardonic smile," but you are beyond caring. There's nothing left to do but call the undertaker and order the flowers.

Total time: under an hour, tops.

That's what it is like to die of strychnine poisoning.

Everything Is a Poison

Mystery fans in particular know that strychnine is a poison. So it's understandable that readers of *The Mysterious Affair at Styles* would wonder why Mrs. Inglethorp is being fed a daily dose of the stuff in a tonic. What could she be thinking?

The answer lies in understanding how physicians look at poisons and what strychnine does to the human body. Because despite the fact that strychnine can kill, for a long time it was used to cure.

Still is, in fact.

Our story starts with Paracelsus, the German physician who during the Renaissance developed new methods for treating illnesses. He started from the standpoint that, as he wrote, "everything is poison, there is poison in everything. Only the dose makes a thing not a poison."

He was not just talking about strychnine or arsenic. Too much of anything is dangerous to the human body. Clean water is safe to drink, but slug down several gallons quickly and you develop water intoxication in which your cells swell as they try to absorb the excess. Breathing pure oxygen for too long causes hyperoxia, damaging the cell membranes and causing brain and lung damage.

So if everything is a poison, the reasoning goes, it simply becomes a matter of finding a safe dosage and learning what good it can do for you.

Even strychnine.

From Quakers to Quacks

Some folks like water,
Some folks like wine,
But I like a taste,
Of straight strychnine.

Strychnine, by The Sonics (1964)

Strychnine is the distilled essence of nuts from the Strychnos nux-vomica tree, found in India, Sri Lanka, Australia, and north-central Africa. The name is derived from the Greek word *strukhnos* for a type of nightshade, but it is more commonly called the poison nut or Quaker button tree.

("Quaker buttons," by the way, comes from the Religious Society of Friends. Their nickname "Quakers" originated as an insult, a play either on their belief that one should "quake before the Lord," or from the habit of some members to tremble during services when touched by the Holy Ghost.)

Healers would grind the nuts and stem bark and use them to give the heart and respiratory systems a boost as well as to treat a laundry list of problems, including dyspepsia, dysentery, paralysis and sexual impotence.

Scientifically, strychnine works as a neurotoxin, binding itself to the neurons that control the muscles and interfering with the electrical signals used to control them. By taking the place of glycine, the organic compound that inhibits muscle action, it causes the poison's characteristic muscle spasms that can end in death by asphyxiation.

Terrible, right? Why would anyone take something that stimulates your body that way?

Ever drink coffee? Tea? Red Bull? Strychnine and caffeine have a similar molecular structure and both block the glycine receptors. There are crucial differences — caffeine doesn't kill you for one — but at low doses strychnine acts as a stimulant.

The modern history of strychnine begins in the early nineteenth century. The plant had been known in Europe since the 1540s, but it wasn't until 1818 that French chemists Joseph Bienaimé Caventou and Pierre-Joseph Pelletier isolated the nux-vomica essence and named it strychnine. They tested it on rabbits and attempted to develop an antidote. Some of their ideas, such as ingesting chlorine water, were as deadly as the drug.

In the meantime, physician Pierre Fouquier experimented with nux-vomica on patients at a Paris hospital. The results, at best, were mixed. One experiment left its victim paralyzed for eight hours, frightening the assistants as much as the other patients. Some who survived the convulsions claimed they were cured and checked out of the hospital before the treatment was completed, or at least before the doctor could stop them.

By 1828, reports of the drug had reached England, and soon British doctors were testing strychnine on all kinds of problems such as intestinal worms, headaches, lead poisoning, diabetes, catatonia and cholera. They injected it into the eyelids as a possible blindness cure, and up the urethra and into the bladder for urinary retention. Surgeons would give it to their patients before the anesthetic was given. Doctors and quacks alike promoted it as a wonder drug, and by the late Victorian period, it slipped into tonics as a pick-me-up.

Accidents Will Happen

Given its lethality in small doses — the equivalent of one-fifth of a standard aspirin tablet was enough to kill Mrs. Inglethorp — it was amazing anyone survived. For example, in 1900, a Dr. C.F. Abraham of Ontario prescribed for "Baby Smith" a mixture of belladonna, strychnine, aromatic ammonium and syrup of tolu balsam, to be taken with a little water every two hours. It's not known how well "Baby Smith" responded to this treatment.

Even professionals ran the risk of near-fatal accidents. In 1896, a medical student wrote to a British medical journal describing what happened when he needed a boost while studying:

"Three years ago I was reading for an examination, and feeling 'run down' I took 10 minims [about 1/50th of a fluid ounce] of strychnia solution with the same quantity of dilute phosphoric acid well diluted twice a day. On the second day of taking it, towards the evening, I felt a tightness in the 'facial muscles' and a peculiar metallic taste in the mouth. There was great uneasiness and restlessness, and I felt a desire to walk about and do something rather than sit still and read. I lay on the bed and the calf muscles began to stiffen and jerk. My toes drew up under my feet, and as I moved or turned my head flashes of light kept darting across my eyes.

"I then knew something serious was developing, so I crawled off the bed and scrambled to a case in my room and got out (fortunately) the bromide of potassium and the chloral. I had no confidence or courage to weigh them, so I guessed the quantity — about 30 gr. bromide of potassium and 10 gr. chloral — put them in a tumbler with some water, and drank it off. My whole body was in a cold sweat, with anginous attacks in the precordial [heart] region, and a feeling of 'going off.'

"I did not call for medical aid, as I thought the symptoms declining. I felt better, but my lower limbs were as cold as ice and the calf muscles kept tense and jerking. There was no opisthotonos [the characteristic arching of the back], only a slight stiffness at the back of the neck. Half an hour later, as I could judge, I took the same quantity of bromide of potassium and chloral, and a little time after I lost consciousness and fell into a 'profound sleep,' awaking in the morning with no unpleasant symptoms, no headache, &c., but a desire 'to be on the move' and a slight feeling of stiffness in the jaw.

"These worked off during the day."

Strychnine at the Olympics

By the turn of the century, athletes were taking strychnine to enhance their performances. Runners and cyclists drank it to boost their endurance. Boxing managers kept a bottle of strychnine-laced ointment at hand to dull their fighters' pain. Football trainers stocked their bags with strychnine pills along with the smelling salts, brandy and other tonics.

In an era before drug testing, such use was not illegal, but it did spark rumors. The Welsh championship bicyclist Arthur Linton was rumored to have died from a drug cocktail administered by his trainer, the notorious "Choppy" Warburton, but the truth is that he died at age 24 from typhoid. However, Warburton did carry with him a black bottle, possibly containing strychnine, that he used to dose his charges during races.

The most notorious use of the drug occurred during the 1904 Summer Olympics marathon in St. Louis, Missouri.

The event was a debacle. Of the 32 runners who started, only 14 finished. One runner rode over part of the course in a vehicle, ran into the stadium and attempted to claim the gold medal before his cheating was discovered.

It was a surprise anyone finished. St. Louis is hellishly hot in the summer. Temperatures that August were in the 90s, with the humidity nearly as high. Thirsty runners could find water only at a tower and a well. They raced over unpaved roads that quickly became choked with dust from the horses and vehicles that paraded with them. Several runners who breathed in too much dust finished the race in the hospital.

The event's only bright spot was that it made Olympic history for being the first in which black athletes participated. It wasn't intentional. The founder of the games, Pierre de Coubertin, had planned the Olympics as "the means of bringing to perfection the strong and hopeful youth of our white race." But the World's Fair was in St. Louis at the time, and two members of South Africa's Boer War Exhibit, Tswana tribesmen named Len Tau and Jan Mashiani, decided to compete. Mashiani finished twelfth. Tau did better by finishing ninth, and he could have won if a wild dog hadn't chased him off the course for a time.

The race was won by Thomas Hicks, an Englishman running for the United States. After 19 miles, Hicks was in first place by more than a mile, but fading fast. When he stopped to rest, his manager leapt from a car and dosed him with brandy mixed with a bit of strychnine sulfate, a.k.a. rat poison. That got him running again, until he collapsed, his face ash-white. His supporters bathed him in warm water and forced down another dose of strychnine, brandy and egg whites. Delirious and staggering — at one point his trainers carried him — Hicks finished first and collapsed. It took more than an hour before he could stand and receive his gold medal.

Thankfully, strychnine no longer appears on the shelf in tonics. But if Mrs. Inglethorp were alive today and in need of a pick-me-up, she could turn to homeopathic remedies sold in pellet or liquid form. Although it would be nowhere near the same strength as her tonic, it would also be nowhere near as lethal.

The Demeanour of Murderers

Charles Dickens

While Charles Dickens did not attend Palmer's trial, he paid close attention to the newspaper reports, and he didn't like what he read. "The Demeanour of Murderers," he told a friend, was "a quiet protest against the newspaper description of Mr. Palmer in court: shewing why they are harmful to the public at large, and why they are even in themselves, altogether blind and wrong." The essay appeared in his Household Words magazine on June 14, the day Palmer was executed. To make the essay easier to read, the longer paragraphs were subdivided, but the text was not changed.

The recent trial of the greatest villain that ever stood in the Old Bailey dock, has produced the usual descriptions inseparable from such occasions. The public has read from day to day of the murderer's complete self-possession, of his constant coolness, of his profound composure, of his perfect equanimity. Some describers have gone so far as to represent him occasionally rather amused than otherwise by the proceedings; and all the accounts that we have seen, concur in more or less suggesting that there is something admirable, and difficult to reconcile with guilt, in the bearing so elaborately set forth.

As whatever tends, however undesignedly, to insinuate this uneasy sense of incongruity into any mind, and to invest so abhorrent a ruffian with the slightest tinge of heroism, must be prejudicial to the general welfare, we revive the detestable subject with the hope of showing that there is nothing at all singular in such a deportment, but that it is always to be looked for and counted on, in the case of a very wicked murderer. The blacker the guilt, the stronger the probability of its being thus carried off.

In passing, we will express an opinion that Nature never writes a bad hand. Her writing, as it may be read in the human countenance, is invariably legible, if we come at all trained to the reading of it. Some little weighing and comparing are necessary. It is not enough in turning our eyes on the demon in the Dock, to say he has a fresh colour, or a high head, or a bluff manner, or what not, and therefore he does not look like a murderer, and we are surprised and shaken. The physiognomy and conformation of the Poisoner whose trial occasions these remarks, were exactly in accordance with his deeds; and every guilty consciousness he had gone on storing up in his mind, had set its mark upon him.

We proceed, within as short a compass as possible, to illustrate the position we have placed before our readers in the first paragraph of this paper.

The Poisoner's demeanour was considered exceedingly remarkable, because of his composure under trial, and because of the confident expectation of acquittal which he professed to the last, and under the influence of which he, at various times during his incarceration, referred to the plans he entertained for the future when he should be free again.

Can any one, reflecting on the matter for five minutes, suppose it possible we do not say probable, but possible that in the breast of this Poisoner there were surviving, in the days of his trial, any lingering traces of sensibility, or any wrecked fragment of the quality which we call sentiment? Can the profoundest or the simplest man alive, believe that in such a heart there could have been left, by that time, any touch of Pity? An objection to die, and a special objection to be killed, no doubt he had; and with that objection very strong within him for divers very weighty reasons, he was not quite composed. Distinctly not quite composed, but, on the contrary, very restless. At one time, he was incessantly pulling on and pulling off his glove; at another time, his hand was constantly passing over and over his face; and the thing most instanced in proof of his composure, the perpetual writing and scattering about of little notes, which, as the verdict drew nearer and nearer, thickened from a sprinkling to a heavy shower, is in itself a proof of miserable restlessness. Beyond this emotion, which any lower animal would have, with an apprehension on it of a similar fate, what was to be expected from such a creature but insensibility?

I poison my friend in his drink, and I poison my friend in his bed, and I poison my wife, and I poison her memory, and do you look to ME, at the end of such a career as mine, for sensibility? I have not the power of it even in my own behalf, I have lost the manner of it, I don't know what it means, I stand contemptuously wondering at you people here when I see you moved by this affair. In the Devil's name, man, have you heard the evidence of that chambermaid, whose tea I should like to have the sweetening of? Did you hear her describe the agonies in which my friend expired? Do you know that it was my trade to be learned in poisons, and that I foresaw all that, and considered all that, and knew, when I stood at his bedside looking down upon his face turned to me for help on its road to the grave through the frightful gate then swinging on its hinges, that in so many hours or minutes all those horrors would infallibly ensue? Have you heard that, after my poisonings, I have had to face the circumstances out, with friends and enemies, doctors, undertakers, all sorts of men, and have uniformly done it; and do you wonder that I face it out with you? Why not? What right or reason can you have to expect anything else of me? Wonder! You might wonder, indeed, if you saw me moved, here now before you. If I had any natural human feeling for my face to express, do you imagine that those medicines of my prescribing and administering would ever have been taken from my hand? Why, man, my demeanour at this bar is the natural companion of my crimes, and, if it were a little different from what it is, you might even begin reasonably to doubt whether I had ever committed them!

The Poisoner had a confident expectation of acquittal. We doubt as little that he really had some considerable hope of it, as we do that he made a pretence of having more than he really had. Let us consider, first, if it be wonderful that he should have been rather sanguine. He had poisoned his victims according to his carefully laid plans; he had got them buried out of his way; he had murdered, and forged, and yet kept his place as a good fellow and a sporting character; he had made a capital friend of the coroner, and a serviceable traitor of the postmaster; he was a great public character, with a special Act of Parliament for his trial; the choice lit spirits of the Stock Exchange were offering long odds in his favour, and, to wind up all, here was a tip-top Counsellor bursting into tears for him, saying to the jury, three times over, "You dare not, you dare not, you dare not!" and bolting clean out of the course[1] to declare his belief that he was innocent.

With all this to encourage him, with his own Derby-day division of mankind into knaves and fools, and with his own secret knowledge of the difficulties and mysteries with which

---

[1] "Bolting clean out of the course" refers to a horse that has run off the course during a race.

the proof of Poison had been, in the manner of the Poisoning, surrounded, it would have been strange indeed if he were not borne up by some idea of escape.

But, why should he have professed himself to have more hope of escape than he really entertained? The answer is, because it belongs to that extremity, that the villain in it should not only declare a strong expectation of acquittal himself, but should try to infect all the people about him with it. Besides having an artful fancy (not wholly without foundation) that he disseminates by that means an impression that he is innocent; to surround himself in his narrowed world with this fiction is, for the time being, to fill the jail with a faintly rose-coloured atmosphere, and to remove the gallows to a more agreeable distance. Hence, plans are laid for the future, communicated with an engaging candour to turnkeys, and discussed in a reliant spirit. Even sick men and women, over whom natural death is impending, constantly talk with those about them on precisely the same principle.

It may be objected that there is some slight ingenuity in our endeavours to resolve the demeanour of this Poisoner into the same features as the demeanour of every other very wicked and very hardened criminal in the same strait, but that a parallel would be better than argument. We have no difficulty in finding a parallel; we have no difficulty in finding scores, beyond the almost insuperable difficulty of finding, in the criminal records, as deeply-dyed a murderer.

To embarrass these remarks, however, with references to cases that have passed out of the general memory, or have never been widely known, would be to render the discussion very irksome. We will confine ourselves to a famous instance. We will not even ask if it be so long ago since Rush was tried, that his demeanour is forgotten.[2] We will call Thurtell into court, as one of the murderers best remembered in England.

With the difference that the circumstances of Thurtell's guilt are not comparable in atrocity with those of the Poisoner's, there are points of strong resemblance between the two men.[3]

Each was born in a fair station, and educated in conformity

---

[2] James Rush was hanged in 1849 for the murders of his landlord and his son. The case was notorious enough for Staffordshire Potteries to produce figures of Rush and his mistress, plus three buildings tied to the murders.

[3] John Thurtell (1794-1824) was hanged for the murder of William Weare over a gambling debt.

with it; each murdered a man with whom he had been on terms of intimate association, and for whom he professed a friendship at the time of the murder; both were members of that vermin-race of outer betters and blacklegs, of whom some worthy samples were presented on both trials, and of whom, as a community, mankind would be blessedly rid, if they could all be, once and for ever, knocked on the head at a blow.

Thurtell's demeanour was exactly that of the Poisoner's. We have referred to the newspapers of his time, in aid of our previous knowledge of the case; and they present a complete confirmation of the simple fact for which we contend. From day to day, during his imprisonment before his trial, he is described as "collected and resolute in his demeanour," as "rather mild and conciliatory in his address," as being visited by "friends whom he receives with cheerfulness," as "remaining firm and unmoved," as "increasing in confidence as the day which is to decide his fate draws nigh," as "speaking of the favourable result of the trial with his usual confidence." On his trial, he looks "particularly well and healthy." His attention and composure are considered as wonderful as the Poisoner's; he writes notes as the Poisoner did; he watches the case with the same cool eye; he "retains that firmness for which, from the moment of his apprehension, he has been distinguished"; he "carefully assorts his papers on a desk near him"; he is (in this being singular) his own orator, and makes a speech in the manner of Edmund Kean,[4] on the whole not very unlike that of the leading counsel for the Poisoner, concluding, as to his own innocence, with a So help me God!

Before his trial, the Poisoner says he will be at the coming race for the Derby. Before his trial, Thurtell says, "that after his acquittal he will visit his father, and will propose to him to advance the portion which he intended for him, upon which he will reside abroad." (So Mr. Manning observed, under similar circumstances, that when all that nonsense was over, and the thing wound up, he had an idea of establishing himself in the West Indies.)[5]

---

[4] Edmund Kean (1787-1833) was considered in his day to be the best tragic actor of all time. "Seeing him act," Samuel Taylor Coleridge wrote, "was like reading Shakespeare by flashes of lightning."

[5] George Manning and his wife, Marie, were hanged in 1849 for killing their lodger and burying him under their kitchen floor. Dickens attended their hanging and was appalled: "I believe that a sight so inconceivably awful as the wickedness and levity of the

When the Poisoner's trial is yet to last another day or so, he enjoys his half-pound of steak and his tea, wishes his best friends may sleep as he does, and fears the grave "no more than his bed." (See the Evening Hymn for a Young Child.[6]) When Thurtell's trial is yet to last another day or so, he takes his cold meat, tea, and coffee, and "enjoys himself with great comfort"; also, on the morning of his execution, he wakes from as innocent a slumber as the Poisoner's, declaring that he has had an excellent night, and that he hasn't dreamed "about this business." Whether the parallel will hold to the last, as to "feeling very well and very comfortable," as to "the firm step and perfect calmness," as to "the manliness and correctness of his general conduct," as to "the countenance unchanged by the awfulness of the situation" not to say as to bowing to a friend, from the scaffold "in a friendly but dignified manner" our readers will know for themselves when we know too.

It is surely time that people who are not in the habit of dissecting such appearances, but who are in the habit of reading about them, should be helped to the knowledge that, in the worst examples they are the most to be expected, and the least to be wondered at. That there is no inconsistency in them, and no fortitude in them. That, there is nothing in them but cruelty and insensibility. That they are seen, because the man is of a piece with his misdeeds; and that it is not likely that he ever could have committed the crimes for which he is to suffer, if he had not this demeanour to present, in standing publicly to answer for them.

---

immense crowd collected at that execution this morning could be imagined by no man, and could be presented in no heathen land under the sun."

[6] Dickens probably was thinking of "Glory to Thee, my God, this night" by Thomas Ken (1637-1711), particularly the third verse:

Teach me to live, that I may dread
The grave as little as my bed;
Teach me to die, that so I may
Rise glorious at the awful day.

About the Authors

George Fletcher (1848-1933) was born in Bromsgrove, Worcestershire. He was educated at Bromsgrove School and earned an MA and an MD at Clare College, Cambridge. He was a member of the Royal College of Surgeons and the Worshipful Society of Apothecaries. He worked as a surgeon at St. Thomas's Hospital, London, and was visiting Magistrate at Pentonville Prison.

Bill Peschel is a journalist who shares a Pulitzer Prize with the staff of *The Patriot-News* in Harrisburg, Pa. He also is mystery fan who has run the Wimsey Annotations for nearly two decades. He is the author of the 223B series of Sherlock Holmes parodies and pastiches, *The Complete, Annotated Mysterious Affair at Styles*, *The Complete, Annotated Secret Adversary* and *The Complete, Annotated Whose Body?* as well as *Writers Gone Wild* (Penguin Books). He lives in Hershey, where the air really does smell like chocolate.

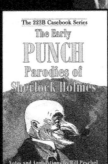
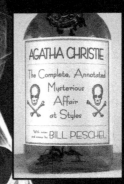

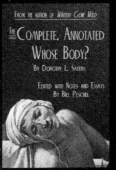

Printed in Great Britain
by Amazon

39947798R00128